TWO WHEELS & A TAXI

Two Wheels & a Taxi

A SLIGHTLY DAFT ADVENTURE IN THE ANDES

Virginia Urrutia

Illustrations by Betsy James

THE MOUNTAINEERS/SEATTLE

THE MOUNTAINEERS: Organized 1906 ". . . to encourage a spirit of fellowship among all lovers of outdoor life."

Published by The Mountaineers
306 2nd Avenue West, Seattle, Washington 98119

Published simultaneously in Canada by Douglas & McIntyre Ltd.
1615 Venables Street, Vancouver, B.C. 2H1

Manufactured in the United States of America

Edited by Jennifer Keller
Cover design by Elizabeth Watson
Book design by Marge Mueller

Library of Congress Cataloging-in-Publication Data

Urrutia, Virginia.
    Two wheels & a taxi : a slightly daft adventure in the Andes /
Virginia Urrutia ; illustrations by Betsy James.
        p.   cm.
    ISBN 0-89886-141-1 : $14.95
    1. Andes Region—Description and travel.   2. Ecuador—Description
and travel—1981-   3. Cycling—Andes Region.   4. Urrutia, Virginia—
Journeys—Andes Region.   5. Urrutia, Virginia—Journeys—Ecuador.
I. Title.   II. Title: Two wheels and a taxi.
F3741.A6U77 1987
918.66—dc19   87-28159
                                                                  CIP

To lovers of mountains—my friends in Ecuador, who know how to temper adversity with laughter and who yearn for the schooling that we take for granted.

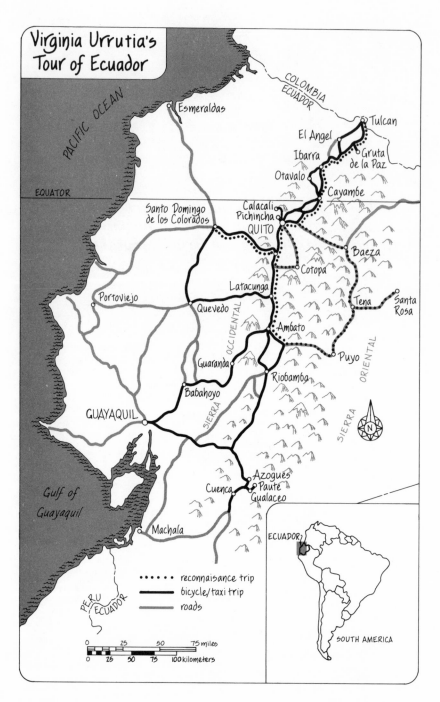

Virginia Urrutia's Tour of Ecuador

COLOMBIA
ECUADOR

PACIFIC OCEAN

Esmeraldas

Tulcan

El Angel

Ibarra   Gruta
                de la Paz
Otavalo

EQUATOR   Cayambe

Santo Domingo   Calacali
de los Colorados   Pichincha
                       QUITO

                                    Baeza

                       Cotopa

Portoviejo   Latacunga   Tena   Santa
                                                   Rosa
          Quevedo

                       Ambato

          Guaranda   Puyo

          Babahoyo   Riobamba

GUAYAQUIL

                                              N

                       Azogues
            Cuenca   Paute
                       Gualaceo

Gulf of
Guayaquil

          Machala   ECUADOR

                             SOUTH AMERICA

PERU
ECUADOR

OCCIDENTAL

SIERRA

SIERRA   ORIENTAL

•••••• reconnaisance trip
━━━━ bicycle/taxi trip
━━━━ roads

0   25   50   75 miles
0   25   50   75   100 kilometers

vi

Contents

1

GRANDMOTHERS MUST BE PROTECTED

"I HAVE KNOWN guys in Peru who were robbed and left in the gutter with nothing on but their shorts," my friend warned when I told him in the cold winter of 1982 that I was going to tour Bolivia, Peru and Ecuador.

I was alarmed. "They wouldn't do that to a woman!"

"Oh yes, women too," he assured me. "Go there alone on your bike and you'll be dead."

No denial was possible. He had lived there and I had never been to South America. Other friends who had never been to South America, and had no intention of going, were equally comforting.

"My friend had a necklace snatched from her very neck in front of her very hotel," one informed me.

"I will just wear my old wristwatch," I replied.

"So-and-so had her suitcase stolen out of her hotel room," was the final encouragement I received from another well-wisher.

I turned to all the books I could find in the library that would tell me about countries in the Andes. Contrary to most travel books, which gloss over dirt, diseases and disasters, the ones I read only confirmed my friends' fears for me. Numerous snakes, unsavory and unsociable, would be lurking about even at high altitudes instead of just crawling about down in the jungles where they belonged. Some were famous for leaping out at victims from behind trees. According to the travel advisories, the malarial mosquito that inhabits the jungles of Ecuador, where I longed to go, plants an intelligent parasite that has learned to resist the most common drugs. The only way I could escape from my friends and take the trip was to tell them that this time, no, I would not take my bicycle.

My friends, however, had not considered the peculiar armor

that protects grandmothers. From the moment my plane landed like a condor on the heights above La Paz, Bolivia, I discovered that a woman alone in South America is not only considered *valiente,* but is treated by guides and taxi drivers as respectfully as if she were their own grandmother. And of course grandmothers must be protected—cheated by all means, but always with courtesy. Her presumed helplessness is a grandmother's best defense against physical harm, if not against fiscal.

Now, months after my comforters had all but consigned me to the morgue, I found myself flying over the Ecuadorian Andes, looking down at the peaks below. The plane, with the abandon of a carnival loop-the-loop ride that had broken away from its moorings, was vaulting with dramatic suddenness over the mountains from the Ecuadorian coast to the high Quito basin—a half-hour flight. Half my trip—Bolivia and Peru—was already behind me and so far I was unmurdered, unraped and unrobbed. However, my arms had been punctured by all the shots offered by the hometown health department, and I wore my most tattered clothes, just in case anyone wanted to knock me into the gutter and strip me down to my underwear, as predicted.

This trip marked the first time I had left the United States without a bicycle either reposing below me in the hold of a plane or waiting to be bought in some Italian or English city when I landed. A bike had always been as necessary as my traveler's checks and passport. It never seemed like a real trip without a bicycle because I never considered that I had toured a country unless I had poked over it on two wheels. Without my bike I now felt naked.

My passion for bicycles began fifty years ago when an uncle taught me how to ride one. After retiring as a geology professor he took up bicycling to study the countryside more intimately. Often I went with him. As I enjoyed a long coast with him behind, I would hear the bell on his handlebar jingling insistently, signaling me to brake to a stop. He would wonder why I had not noticed the granite boulder in a nearby field and we would pause while he gave me its geological history. His slow-moving two wheels let him trace vestiges in the countryside of past floods, earthquakes and deep freezes. Whenever we came to a hill, even a small one, he would order me to dismount. Walking would use different muscles, he said, rest the ones that had been pumping, and I would be less tired at the end of the day. I discovered he was right. After many miles of cycling, my knees needed no bending exercises to get rid of stiffness. Although my uncle walked slowly up all hills, he could easily do a "century" (one hundred miles a day) long before the ten-speed was invented.

After a summer of wheeling over the countryside with him, my addiction to the bicycle was beyond cure. In the years that followed, it only got worse. I normally suffer no symptoms so long as I am either taking or planning to take a long bicycle trip. And for more than thirty years I have done just that—always alone. I have bicycled over the Swiss Alps, above and beside the Norwegian fjords, over the roller-coaster pitches of New Zealand, across the flatlands of Holland, along the valley of the Po, through the snarl of London traffic, and in and out of a weaving line of Sunday drunks in Yugoslavia.

In the course of these adventures, I learned that the slow-moving bicycle is an instrument for observation. It brings about a marriage with the land, allowing the rider to discover what covers it, what elements assail it, who moves and works upon it. Only walking can bring about a closer relationship. My curiosity has been exceeded only by the curiosity of the people I meet along the way, who wave in surprise as I pedal by alone, wearing not shorts and helmet but a skirt, jacket, necklace and floppy hat, as if I had not yet left the Victorian age. Onlookers stop their work or gossip, rush over to look at my map, which might be spread across the handlebars, and cluck happily when I point out the route already traveled in their country. Their curiosity satisfied, they wave me off with blessings and encouragement. If a traveler wants to meet people, let him mount a bicycle, pedal slowly, stop for lunch—which invites gestured conversation—or occasionally pull out a map, which speaks any language. Even better, if the bicyclist is lucky enough to be slightly lost, a flock will gather at once, each member offering a different idea of the best way to get to where he wants to go.

Because of the biking habits of strolling and stopping formed with my uncle, I am an oddity to the modern cyclist in aerodynamic uniform and helmet, who zips about on his multi-speed with head down, legs pumping like accelerated pistons, lungs puffing as he attacks hills. I am also prone to such deviant behavior as walking my bicycle through crowded city traffic, wearing skirts on long trips so that I'm dressed for dignified places such as cathedrals and tearooms, poking along at an average speed of seven miles per hour and

touring on a well-crafted one-speed that can be put on trains and planes without suffering more than a slightly askew and easily repaired fender. When the baggage attendant hands me the bike and wishes me good luck, I can pedal off at once. Nothing has been damaged, and nothing needs to be screwed back into place—except perhaps the pedals. If I put plastic protectors between the tire and tube, the bicycle is almost maintenance free (a good thing because I could not even pass the all-thumbs mechanical test).

Even so, bicycling in South America, whether cruising over the Chilean desert or cutting through an Andean pass, seemed a formidable undertaking. Hills and mountains were not in themselves formidable; I merely had to go over them. What daunted me was the aloneness I would suffer in those mountains. Not since I had braved bears and brigands while pedaling through the Rockies years before had I slept out alone. Since then, I had become devoted to beds and baths. But in the Andes, hotels catering to such devotions were hundreds of miles apart. I had also become used to a leisurely sight-seeing pace that never lets me accomplish more than fifty miles a day on my one-speed bicycle, whether the road runs up or down, is graveled or paved.

As the plane glided down toward Quito, I looked more closely at the mountains below me, searching for roads to ride on or villages for a safe rest at night. I could see nothing but a primordial chaos of brown mountains—a disorderly world still in the making. Rising above the chaos were a few snow-topped peaks, haughtily striving to bring majesty and order to the upheaval around them.

"If I were going to bicycle in South America, I would want a military escort," was the last heartening observation another friend had made before I began my trip. As I turned away from the window of my plane and my vain survey for bike routes, I sighed. We were now above Quito. From under the seat in front of me I pulled out my tiny suitcase, purposely too scruffy-looking to attract any but the most destitute of thieves.

What I had not foreseen as I looked out the window was that a long and sometimes unruly parade of adventures—mishaps with those who cheated and security with those who did not—would convince me that a bicycle trip was possible even in the Andes. What I would not have believed was that in less than a year a slightly daft seventy-year-old lady bicyclist would be coasting in terror down those mountains, her knuckles white over the brake levers, heart pounding, not expecting to reach the bottom of the hill alive. Even less could I have foreseen that an escort for such an adventure would materialize. Though not from the military, he would offer as much protection as a man armed with a machine gun.

2

THE THIEF OF THE MIDDLE OF THE WORLD

THE BEST WAY to come to Ecuador, a native of the country told me, is to come without anything reserved ahead of time. If that is the best way to arrive, I arrived in the best way.

My travel agent wrote to a hotel that I had picked out of a guidebook, but the hotel had never answered. Feeling like a chartless mariner, I stepped out of the Quito airport to be hit with cultural shock in reverse. No battered taxis with molting paint and broken windshields, like those I had seen in Bolivia, waited in front of the building. Instead, I saw shiny yellow taxis with uncracked windshields and without so much as a hair of a scratch. I approached the one with the most honest-looking driver, and soon we were darting through Quito traffic, through wide streets that looked almost scrubbed, past white buildings.

"What a rich country!" I remarked to the driver and he proceeded to expound on its virtues: everyone has everything he wants to eat; everyone buys all he wants; there are few delinquents; the country is rich in oil. I later learned that this was quite exaggerated, but at the time I was comforted.

"Do you need money, Senora? There is an exchange right near here. I will wait for you." He drove into a wide parking lot in front of a covered shopping mall.

"The *cambio* is just inside, Senora," he said, pointing out a front entrance. I hurried into it and soon found the bank. Above the teller's wicket was a notice warning me that the *cambio* would be closed for three days for the New Year's holiday. Guessing hastily at how much money I thought I might need, I exchanged some traveler's checks and hurried back to the taxi to find the driver wiping fingerprints off the shiny yellow hood. I crawled into the back seat as neatly as possible.

"What is the name of your hotel, Senora?" he asked.

I told him. He shook his head.

"Ah, si!" he said. "There is no hotel there now. They closed it. The manager died or the workers quit. I am not sure what happened, but it was not a good hotel. I will take you to a better one."

Within minutes we had rolled up in front of a small, first-class hotel. A bellboy ran down to greet us before I had time to crawl out of the cab. After severely admonishing him to take good care of me, the driver left me there with a bow, as if I were visiting royalty.

Carrying my tiny suitcase, the bellboy helped me to my room and pointed out all its amenities, including a spotless bathroom with a superfluity of white towels.

After he left, I walked over to look out the sixth floor window.

The roofs stretched in geometric zigzags to the Andes in the east, to pyramidal Mt. Cotapaxi thirty-five miles away, shooting skyward above the green mountains ringing the city. Below, the streets looked peaceful, inviting exploration. I had arrived in Ecuador without plan but not without means—two-thirds of my money as well as nearly half my time remained. My plane back to the United States was twelve days away. Could I be lucky enough to explore Ecuador, as I had in Bolivia, in a taxi with a reliable driver who would let me stop to root about and photograph?

A day's investigation convinced me that an organized tour was the most expensive way to see the country. A public bus was the cheapest way to *go,* but a taxi was the cheapest way to *arrive.* In South America, there seemed to be a wide gap between going and actually arriving where you wanted to be. Dusty buses, painted pink with blue scalloped trim, bearing such names as *Santa Teresa* or *Maria de la Concepcion,* which should guarantee protection, bounced over the countryside while cardboard saints and other pious baubles danced above their windshields. But such divine assistance did not keep passengers from waiting hours for a flat tire to be repaired or for a spring to be tied together with bailing wire. My spirit of adventure was limited by wanting to arrive.

The next morning I told the senorita at the hotel desk that I wanted to meander through the ancient part of Quito, which had been left intact from Spanish colonial days, so they claim.

"It is too far to walk. Take a taxi," she advised me.

A shiny yellow taxi, just for that purpose, was waiting in front of the hotel; the driver all but pounced upon me. Gladly he would take me to the old town at his usual rate of 300 sucres an hour, about $4.60. This was a good price. When we got near Plaza Independencia, dead center of colonial Quito, we saw that it was anything but dead. Traffic was dashing helter-skelter in all directions and cars were jammed into all the parking places. My driver did not seem to know where to put his cab. Clearly he had no intention of squeezing it in somewhere or of running around with me. Immediately he wanted his fee of 350 sucres so that he could return to his post in front of the hotel. I looked in my purse for the money and found only a 1000-sucre bill and small change amounting to 150 sucres. I handed him the bill.

"Do you have change, senor?"

"I have no change," he answered quickly, without even having to look in his pockets. "Buy something," he urged, pointing to the nearest opening in a wall through which we could see a shop and an array of woolens. I ran in and flourished my 1000-sucre bill in front of the shopkeeper. "Senora, have you change for my taxi?"

"No!" she shot back with a quick shake of her head. I hastily picked up a pair of wool mittens and held them out to her with the money. She hardened into granite.

"Too little!" she snapped and turned away from me.

Completely perplexed, I returned to the taxi driver, but he saw no problem.

"You can pay me the 150 sucres now, Senora," he suggested, "and then I can come back to the hotel at two o'clock and get the rest of the money."

"Very well," I agreed happily. "And when you come back to the hotel, you can take me out to the 'Middle of the World.' " At this suggestion, he shook my hand enthusiastically.

Fine, I thought to myself as he drove off. The "Middle of the World," as they call the equator in Ecuador, is only a fifteen-mile drive north from Quito and it will be a good test to see if he is a reliable driver to take me all over Ecuador. Surely he must be honest himself to trust leaving me here when I still owe him 200 sucres.

It was the day before New Year's. The country and city were getting ready for a weekend holiday. Stalls in the street markets were heaped with masks to be worn by the celebrants who would cavort in the streets that night. Hurried shoppers haggled over fruits and vegetables piled on stalls in narrow alleys. I stepped cautiously over

the broken pavement of the old streets and, anxious to avoid being slaughtered by maniacal motorists, sought out crossings where policemen in brown uniforms and white gloves were vigorously waving at the traffic to quell it into submission. I squeezed and wiggled my way through the crowds, occasionally retreating to peaceful pews in shadowy old churches heavy with mustiness and stirring with the whispering and shuffling of many worshippers.

By noon I was making my way by foot part way back to my hotel, planning to take a taxi as soon as I emerged from the old city. I was cutting across Elejido, the central park of the city, when bang! I twisted my ankle and went sprawling, landing hard on both knees. At Quito's altitude of 9,250 feet, a stranger can suddenly become light-headed and fatigued. Although I suffered no more than broken, bleeding skin and two ruined stockings, a minor shock surged through me. Close to fainting, I made my way half a block to the nearest taxi.

"Fifty sucres to your hotel," the driver informed me pleasantly. He then spent the short distance back to the hotel telling me how I should take care of my bloody knee with salt and hot water. Good advice, except when I got back to my room I had to substitute soap for salt.

At lunch I thought I could get my 1000 sucres changed so that I could pay my first taxi driver the 200 sucres I owed him as well as the fee for the trip to the Middle of the World. That thirty mile round trip should not be much more than an hour—300 sucres. But I ate too much and I had to charge it to the hotel. "By now he must have change himself," I thought. "I will pay him everything when we get back from the Middle of the World."

At promptly two in the afternoon the taxi driver to whom I was indebted showed up, and we headed north to the equator.

"I want to stop for my wife," he half-asked after a few minutes and I nodded, thinking it would be interesting.

I was wrong. During the afternoon, I would discover the stupidity of my assenting and he would discover, too late, the stupidity of his asking. He did not know, of course, that he was being tested as a tour guide for Ecuador and I began flunking him point by point, with every mile. After we finally gathered his wife and little boy, which took nearly an hour, it soon was apparent that I was only being taken along incidentally. We made a number of stops for purchases for the child; parked to see a wrecked car; paused at a stand selling wine, which I refused to buy; stopped for soda pop, which I was expected to buy; detoured on errands for his wife when she could interrupt her chatter long enough to give instructions; took a circuitous route in every direction but north, which was where the equator was supposed to be; and had our progress frequently halted by scores of children in New Year's masks who were holding ropes across the street and demanding coins as passage. The only thing going straight about the trip was the line at the equator, which we finally reached, after two hours, at about four o'clock.

I headed for the monument marking the Middle of the World but a man with a Polaroid camera continually obstructed my passage. He followed me as closely as a cat that rubs against your ankles and makes you stumble. I told him emphatically that I did not want my picture taken in front of the monument. Scowling, I refused to open my purse to buy snapshots of the little boy, whose picture he had succeeded in taking. After much argument with the photographer, the driver, sulking, had to buy them himself.

I began thinking of the driver, who had never introduced himself, as *tonto,* or blockhead. He continued to fail his test on the way back to the hotel, where we arrived at six o'clock after sundry delays and deviations. Foolishly, I had not agreed upon a price before we set out, unless he still thought it should be 300 sucres an hour. I still had the unbroken 1000 sucre note and he claimed to be utterly lacking in sucres. My knee was smarting and so was my temper. We quibbled a while and then he snatched the 1000 sucre note from my hand and said that this would pay for what I owed him, as well as the trip to the Middle of the World. Off he drove. I was defeated.

Blazing, I walked up the hotel steps to the senorita at the desk.

"We went to the Middle of the World," I began. "He took all his family along and I paid him 1000 sucres." I was too weary with my throbbing knee to explain that I already owed him 200 sucres.

"You should not have paid him the 1000 sucres!" She also blazed. "It was your time, not his. He is not supposed to take his wife along. I will tell the hotel manager."

"Yes," I admitted. "I was a *pendeja*"—(put politely, a damn fool)—"But he is a *pendejo,* too. I am looking for a driver to take me all over Ecuador and he won't do." I now would have to try out another driver, and the next trip I hoped to take was to see the market of the Colorado Indians at Santo Domingo, eighty-five miles southwest of Quito.

"Senorita, will you find me an honest, dependable chauffeur-guide to take me to Santo Domingo Sunday?" It was now Friday.

"Yes, Senora. There is another chauffeur with the hotel who is very serious, very honest. I will talk to him." She was eager to help me and I went off to a late supper in a hopeful mood.

A few hours later I had convinced myself that my knee would heal without my having to buy a pound of salt and that I should venture out into the streets to watch the New Year's celebrations. I could have been in New Orleans at a cut-rate Mardi Gras. Masked people, most reeling dangerously, filled the central boulevard, Las Amazonas. A parade weaved in disorderly fashion down the boulevard, towing raggle taggle floats: some crude, some obscene, and some really amusing. One was urging *Abajo con la Inflacion*—"Down with Inflation." It carried a monstrous one-eighth-sucre coin, which would be worth something if inflation had never started in the first place. Long before midnight I trudged back to the hotel.

The afternoon of the next day, New Year's, as I stepped across the lobby, the senorita at the desk called to me.

"I have found a driver for you," she said. "He is not from our hotel. He is from a different hotel but we exchange. He cannot speak English, but he is very serious, very honest. He will take you to Santo Domingo tomorrow for 2800 sucres. Is that acceptable?" She wrote the amount and his name—Angel Godoy.

3

SENOR GODOY

THE NEXT MORNING I was in the lobby a little after eight. Restless to be off, I kept looking at my old wristwatch, impatiently waiting for eight-thirty to arrive, the time Senor Godoy was supposed to appear. Precisely when the minute hand was at thirty minutes past the hour a man jumped over the outside stairs two at a time and hurried into

the lobby. He looked about quickly and then saw that I was the one expecting him. Face bursting with smiles, dark eyes twinkling, he extended his hand in a cordial greeting. A billed cap covered black hair cut in a 1940s crewcut style; his light polyester jacket and slacks must have just left the ironing board. Stocky and shorter than my five feet six inches, with the vigor of a man not yet forty, he looked as if he could roll a mean bowling ball, swat a baseball, slam-bang his way down a soccer field, or sock a volleyball over the net with a loud crack.

"It is not a long trip to Santo Domingo, Senora," he explained after shaking my hand vigorously. "We will see the market of the Colorado Indians and come back after lunch." As soon as we were outside in his Peugeot taxi, yellow and shiny as usual, he wanted to know all about the "Thief of the Middle of the World," as I had begun calling the driver who had flunked my test.

"Es pendejo," he agreed. "He does not know the tourists." It quickly became apparent that Senor Godoy did. He showed me a printed list of the prices that he and his hotel charged for all trips out of Quito. In case he should try to charge me more than the 2800 sucres we had agreed upon for the trip, I put the little piece of paper on which I had written his name and price on the dashboard. It was an unnecessary precaution. By the end of the day I was convinced that he was the most honest taxi driver in South America. Not only that, he bubbled merrily with a sense of humor as contagious as measles. A mild joke between us brought on a gentle drizzle of chuckles. A major comedy like my getting hopelessly tangled in the seat belt brought on a tempest of howls.

As we left Quito, rolling south over jade-green hills, patches of blue sky were trying to push through the steel-gray clouds. I wanted to tell him in Spanish that in our country we say that there is enough blue to make a Dutchman's britches, but I got stuck on the word for Dutchman. His chuckle sounded like rain splashing down a drain.

"Here we say 'enough blue to make pants for Saint Peter'." Just at that moment we passed a rickety bus called *San Pedrito,* baby Saint Peter. "Without pants!" he exclaimed and we went off into a hurricane of howls.

At first I began to consider myself quite a wit. I saw a ragged, emaciated burro beside the road and commented in deliberate Spanish, dropping each word like a stone, "That poor little burro. He has no flesh on the bones. He has only skin on the bones." This brought on a windstorm of merriment, yet I had been making no joke. Deflated, I concluded that my American accent was what was adding to the fun. However, he nearly had to stop the car when I pointed out a huge man in billowing pants and remarked, quite wittily I presumed, "That big stomach! He is wearing the pants of Saint Peter." Later that day, the sight of a bus banging along, covered with dust and held together only by faith brought on a cyclone of hysterics. Its label in front proudly claimed it to be "Super Taxi" and, in case there was any doubt about its merits, on the back window, scarcely visible through the grime, was another label boasting that it had *Servicio de Lujo*—"De Luxe Service." To Senor Godoy and his spotless, golden taxi, to call such service "de luxe" seemed preposterous.

All went well as we dipped and shot up like a looping carnival ride through the mountains of the Sierra, colors of green and brown blurring together like patterns in a paisley shawl. Still I could not resist looking closely at the highway to see if there were shoulders wide enough for a bicycle, to assess the smoothness of the pavement, and to judge the amount of traffic. Once we did pass a young man pedaling along and I was envious.

"If I were only a man," I thought. "If it were only safe for a woman to bicycle in South America!"

In less than an hour we turned west away from the brown and green fields like paisley shawls. At the top of a high hill we abruptly dropped down into subtropical country, covered now with all-green shawls. Suddenly we came upon a line of waiting cars.

Landslide! The single line of traffic was pinned between the mountain on the left and the chasm on the right. We had to stop, and the upturned corners of Senor Godoy's mouth turned down, with no visible hint of the familiar chuckle. Bulldozers already were gnawing away on the mountain of dirt that had fallen down over the entire roadway, but the obstruction looked so impassable that I wondered if it would be worthwhile to wait for it to be cleared away.

"I have confidence in you, Senor," I told him. "You decide what we should do. How much time will this take?"

"Only two hours," he answered without hesitation.

"Was there a person underneath?" I asked.

"No," he answered and shook his head. Meanwhile, as if they had dropped from the sky, Indian women appeared with bowls of stew for sale. They padded from car to car with beguiling smiles, lifting up a spoonful to tempt us. "A little bit warm," they coaxed.

Heedless of the threat that more of the mountain might fall down upon them and instantly adjusting to the situation, people poured out of buses and cars and began crossing back and forth over the heap of earth, soon wearing down a path. Drivers of now empty buses that had been on their way west to Santo Domingo turned their huge machines around, all but knocking the crowd off the road. Announcing that they were heading back to Quito, they took in the passengers from Santo Domingo who had crossed the landslide and wanted to continue their trip. In the other direction, passengers from Quito crossed over the landslide and took buses that were now turned around and heading back to Santo Domingo. All this went on for two hours, just as Senor Godoy had predicted, until the mountain of rubble had been sufficiently excavated by the bulldozers to let one lane of traffic through. The instant this happened, one driver who had just turned his huge empty bus around for Quito, somehow managed to turn it around again for Santo Domingo, pushing and squeezing the crowd out of the way. In seconds his former passengers scrambled over the slide again and climbed back into the bus, placidly confident that they would reach Santo Domingo. Senor Godoy, worried about his passenger, grimly watched the bulldozers. When he saw that the passage was almost cleared, he ran back to the taxi, jumped in, and we began to burrow our way through the mob.

"We will not see the market, Senora." He was apologetic. "It will be over now. But I can take you to a home of the Colorados."

"Do not worry, Senor." I wanted to put him at ease. "The home will be even more interesting."

We soon reached the town of Santo Domingo, but hurried

through without stopping until we came to a dirt road leading off the highway into thick tropical bush. We bumped along for a short way and then turned into a lane ending at a hut. An Indian, half asleep, walked out to greet us. The sight of him was startling. *Colorado* means ruddy or red, and this man lived up to the name. The top of his head was covered with vermilion-colored clay molded into a triangular shape, shingle-stiff and sticking out like a large bird beak over his forehead. The guidebook had described the Colorados, both men and women, as wearing paint and little else; but the guidebook's writer evidently had not visited them for some time. This man at least had succumbed sufficiently to civilization to be decently clothed. From waist to knees he wore a wide cotton band with red, white, yellow and green horizontal stripes, which, along with painted red stripes on his body, covered his nakedness even more than necessary.

His costume was rivaled in brilliance by the red fuchsias, many-colored orchids and huge golden cup-like blossoms of *copas d'oro* that festooned the greenery in the plantation surrounding his hut, a small clapboard structure with a thatched roof. I peeked inside and saw a dirt floor.

"Can we go inside, Senor?" asked Senor Godoy, who had noticed my inquisitive look.

"No, the senora is taking a bath." His sleepy face showed no animation.

A woman, wearing only a skirt and brassiere, eventually came out. Husband and wife agreed to pose for a picture, resigned to being curiosities whom people would pay to photograph. A hint of a twinkle came into the man's eyes as he looked directly at the camera, but the woman stared away wearily. Perhaps she had reason to be tired. Near the house were lushly growing plantings of bananas and pineapple, all requiring weeding and hoeing. The man pointed them out proudly to us before we left.

After we had lunch at a patio restaurant in Santo Domingo, it was a quick two-hour trip back to Quito. Unimpeded by landslides, I was back in my hotel before dark.

I was jubilant. If the day's trip had been a test of the driver, Senor

Godoy had passed without even knowing that he was being tested. He cared for me as if I really were his grandmother. When we stopped at a fruit market or ice cream store, he would trot back with something that he thought the senora might like to try, applying no pressure on me to give him a treat. The tip for the waiter at lunch? He suggested an amount less than I had thought necessary. The agreed price for the trip to Santo Domingo? It was all that he asked. And change? He had plenty. I asked him to come the next day to plan a tour of Ecuador.

Early the next morning Senor Godoy and I sat down in the lobby of his hotel with a calendar before us, and planned trips for my remaining eight days in Ecuador, including an itemized account of the total cost. I was encouraged. Even buying two hotel rooms, a double set of meals and paying his daily fee for each trip, the total cost was less than that of one day's car rental and gas back home. The parking fees and gas for the taxi would be his responsibility.

We would go first this same morning to the market at Ambato south of Quito, a short day trip. Tomorrow we needed time to make arrangements for subsequent trips: a two-day trip north to *la frontera* (the frontier with Colombia), and a three day trip east to the jungle. If possible on the last day in Ecuador we would go to Mt. Cotopaxi.

"We will travel in two zones of the country, Senora," he said, proud to explain its geography. "We are going to Ambato and *la frontera,* both in *La Sierra,* and the jungle, which is in *El Oriente.* Santo Domingo, where we went yesterday, is in *La Costa.*"

The Andes, running north and south, divide Ecuador into three distinct regions. *El Oriente,* or jungle, is below the Andes on the east. It is a large area, sweltering and humid, bordering Colombia and Peru. *La Costa* is on the west. It is a narrow coastal plain extending from the Andes to the Pacific Ocean and is also sweltering and humid. *La Sierra* is the Andean region itself. Like twin spines on the country's back, two parallel ranges of the Andes cut across Ecuador from southwest to northeast, forming the Eastern and Western cordilleras. Between the two cordilleras are valleys, called "basins," which are separated from each other by high mountains. The Sierra has a spring-like climate. Ecuadorians, no matter which zone they live in, consider the climates of the other zones quite inhospitable. Those in the Sierra call the Oriente and coast insufferably hot. Those from the Oriente climb out of their jungles to visit Quito and complain that they are freezing.

We were soon rolling through the Sierra to the Indian market in Ambato, 105 miles south of Quito, where everything that a merchant could grab by at least two legs was sold alive. Puppies, kittens, guinea pigs, and chickens were cackling, squeaking, mewing or whimpering. A tiny baby girl, unrestrained by swaddling clothes of any kind, was lying in a box on a pile of rags kicking her legs happily, somehow avoiding being sold by accident.

Carrots, cabbages, potatoes, beans, fruits—and everything else that could be grown in the Sierra—were piled on tables under huge tents. Senor Godoy, with a cotton flour sack slung over his shoulder, went from one vendor to another, haggling for fruits and vegetables. He would cajole; the portly Indian lady presiding over the pile of produce would scowl; he would plead a little and she would relent a little, until finally an extra carrot or two would be tossed into the sack. He refused to buy a rabbit, which he said his wife loved, because the price was too high. That disappointed me. I was curious to know how we would get back to Quito with a terrified rabbit kicking in the back seat.

The bargaining was more than a casual exercise in psychology. Senor Godoy had a family of four boys, whom he called his *hombres*.

"They are little fatties," he grinned, a compliment in a land of thin children. "They jump all over me when I get home. 'Papa, papa, what is in the sack? Bananas?' they ask. They eat bananas and bananas and then they want dinner, too."

The oldest was eleven and the youngest was three, and when they were not eating or going to school, they were playing ball. He had given each one a soccer ball for Christmas.

"Oh, the broken windows," he moaned and chuckled as he held his head in his hands.

After our day of staying in Quito to make arrangements, we

started our two day trip north to *la frontera,* about 165 miles away; but the trip nearly ended ninety miles north of Quito. As we were zipping through the green and rusty mountains, we were puzzled by a long line of cars waiting at a gas station. Apprehensive, Senor Godoy jumped out of the cab and ran over to the station attendant. He learned that the public employees who deliver gas to the stations were on strike, and that shortly the whole country would be out of gas. We would not be able to get back to Quito if we went to the frontier; nor would we be able to make the trip to the jungle, for which I had paid a substantial non-refundable deposit.

I settled back in the cab, confident that Senor Godoy would find a solution if one existed. He did. After a frantic half hour of pushing the cab through lines at several stations, he had managed to get eight gallons of gas when every other driver had only gotten five. He had plans to dicker with a Quito friend who could get him enough gas for the jungle trip.

Reassured, we followed the rising and falling road north until, late in the afternoon, rolling black storm clouds bruised the intense blue above us as if all the Sierra were setting a stage scene for a tragedy. I was thrilled with the pageant in the sky, but Senor Godoy paid no attention. He was absorbed in the soccer match coming over his car radio.

"Oh, Senor. What a pity. If you were not taking me to *la frontera,* you could see the soccer game."

The smile vanished and he pulled himself up straighter behind the wheel. "Senora, in all my life I have only gone to the cinema two or three times. We have television at the house but I do not watch much. I want to be with my sons and educate them. I prefer to work." Having provided work rather than a soccer match, I felt virtuous.

There were no long lines at the gas stations when we returned from the Colombian frontier. Women with empty cans laughed by the gas pumps as they filled their cans with gas for cooking fuel.

"Ah, Senor Godoy, if there is no gas, the revolution comes," I observed, not needing much astuteness to predict such a possibility.

"Senora, you understand!" he whooped. But the strike was

now over for sure, so next day we could be off to the jungle.

The road to the jungle climbs over the Eastern Cordillera and descends to the gentler slopes of *la selva,* the tropical area between the Andes and the Napo River. So we started out early in the morning, climbing up the rocky road that slices through the Eastern Cordillera. We quickly reached the summit at 13,000 feet. The top of the pass was marked by a blue-robed Virgin encased in glass. She was there for a good purpose, as if to warn: "Abandon all hope who drop off here." Senor Godoy, however, passed by her without so much as a nod of the head.

Suddenly we were dropping, almost headlong, twisting in and out, a mountain above us on one side, a bottomless abyss on the other. After plunging a few miles, the road was less steep but more dangerous. A layer of mud, one foot thick, oozed to the edge of the precipice. Senor Godoy drove so easily over the road, now slippery as soap, that I had no more sense than to suggest he stop for a photograph.

"No, Senora. If we stop, we do not start again. Only the music on the radio keeps me calm."

The music might have pacified him as he contended with the dangers of the drive, but the scenery excited me. Somehow I was not worried about skidding off the road and dropping to the center of the earth.

"You are so tranquil, Senora," he commented. "You are not nervous."

I could imagine that many other tourists would be on the verge of hysteria in such a situation, but my faith in Senor Godoy's driving was complete.

By lunch time we had reached the little port of Misahualli on the swift flowing Napo River, still icy after tumbling down from the Andes. "Port" in this case means that dugout canoes with motors were lined up on the riverbank waiting to carry passengers downstream. Since the river was the only highway into the jungle, Senor Godoy paid the *patrona* of the restaurant where we ate to watch the cab for the two days we would be in the jungle. There was also a "check-point Carlota" near the river, a woman who checked my passport and wrote down a resume of my life before she released us into the jungle. While I was trying to think of my age in Spanish, Senor Godoy, whose mind stored data like a computer, informed her that I was a sixty-nine-year-old teacher who had retired in 1974. He had supplied her with all other desired information before I could think of the correct dates in English.

We walked to the edge of the river and chose the strongest canoe with the most intelligent-looking operator, a necessary precaution as we soon found out. Once pushed from shore, the fifteen-foot canoe shot downstream, dodged rocks and logs rearing up from the shallows, bounced and banged over rapids, and scarcely missed boulders hidden by deeper water. We were only one degree below the equator, but the wind off the chilly water made me shiver. I wanted my jacket, but I had left it in the trunk of the cab.

Senor Godoy, knuckles white, held tightly to the gunwales as we took what amounted to a white water rafting trip.

I asked him later, "Did the trip in the canoe bother you?"

He paused before he could answer. "Yes, Senora, I was afraid. One time when I was young I was swimming. I got caught in a whirlpool. I almost drowned. Before we came here, I said to my wife, 'I cannot go, I cannot go.' But she said, 'Nothing will happen.' Yes, Senora, I was afraid."

After three hours, we had dodged the last rock and were turning shoreward. Soon the canoe slid onto a narrow sandy beach. In a clearing on a bank high above us, we saw our jungle hotel, a large white one-story building, which we reached by climbing two long flights of stairs. We were grateful to find that it had all the amenities of civilization, including meals, private bath and a shower that ran at the same temperature as the outside air, which meant warm.

Next morning the *patrona* of the hotel persuaded us to go on a *caminata,* or long walk, into the green, dripping gloom of the jungle, which, unlike the hotel, made no concession to the amenities of civilization. A guide, armed with a machete, cut our way through the wall of rampant vegetation. We slid down slimy banks, grabbed hold of tangled branches to pull ourselves up grease-slippery hills, and swung across gulleys on lianas. The jungle had everything that nature documentaries on television had let me to expect: umbrella ants marching to and fro in disciplined ranks; blue butterflies fluttering in places where shafts of sunlight cut through the leafy canopy above us; a coral snake with purple, yellow and red bands; soft tree trunks that spouted pure, cool water when the guide cut a hole in them.

For two hours we wallowed our way through the jungle ooze until I thought I could no longer slide down or be pushed up any more. Just then I saw something that the television programs had not warned me about: a waterfall, some ten feet high. Unless I wanted to remain in the jungle for the rest of my life, I would have to climb over it. There was no other way out. There were toeholds in the rocks on either side and, spreading myself over the cataract, I tried to slip my hands and toes into them. But the waterfall knocked me down to the bottom again. I was worse than the legendary frog trying to hop out of the well. I went up the waterfall two feet and fell back down two feet. At last the guide pulled from above and Senor Godoy shoved from below until, soaked and gasping, I was yanked over the top. All of us were hysterical with laughter. Even greater was my relief when we walked a short distance from the waterfall and stepped through a curtain of leafy branches into the clearing behind the hotel, just in time for lunch.

While we had been slogging our way through the jungle, a canoe heading to the port upstream had hit a rock and overturned. Two people had drowned; four passengers had been able to buck the swift current and swim to shore. We would need a canoe to get back to the port ourselves and I thought of Senor Godoy's fear of drowning.

Early next morning we sat on the hotel porch and anxiously scanned the river for a canoe. The canoes are hailed like taxis by passengers on the shore, and soon we saw one putt-putting along in the middle of the river.

"Is that a good canoe?" Senor Godoy asked the host of the hotel.

"Very good," he answered.

After we climbed in it and started upstream, we discovered that the host knew nothing about it. Its motor failed repeatedly, threatening to set us helplessly adrift downstream. Senor Godoy's white fists

squeezed continually on the gunwales until we finally beached at the port more than four hours later. We had chosen the worst canoe on the Napo.

It was a long drive back to Quito, though we chose a safer road than the one we had taken three days before. We did not reach my hotel until after dark.

The next day was my last in Ecuador, and Senor Godoy and I drove forty miles southeast to a road spiraling up the lower cinder slopes of Mt. Cotopaxi. Leaving the taxi perched on a flat place, we climbed a few yards toward the summit, 19,347 feet high, glistening white far above us.

Later, as we drove back to Quito, I thought how well Senor Godoy had taken care of me: he had saved me fifty dollars on the jungle trip by making arrangements himself instead of going to a tour bureau; he skillfully avoided weaving drunks or cars charging toward us without lights when we had to drive back in the dark from the jungle; he suggested tips for waiters that were less than I would have given. Most surprising was the last gesture—pulling taffy from his pocket when the altitude and powerful wind on Mt. Cotopaxi had made me ravenous for something sweet. "I had foreseen this," he chuckled.

"All our trips pleased me very much," I told him, as we neared my hotel. My words were inadequate, limp.

"I did the best," was his simple explanation.

He deserved a good tip and I had put aside sucres for that, but I wanted to do something more—something for his boys. At first I had thought of footballs, but his family did not need more broken windows. Then I remembered when we had gone only a few miles on the first trip, Senor Godoy had asked me if I had a big house.

"Do you have many books in the house?" he asked next. He was impressed when I said yes. Now I had an idea.

"Senor, do your boys like to read?" I asked. His whole being sparkled and he nodded vigorously.

"It would please me to buy books for your boys."

He stiffened. "Senora, the boys have all the books they need in the school. We have periodicals in the house. I want them to work hard and to be very serious in the school." He paused and the stiffness relaxed into wistfulness. "Senora, you have had books all your life."

It was too late to explain that I always gave books to children. I could not have hurt his pride more if I had asked if his boys needed shoes.

The next morning was still black when I went down to the lobby to get a taxi for the airport. My baggage had expanded from a tiny plastic suitcase to a llama wool *bolso,* or bag, stuffed to bursting with an alpaca blanket, three bulky wool ponchos warm enough for the Arctic, a multicolored Indian cap, an embroidered wool dress, and a hand-woven belt. I waddled out to the taxi stand in front and discovered that the only available taxi was manned by the Thief of the Middle of the World, who was snoozing behind the wheel. Revenge is sweet. After my complaint about his outrageous behavior as a driver, the hotel management, losing no time, must have demoted him to the night shift. I roused him and, in a severe tone, asked him the rate to the airport.

"One hundred fifty sucre," was the quick reply.

Quite loudly I asked the bellhop, who was standing near, "Is that the correct amount?"

"Si," he nodded.

"Taxi for the hotel," my Thief of the Middle of the World announced curtly as we drove off. I stiffened defensively. We had not gone very far when he saw a store that was open. "Oh, Senora," he begged. "I want to buy milk."

"No! No!" I all but shouted. "I have to go to the airport." When he pulled in front of the terminal, we both jumped out.

"One hundred fifty sucre," he snapped, "and nothing more." I paid him and he started to get back into the cab.

"But my things are in the trunk!" He quickly retrieved them for me and sped away. I was relieved to see him go before he caused some final disaster.

Later I looked out the window of the plane at the land of Ecuador disappearing below me—the crumpled heaps of mountains, the checkerboard fields, the snow-crowned peaks lined up in parallel rows. I tried to pick out the roads Senor Godoy and I had traveled. Yet I had the thirsty feeling a person has who has only half-drunk his morning cup of hot coffee while walking about the house, and then has put the cup down but can't remember where. The trip to Ecuador was only half-consumed. Still thirsty, I would not be satisfied until I had really seen the country, until I had bicycled through the valleys and mountains I saw below.

4

THIS WILL NEVER DO

ONCE BACK HOME, it hit me that I could get close to those mountains and valleys of Ecuador, drifting through their grandeur as slowly as I wanted on my two wheels. I had already found the perfect escort, Senor Godoy. In his taxi he could hover near, rescuing me if I got stranded between hotels. I felt he would protect me again as if I were his own grandmother. Immediately I began plotting ways of convincing him to act as my support vehicle. The idea excited and enslaved me. I spent an evening translating an article a reporter had written about my past bicycling adventures. It had appeared in the Portland *Oregonian* a few months before. I stuffed the article, its translation, and a letter of gratitude to Senor Godoy into an envelope. The attractive, fat envelope must have tempted a thief in the Quito post office, who perhaps thought it had money in it. My letter never arrived. I found out later that thieves were plundering many letters and packages, especially those from the United States around Christmas time.

Two months passed but my determination to go back to Ecuador did not. I wrote another letter to Senor Godoy, describing the pleasant time he would have in his taxi reading or snoozing while he was waiting by the side of the road for me to catch up on my bicycle. This time the thieves in the post office had either been hung or otherwise eliminated and my letter did arrive. Soon I got an answer.

Senor Godoy was anything but reluctant to be a support vehicle for my bicycle. "Receive my most cordial greetings," he wrote, beginning in the style that courtesy dictates for Spanish letters, "and my desire that this finds you very well in both health and life." After all these formalities, he assured me that he would be very pleased if I returned to Ecuador. There would be no problem for him, and his "super taxi" would be "at my orders" whenever I would like to go and wherever I would like to go. In fact, he expected me and my beautiful "machine of two wheels." If I wanted to bring an *amigo* or *amiga,* I could go more cheaply, he suggested, as the cost would be divided between us. All my *amigos* were married to my *amigas,* I regretfully informed him.

The planes bearing the letters between us may have flown in the air, but I was so excited to hear more from him that it seemed as if they were trudging upon land instead. Could I go to the Galapagos? He would make economical arrangements for me. What would I do with my bicycle while I was in the Galapagos? No problem—he would keep it at his house. What were the distances and altitudes? No problem—he would proportion all for me. I wanted a map—he would have it ready. What would my expenses be? "I will be considerate," he wrote. I knew from my experience with him that I could trust him to give me a fair price.

In short, for him there was no problem, no matter what. Senor Godoy may have been without problems, but I had a few. I had to change airlines, and the new airline refused to take my bicycle unless it was boxed. Nothing could have been more complicated than hauling a boxed bike through two plane transfers across two continents and an ocean. I would have to buy a bicycle in Quito. A phone call, marvelously brought about by direct dialing, summoned Senor Godoy from his taxi in front of the hotel in Quito.

"Senora, *com'esta?* How are you?" he shouted happily, making sure his voice carried over the two continents and an ocean. Yes, he would meet me a day earlier, he said, as he took note of the flight number and hour of arrival. Yes, we could buy a bike in Quito; there were many bikes at various prices.

"At various prices?" I asked.

"Yes, at various prices," he repeated. As usual, there would be no problem. I had a happy vision of showrooms filled with shiny bicycles, presenting a choice of models and a choice of prices.

Two weeks later my plane was circling for a landing over Quito. For the first time in all my traveling I was to be met at the airport by someone I knew. At least I hoped I would be met. The plane was arriving an hour ahead of the scheduled time. "Senor Godoy doubtless will have phoned the airport to confirm the time," I thought. Doubtless he had for there he was, beaming from head to foot as he waited for me to clear customs.

"Com'esta!" he exclaimed, grabbing my small plastic suitcase and propelling me toward the taxi.

We began catching up on news as we motored toward the city center.

"Senora, you have been practicing Spanish with someone," he commented. I was pleased that he thought my language improved, but I had to admit that I had accomplished it by talking to myself: by muttering in Spanish as I went about my house, by uttering uncomplimentary opinions about other drivers as I went about in my car, by keeping up a constant rumble in this foreign tongue and hoping that my behavior would alarm as few people as possible.

"How are the four *hombres*?" I asked.

He began to laugh heartily. If it had not been necessary to keep both hands on the steering wheel, he would have clapped them to his head.

"There are five, Senora. *Cinco hombres!*"

"Cinco!" I exploded. I had not expected this news because I had not been advised of its possibility.

"Si, Senora," he chuckled. *"Cinco hombres.* A girl does not come." The baby who had failed to be a girl had arrived in March and was now eight months old.

When we got to my former hotel, I saw that the staff had changed, so I did not get the welcoming handclasp I had been vain enough to expect. Instead, Senor Godoy escorted me to my room to make sure that everything was ready and then trotted briskly back to the desk to inform them that everything was *not* ready. The bed was unmade and the bath was untowelled. But there were other rooms, even if I had not paid in advance. Before Senor Godoy left, he outlined the two things that we must get done the next day: we must buy a bicycle and make final arrangements for my ticket to the Galapagos Islands. It was the one day shops would be open before the five-day holiday celebrating the Day of the Dead, November 2.

If Senor Godoy agrees to arrive at eight-thirty in the morning, that is the time he arrives. Just like the moving figures in a medieval clock who march forth stiffly at striking time, he rolled up in his yellow taxi, back erect behind the wheel, cap jutting over his face, precisely on time like clockwork.

Quickly we drove down to the wide Avenida Amazonas, a street flanked by expensive shops, airline offices, and travel agencies. We went into the agency that had my airline ticket to the Galapagos, as well as instructions on how to find my "economy launch" once I got to the islands. The trip was so much more economical than I expected that I inquired timidly of the agent if the launch would really be safe.

"Of course," she smiled. "Very safe. You will have a wonderful trip." I found out later that being "safe" did not include a life jacket for the rough crossing to the shore in a tiny motor boat.

An economical launch? Si! An economical bicycle? No! The prices for bicycles were "various," as Senor Godoy had said, but all variously high. For several hours we crisscrossed the city, alighting on every shop that had bicycles. We usually found only three or four, all for men, mixed up with a motley assortment of things that had nothing to do with bicycles like large appliances, small kitchen appliances, and furniture. There were many mud-hopping "choppers" for men and women, such as small boys use at home for jumping curbs and bouncing over neighbors' lawns. There were also a few exorbitantly priced ten-speeds and some cheaper one-speeds disguised as ten-speeds with their turned-down handlebars and narrow tires. But they were all for men.

By late morning we found a shop that displayed one bicycle, among other things, in its cluttered windows. We walked in, passed the acre of furniture and stuff we had no interest in buying, and discovered a lady's bicycle standing alone in a herd of large men's bikes. It had five gears, its tires were scrawny, and it looked as if it would disintegrate after bumping over the first cobblestone. A middle-aged

salesman walked toward us with stiff dignity, exposing a mouthful of
rabbit teeth as he offered a half-smile. I looked the bike over critically, testing its brakes, pinching its fragile tires.

"It is from Taiwan," the clerk explained proudly by way of recommendation. "It is 14,700 sucres." At $180 it was more expensive
than the beautifully crafted bicycle I had bought in Milan and intended to bring here.

"Senor, you have the only woman's bicycle in Quito," I said.

"I know it," he grinned, baring the teeth.

Senor Godoy pointed to the tires. "These are not good, Senor.
Would you make a discount?" The clerk displayed his dental array in
a scornful grin. Of course there would be no discount. We left. We
soon found another shop selling stoves, kitchen cabinets and a few
bicycles, again all for men. One sturdy model from Brazil was like
one of the men's bikes I had just seen in the other store, but it was

selling at a discount, nearly 2000 sucres, or twenty-five dollars less. I held it against me. Even with the seat lowered completely, it was still high, and I had brought nothing but my full bicycling skirts along, only comfortable on a lady's bike.

Senor Godoy felt the machine in all its vulnerable areas and seemed to approve. It was stout of tire and frame, but I did not feel as if I could have a love affair with it, as had been the case with all the bikes I had bought on European trips. Senor Godoy sensed my doubt.

"Let us go back to the man with the teeth," he whispered. "Let us look again."

We trotted back down the street to the store of "The Teeth," the not quite flattering name we had given to the salesman there. The Teeth saw us come in and moved toward us with the look of a person who is sure that his victim is about to succumb. Again Senor Godoy tried to coax a lower price; again I examined the lady's bike and saw nothing but eventual broken spokes, flat tires and gears that would never work. We murmured something about thinking it over and left. The Teeth clearly wanted to say, "You'll be sorry."

As we walked back to the store of the discounted Brazilian bike, I brightened.

"With what I save on that bike on sale, I can buy a pair of pants," I told Senor Godoy. His face brightened at that idea. Back at the store of the bargain bike we found it still resting in its corner. We asked the teenage salesman to lower the seat as much as possible, since I had lost the knack of dismounting by throwing my leg over the rear wheel when I came to a stop.

"We return after lunch. Be sure it is completely ready by then," cautioned Senor Godoy.

Now all I needed was sucres. Immediately Senor Godoy ran up and down the street on a spy mission to locate the best exchange for my traveler's checks—not all banks were in agreement. When I took my checks out of my purse at the bank, my passport was not in it. I had forgotten to remove it from its place for safekeeping, which was down my neck. With some squirming I fished it out while Senor Godoy watched with embarrassed amusement. Later he told me not to let anyone know I kept money or passport there. If necessary, he would pay for purchases, and I could reimburse him when it was convenient.

After lunch, exhausted after having examined every bicycle in town, I was ready to settle for pants at the first store. My only requirements were that they fit and not be purple. Modest as those specifications were, I had to case three stores before I found a rack holding pants that even approached suitability. I picked out a black pair and tried them on, putting the big part of them in back, since that was the biggest part of me. I noticed that Senor Godoy and the clerk were whispering in a corner. I assumed that my driver was merely acting as my press agent, informing the clerk, as he had his family and the travel agent, that the seventy-year-old lady was going to bicycle through the Andes. The clerk was presumably replying, as all the others had, that this was not possible at that altitude for a seventy-year-old lady.

"These are all right," I announced with relief. And shortly we were marching back down the street to the furniture and appliance store to collect the bike. Yes, it was completely ready, according to the young boy who served as mechanic. I went over it dubiously, testing the brakes, worrying about the too-high seat, and feeling no affection.

"Try it," I asked Senor Godoy as we left the store. He got on and proceeded uncertainly down the sidewalk.

"It is well," he concluded after getting off, "but I have no experience with bicycles."

He wheeled the bike down the street to the cab. He then picked it up and raised it to the borrowed baggage rack on the roof, securing it with numerous straps, all of which had to be unfastened when he reached my hotel. Taking the bike down, he carried it into the lobby, past the admiring eyes of the bellboy, who wanted to know how many gears it had. He wheeled the bike to the elevator, which was so small that a yardstick would have had difficulty fitting itself in crosswise. But Senor Godoy was a practical man undaunted by the limitations of the yardstick. He upended the bike, pushed it into the elevator on its back wheel, and we squeezed ourselves in beside it, holding our breath for an ascent of four floors.

Once alone in my room with this unloved beast of burden, I walked all around it and felt truly depressed. I turned it upside down and spun the wheels around. There was something wrong with the front wheel. It wobbled drunkenly.

"Mistake number one," I sighed. "I should have boxed and packed my Italian bike down here. This will never do."

5

DAY OF THE DEAD

ON THE DAY OF THE DEAD, November 2, Indians all dressed in white pad softly to the cemeteries with baskets of food on their heads, spread the food out on family graves, and ring bells to call the dead to join in the feast. At least, this is what I had read in travel books, so I wrote to Senor Godoy much earlier that I must be in Ecuador in time to watch this festival.

"Yes," he answered, "but the people visit the tombs of the departed in black clothes, not white. It is something interesting in the country, these customs, and I think you are going to enjoy it very much."

All Ecuadorians on the Day of the Dead bring flowers to cemeteries to decorate graves, but only the Indians come with baskets of food. What do Indians really believe will happen when they implore the dead to join them for the feast? No anthropologist, apparently, has succeeded in loosening the truth from the Indians, who visit the graveyard wrapped in their legendary stoicism. The Quito morning newspaper on November 2 had published a long article about these customs, which the Ecuadorians also find interesting. The article described the graveyards in Calderon, a few miles north of Quito, but Senor Godoy thought we should go first to Saquisili, an Indian village about sixty miles south of Quito on the Pan American Highway. There the customs were even more colorful, he said, and no outsiders were there to observe them.

We left the bicycle in the room so that we could get to the cemetery early, before the celebrants were too far gone with celebration or left the cemetery altogether. Later in the afternoon, Senor Godoy told me, the drunks on the highway would form a continuous, wobbling wave of traffic, threatening death at every curve.

El Dia de los Defuntos, the Day of the Dead or literally, "Day of the Defunct," was the start of a five-day holiday in Ecuador, from Wednesday through Sunday. Stores, banks, and public buildings were bolted and silent as death, but not the highways. Even with our early start we found cars packed on the road south. Senor Godoy alternated his usual chuckles with worried remarks about the traffic.

"There are many drunks. We must not stay too late. It is very dangerous," he kept repeating. I understood.

I remembered the trip back from the jungle last year when we got caught by darkness, which drops without hesitation or mercy at six sharp at the equator. A black bicycle or two wobbled along beside the highway. Several drunks, heaps of unconsciousness in the ditches, were reduced to harmlessness but posed a problem for their hovering families, who could not figure out how to dispose of them. Not so harmless were the drunken drivers weaving toward us without lights. "How would you like to drive on the highways of Ecuador at night?" Senor Godoy asked, still able to chuckle merrily.

"It would be worse if I were driving and you were the passenger," I suggested. He whooped. He said that being a passenger in the car while someone else was driving made him highly nervous. I understood that, too.

The street leading to the cemetery in Saquisili was thronged with Indians in black, padding along with baskets on their arms, not on their heads. Delicately, Senor Godoy managed to park the cab without hitting anybody, and we squeezed our way up the street past numerous stalls with flowers for sale, both real and plastic.

The cemetery looked like a stirred-up anthill, swarming with people enjoying the commotion and attending to sorrowful duties with uncommon cheerfulness. Senor Godoy was the only non-Indian. I was the only Anglo-Saxon, a self-conscious observer.

Near the gate, the tombstones and graves were heaped with flowers in extravagant rebellion against the bleakness of death. Flowers circled tombstones, flowers hung from crosses, flowers ringed or covered the dusty mounds, leaving just enough room for wine and food, brought to entice *los defuntos* to the surface. A lady in sparkling white reverently laid more flowers at the base of an equally white tombstone. Her black-eyed child, festive in her best red dress, studied me solemnly as I took her picture. Her mother, far from being suspicious of the camera, encouraged me. The child was beautiful, we agreed.

The crowd formed a tight mass in the middle of the graveyard, and the smell of wine and brandy was even more concentrated. The "defunct," probably hoping to spend eternity in peace, would scarcely have room for their bony elbows if they rose for nourishment. With difficulty we squirmed between the bodies of the living and the graves of the dead and stopped before a family huddled beside a tombstone. Wrapped in black shawl, a man sat cross-legged and bent over the sand mound where *el defunto* was reposing. He rang a little bell and, in a soft pleading voice, sang repetitive prayers, which he kept track of by making marks in the sand in front of his knees. His wife, dazed with drink, dozed beside him, her head wobbling over her breast. The rest of the family nodded in time to his prayers and chewed on greasy pieces of chicken.

Sober and businesslike, a boy went from grave to grave with a pail of whitewash, bargaining with the survivors for a price to renew the abode of the dead. His work was well advertised by the gleaming white edifices he left behind him. He came to one family and regarded their tattletale-gray property critically. His price was too high, they answered firmly. With equal firmness he argued that it was too low. They waved him off impatiently. After all, someone else would come along with a pail of whitewash at a better price, and then the departed could go back to sleep for another year, his earthly resting place freshly camouflaged.

A boy about twelve, with a small paintbrush held skillfully between his fingers, was on his knees before a tombstone. He was slowly blackening the washed-out letters that chronicled the vital statistics of the resident underground, and also expressed the hope that at last the departed would rest in peace with the angels in heaven. Not unnerved by the crowds bumping themselves about him, the child traced each letter boldly and did not slip a wisp from the lines and circles. His work shone.

Other children, so solemn that it did not occur to them to play or romp, comprehended all too well the mystery of death and sat close to their parents for comfort. Senor Godoy studied me as I watched the children.

"Do you have regrets for the Indians, Senora?" he asked. I nodded. The spectre of poverty cast a greater shadow than the spectre of death. The dead, for all I know, were rising up at the ringing of the bells to eat, drink, and be merry. The liquor-laden air was powerful enough to knock out a wraith.

We wandered about in the warm sunshine, permeated with the smell of brandy and sweat. I took numerous pictures, which instead

of causing resentment, attracted people to me. Many came with gentle smiles to ask if I would take pictures of a particular grave loaded with flowers. They would pay, they said. When I explained that I did not have a Polaroid, they turned away, quite disappointed.

Looming near the center of the cemetery was a gleaming white vault, open in front. It housed the departed in orderly rows of boxes all labeled fastidiously and dripping with wreathes and bouquets. A priest, in vestments also gleaming white, was reciting prayers on behalf of the family crowded beside him. "The rich," Senor Godoy explained superfluously.

Nearby, almost pushed out of view by the crowds, a family huddled over a wine bottle and small spread of food. The grandfather rang a bell, keening softly on one high note, finger-marking the prayers in the dirt in front of his folded legs. Tears ran down his sun-hardened cheeks. His small grandson sitting beside him reached up and wiped away each tear with the back of his hand. The old man rang his bell, sang his melancholy one-note dirge, and scratched another mark in the dirt with his finger. The tears flowed, and the boy gently wiped them away. For the many minutes we watched them, the rhythm of weeping and wiping never stopped.

After a time we squeezed our way through the crowds into a far corner of the cemetery. Only a dozen or so Indians, drab as the brown dust around them, rested near infant-sized mounds, unmarked except for small wooden crosses. They were bare of flowers, bare of food and drink. The Indians smiled at us quietly, unembarrassed by the bareness. I only hoped that heaven had not forgotten that the last would be first.

Near them a small man, obviously a foreigner, was reading the Bible to a small group gathered about him. He nodded and smiled when he saw us, slapped the Bible to make a point, and continued reading without pause, except to slap the Bible, make other points, and look around for signs of conversion. The almost numbed group listened courteously, perhaps welcoming a diversion that did not force participation.

is Protestant," Senor Godoy whispered.

e Protestants do well here?" I whispered back. He shook

said. Neither of us could present statistics.

ere still streaming into the cemetery when we picked
to the plaza of Saquisili, past plastic flowers, real
water jugs of earth-colored clay with fat middles and
s, and untempting knickknacks spread out on the
shaky tables. As we walked by some soft drink ven-
lled out in what I presumed to be their best English:
"

aining of aching shoulders, Senor Godoy sat down on
the raised center of the plaza. He believed he was coming
he grippe. I sat down too, complaining of nothing but
eas assaulting my ankles.

of the dead," he chuckled, never too indisposed for a
comes up from the tombs but the fleas. They ring
defunct do not come—just the fleas." I scratched
t a happy time the fleas were having after discov-
unoccupied territory of my legs.

d by with his wife, who had a baby in a shawl
pack. The father stopped and poked a bottle of color-
less liquid into the baby's mouth.

"Do not give it brandy," Senor Godoy scolded. "It is water, Senor," the man answered uneasily. "It is only water."

Except for dropping its cap on the ground from time to time,
the baby seemed sober enough. Its parents at least were walking in a
straight line.

Many were not. One man, supported by his two sons, was indulging in a luxury of weeping, loudly reciting his woes as he wobbled along. Completely unembarrassed by the lack of a bathroom, a
woman spread out her acres and layers of skirts as she squatted
down on the ground to relieve herself. She got up, wiped her wet
right ankle with her left and then her wet left ankle with her right,

and walked on as if nothing unusual had happened. I conceded that she had a convenient costume for such emergencies. As far as I knew, there was only one ladies' restroom, outside of a hotel, on all the 300 miles of road south between Quito and Cuenca.

When we finally drove back to Quito, prayerfully avoiding the oncoming drunken drivers, Senor Godoy was without chuckles. By now it was obvious that he was coming down with the flu. He could scarcely muster an *"Hasta manana"* when we reached the hotel.

"You are sick, Senor," I said. "You need to go to bed."

"I will be be well tomorrow," he assured me weakly.

He said he would get an injection, the miracle cure in that country for every ailment one might get. As he left, he did manage to say that the restaurant across the street from the hotel was advertising *colada morada,* an Ecuadorian dish, and I should try it. He would be at the hotel at 8:30 in the morning, he repeated. Off he drove, looking as if he would never recover.

I had read that *colada morada* is the traditional dish for the Day of the Dead, and my appetite was aroused for something tasty. The guidebook wisely did not describe the dish. I walked across the street to Mama Clorinda's restaurant, advertised as *muy tipico,* or very typical, of the country, and sat down at one of the three tables in the small room. The bare wooden tables, scrubbed clean, would seat four at most. A lady was making coffee at the bar squeezed against the wall in back of the restaurant. The red and white checkered curtains at the little window in front, the Italian-sounding name "Mama Clorinda," and the coziness of the place all made me expect pasta.

"Colada morada," I told the waitress boldly when she came to the table. In minutes she brought back a small plate on which was a lonely, flat, unleavened biscuit.

Beside the plate she put a glass of warm purple juice, which she told me was from the mora berry, a fruit of the mulberry family. She indicated that I was to dip the biscuit into the juice, but such instructions were unnecessary. I was forced to soak the dry biscuit in order to swallow it without choking.

While I dispiritedly dipped and swallowed, I looked over to a table near the front window where a father was sitting with three children of descending heights. He organized his charges with the efficiency of an army sergeant combined with the gentle no-nonsense of a kindergarten teacher. I wondered what had forced him to take on his brood single-handedly. Had his wife left? Was she dead? He looked too cheerful for either of these possibilities. "I know," I said to myself. "His wife is in the hospital having number four."

Just then the waitress came up to speak to him. I only caught the word *panzona,* which means "big stomach" or pregnant woman. The man smiled and said yes, she was in the hospital with her new baby, which pleased both of them.

The word *panzona,* used by an Ecuadorian, surprised me. I thought that it was a term peculiar to Mexico, and unknown here. Once when I happened to use the word with Senor Godoy, he erupted into one of his more impressive tempests of laughter. He had not heard the word before. *"Panzona! Panzona!"* he howled. He told his wife and said she sailed off into hysterics, too.

The *colada morada* choked down at last, I left. I felt that I had done fitting penance for a month of sins, and had paid my respects to the dead at the same time.

That night all the noise of the city came through my open hotel window—cars screeching, drunks shouting their way up the usually quiet street, the hotel taxi driver laughing boisterously with the doorman, all the dogs for blocks around barking at everyone and at each other. The guidebook had said that Quito was quietly in bed after ten P.M., but that night everyone was noisily out of bed. It was a long time before I fell into a sober sleep.

A short time later I was startled out of it.

Angry shouts, screeching car brakes, and loud fighting had exploded in the street below me. I hopped over to the window to see what all the uproar was about. Two cars had pulled up to the corner across the street. The drivers, who left their motors running, jumped out to assist, push or argue with an Indian woman carrying a large basket. In the blur of movement and voices I could not tell what was happening. I could not understand a word of the shouts. A man in uniform also ran over to argue or assist, but he was only the hotel doorman and soon returned to his post on the front steps. After a few minutes the cars drove off, leaving me as puzzled as ever. The woman staggered over to the wall surrounding the corner house, and sank down against it. She wrapped her poncho about her and let her felt hat fall down over her face. A small boy, huddled up in a jacket, his hands in his pockets, now took form out of the shadows. Shivering, he came over to stand in front of her. She said a few words to him and again let her head drop over her poncho.

"Is she drunk or is she just getting an early start on a place to sell flowers?" I thought drowsily as I went back to bed.

Soon I heard a crackling sound and again ran to the window to watch what might be firecrackers. The boy had broken bits of wood over crumpled paper in the street and had lit a fire. Sitting down on the curb, he held his hands above it for a few minutes and then ran back to the woman to get more sticks. She dozed on under her hat. I left him there, adding more sticks, rubbing his hands over the fire, waiting for his mother and the morning. The barking dogs had finally quieted down, but were aroused again by choruses of crowing roosters living in the city. At daylight, still perplexed, I crossed the street to see if there was a flower stall or some other clue to last night's mystery. The corner was deserted. Nothing remained but little bits of charcoal near the curb. The guard on the hotel steps did not seem to remember what had happened. It was too ordinary—just a drunken mother unable to get home.

The senorita at the desk, who could not enlighten me either, kept saying, "Poor little boy! Poor little boy!" Like many here, he was a child without childhood.

6

THIEF OF THE TUBE

NEXT MORNING, restored as expected by the miracle injection, Senor Godoy zipped into a parking spot near the front steps of the hotel. At precisely 8:30, he bounded into the lobby where I was waiting, greeted me with a chuckle, and followed me up to the room to help carry down the ponderous bike from Brazil.

"Today we test the bicycle, Senora," he announced briskly. "We will go to the Middle of the World."

I looked skeptically at the bulky man's bike I had bought and knew that Senor Godoy had a good idea. We did need a shakedown cruise. The monument at the Middle of the World was only fifteen miles north, and the road was paved all the way.

We wheeled the bike the few feet from my room to the elevator, again stood it on its back wheel, and repeated the squeezing and protracted breath-holding that we had gone through before. We held it tight against the elevator cage for a descent of four floors. With aplomb Senor Godoy wheeled the bike through the tiny lobby while the clerk at the desk that morning, who was an enthusiastic bicyclist, smiled approvingly.

Once on our way, Senor Godoy surprised me by starting off in the opposite direction.

"We must get air in the tires," he explained. "I know a friend who will be open today."

I groaned. Before driving off, we had strapped the bike to the luggage carrier on top, tightly enough to withstand a hurricane. To fill the tires we would have to loosen it again and replant it on the ground.

"No problem, Senora," he said cheerfully. "I can fill the tires with the bike on top of the taxi."

We drove into the shop of his friend, Senor Borge, which was not a building at all, but an uncovered lot enclosed by a high wall. In a corner was a small workshed, and through the door I saw tools scattered about. In the middle of the lot Senor Borge, watched by two small boys, was operating on a disabled car. Senor Godoy greeted him briefly and then pulled a long air hose over to the taxi, opened the rear door on one side to get a foothold to reach the roof, and proceeded to pump air into the front tire of the bicycle.

After two squirts of air, I yelled, *"Basta*! Enough!"* He paid no attention and went on pumping in air. In one second—bang! The noise must have aroused all the holiday drunks in Quito. "I told you enough," I groaned. He looked heavenward and was either praying or swearing.

Grimly we unloosened the many straps, lifted the bicycle down onto the ground, and in no time he had the wheel off and the tire and tube wrested from the rim. The tube was so blown apart that it could not be repaired. Only a new tube would serve, Senor Borge advised, and told us where we would find the one bike shop that would be open that day.

We hopped into the car and soon arrived at what was a genuine bike shop, ten feet wide, unenclosed in front. There were two or three bikes for sale just off the sidewalk. Assorted tubes, tires and tools were on shelves behind a side counter; and in a black cavern in the rear of the store was the repair shop. We bought two new tubes and zipped back to the open-air empty lot that served as Senor Borge's garage. Changing tires Senor Godoy knew well, and in minutes the tube was in the tire, the tire was back on the wheel, and the wheel was back on the bike. "Ah!" I sighed happily. The tire, unfortunately, was sighing too, but not so happily. Senor Godoy kept feeling it critically.

"I do not understand," he said. "It is losing air."

Again wheel came off bike, tire came off wheel, and tube slipped out of tire. Senor Borge immersed the tube into a tub of water. Air bubbled to the surface out of a tiny hole.

"A new tube and a hole. He is a thief!" I cried. The men laughed heartily. "Let us go back," I insisted, assuming that defective merchandise would be replaced. The two men shook their heads and laughed all the more. Resigned, I found my repair kit in the taxi and gave Senor Borge a patch and glue. Again the repaired tube, tire, and wheel were put on the bicycle. This time while it was still upside down, we spun its front wheel to check for alignment. Aligned it was not. It spun around giddily no matter how they tried to adjust it to dead center.

"The problem is here," suggested Senor Borge, pointing at the spokes. Spokes were something I always let the bike shop at home contend with and, luckily, spokes always behaved perfectly for me in foreign parts. Here in Ecuador they decided to misbehave. All the men and boys on the car lot professed great innocence in the matter of bicycle spokes.

The bike was set upon its wheels again and I took it out for a test ride around the block. The seat, even placed at its lowest limits, was too high for comfort but I could get off without tumbling by planting my right foot firmly on the ground and carefully lifting my left leg over the rear wheel. The wheels at least went around.

"It serves," I announced when I returned.

Immediately we set out for the Middle of the World, after deciding that I would follow Senor Godoy until we made it through the city. Slowly he drove away, keeping me in his rearview mirror while I pumped furiously to keep up with him. We reached the main avenue bordering the central Elegido park and I discovered that the people were not staying home on this holiday as they should have been. The street was packed with darting automobiles. Senor Godoy suddenly whipped up to an overpass at the end of the street, all the other cars whipping up after him. Only inches were left between the traffic and cement guard wall. I dismounted at the bottom of the ramp and yanked myself and the bike to a neutral zone on the sidewalk. Senor Godoy promptly backed down the ramp, snapped the car into a parking spot and jumped out in alarm.

"What problem do you have? What happens?"

"It is too dangerous," I answered. "I cannot follow."

In cities like London or Vienna, I had always led my bike over the sidewalk when traffic was dangerous and, guided by a map in hand, had been able to choose quieter streets. To follow Senor Godoy through the chaos of Quito's principal avenues was a kamikaze trip. With surprising cheerfulness, Senor Godoy lifted the bike up to the luggage carrier, and again moored it with its assortment of straps. Fifteen minutes later, after we had snaked through traffic to the edge of the city, we unfastened all the straps again, lifted the bike down, and off I started.

It was easy. The road drifted down toward the equator, the few cars passing were not intent upon mayhem, and I floated pleasantly along until the hill dipped to an end in a small valley and the road started climbing. I wiggled off the bike seat, lifted my left leg over the rear wheel, and started to push the bike up the hill. Senor Godoy, who must have been tagging me closely, pulled up just ahead of me.

"Are you well?" he inquired anxiously.

"Very well," I puffed, realizing that the sun was boring down directly above me and that I was at an altitude of about 10,000 feet. "It is the heat that bothers me."

"One thing," he pointed out. "The monument is right ahead, but I can care for you better from behind."

This disturbed me. He was creeping along a few yards behind, off the road as much as possible, but still fair game for a tipsy driver to rear-end him. I winced each time I heard the squeal of brakes.

Crawling when he normally would be darting would pull nerves taut and his tension sent waves to me like the humming of a telephone wire. Finally we reached the parking lot near the monument, and he laughed when I pedaled up to him.

"How is it, Senora?" I was fine, I assured him, feigning coolness. Yes, I would soon get used to the altitude and heat.

The plaque on the obelisk at the Middle of the World marked our position: 0 degrees 00 minutes 00 seconds latitude with an inclination of 6 degrees 38 minutes east. Half of Ecuador swarmed around the monument, faces warm with joys of sun and holiday. A tiny boy trotted up to the bicycle, patted its tires and wiggled with delight when I lifted him up to the seat. He kicked his small heels joyously as Senor Godoy and I held him in place. We wheeled him among the crowd, around the monument, crossing from one hemisphere into another several times. After a while I tried to lift him off, but his legs squeezed tightly against the saddle. He was determined to stay there forever. I looked around for his mother, who had vanished, and had a moment of panic. Would we have to take the child on the bicycle all over Ecuador? In a few minutes, quite unconcerned, she waved across to us from a different hemisphere, then slowly returned to reclaim the child with cuddles and words of thanks.

"There is another monument, Senora," said Senor Godoy as he bustled off to the cab. We fastened the bike to the top and followed a serpentine westerly road that wound its way across the invisible equator and climbed high above the plateau on which the principal monument stood. In a few miles we reached the top and again detached the bike so that I could pedal along the road, which had now flattened out or, more correctly, slowly started to slip into the next hollow. I lumbered along until we reached the village of Calacali, tucked in between high hills. A church, a couple of bars and a store or two bordered three sides of the town plaza, but the pride of the place was a five-foot high obelisk, which informed us that we were again at 0 degrees and 00 minutes latitude. A plaque at the base of the obelisk written in French gave credit for all this information to Charles Marie La Condamine, the redoubtable French geographer who clambered over the Ecuadorian Sierra in the 1740s to measure the mountains and locate the equator. His scientific mission was to measure the distance corresponding to one degree of meridian at the equator. After accomplishing this, he continued climbing over the country until he reached the Amazon. He made the first scientific exploration and maps of that river colossus before returning to Paris to write about his South American travels. His writings included treatises upon the necessity of inoculation. He must have measured everything in sight. Later he made meticulous measurements of the buildings in Rome to determine the length of the ancient Roman foot.

I flopped down with my bicycle in front of the monument and Senor Godoy took a picture. I must have resembled a well-used mop.

"I think this will be a joke," he chuckled. Life for us on this five-week trip would consist of a happy diet of jokes, or *chistes,* as he called them, that made us laugh with the senseless abandon of schoolchildren.

There is the old story about the penitentiary inmates who had been treated to the same jokes year after year by visiting entertainers. Finally the jokes had gotten so well known that the literally captive audience had assigned numbers to the jokes so that all the speaker would have to do was yell out, "Number 302!" and everyone could laugh heartily. We got much mileage out of our jokes, too. Instead of numbers, simple things recalled them, such as the sight of a dusty bus lumbering along the highway. We remembered how we had seen one just as decrepit last year which advertised "De Luxe Service" on its filthy back window. "*Servicio de lujo*," Senor Godoy would call out each time we saw one and we would laugh all over again. Such hilarity as ours cannot be explained to sensible people.

The road that had gone up now went down and I started on it back to Quito, zigzagging across the invisible equator. I squeezed my brakes fearfully and tried to control the wobbling front wheel, which had independent notions about exploring what was over the brink on the right side of the road. At first the bulky bike from Brazil descended with so much deliberation that I had to pedal even going downhill. As the hill steepened, I grew more alarmed with each shaky revolution of the front wheel. I had to tack to the left, like the skipper of a sailboat, to go straight. Only by luck did the bike and I reach the bottom of the hill simultaneously and upright.

"The front wheel is no good, Senor," I said, making wobbling motions with my hand. With this news, the grin on his face vanished. Two days of holiday before I was to go off to the Galapagos and all stores were closed. We shoved the bike into the trunk, having decided by this time that this was much easier than lifting it countless times to the top of the cab, and spun off toward Quito. We saw one tiny shop along the way, hidden in a hole in a wall. It was open but too busy to correct deviant spokes.

"We must go to the thief of the tube again, Senora. Is that all right?" It had to be. The gentleman who sold leaky bicycle tubes seemed to have the only shop that worked exclusively on bicycles. This perhaps made him the best in town.

After half an hour we drew up in front of his shop, which was still not closed. Senor Godoy hopped out of the cab and started negotiations, politely addressing the thief of the tube as "maestro." He came running back in a few minutes.

"The thief of the tube says that he has no help today. His boys are playing ball in the park. He has no time."

I stiffened. "Tell him I will buy the tool to fix the spokes. Ask him how much it costs."

His face fell slightly. "I do not know how to do it, Senora."

Neither did I, but I was determined to try, even if I had to stay up all night tinkering and spinning the wheels. Back he ran and soon returned with the news that the tool would cost 180 sucres. I handed him the bills, but after a quick round trip to the shop he stuck his head through the front window of the cab and happily announced that the thief of the tube would fix the spokes.

I leaned out the cab window. "Now does he want more money?" We snorted. Fixing the spoke was more profitable than selling the tool. I gave him one hundred sucres more and only had to wait ten minutes before Senor Godoy returned triumphantly with the bike. He had supervised the entire process, making sure, I hoped, that the bicycle would return with no vital organs missing.

"It is well, Senora. The thief of the tube said you were right. You cannot mount the bicycle with this problem." He went on to describe the machinery the "maestro" and "lying thief" had used to operate on the spokes.

"Tomorrow we will test the bicycle again, Senora. We will go to Mt. Pichincha. There is a road with a downhill all the way."

Yet that night I lay in bed with uneasy premonitions. Hills did not worry me. With Senor Godoy and his taxi lifting the bike and me over mountains I didn't need to wish for downhill all the way. I expected climbing hills to be easier than it had been on any other trip. What worried me was the bike parked at the foot of my bed. What other breakdowns would it suffer? Never before had I started out with a bike that did not endear itself to me at once.

"Oh well," I thought as I finally began to drop off to sleep. "I have always worried in bed the night before I started out on a trip."

7

SHAKEDOWN CRUISE

THE NEXT MORNING Senor Godoy escorted the bicycle into the elevator, through the lobby, and out the front door. The senorita working the morning shift at the desk had not seen the bicycle before. As we nonchalantly wheeled the bike through her lobby, she stared at us, not in open-mouthed surprise like the others gathered there, but with scowling hostility. Why she thought a bicycle would bring greater disgrace to her refined hotel than the stacks of mountaineering gear that other guests often piled in the lobby, I don't know. Nonchalantly, we escaped the black cloud gathered in her face, stuffed the bike into the trunk and headed west.

I was thrilled to go up to Pichincha, 15,696 feet, an old volcano that lords over the northwestern skyline of Quito. Pichincha has a malevolent past and an uneasy future. Since the Spanish conquest five eruptions have been recorded. In 1566 the volcano disgorged its contents, burying Quito under three feet of ash and stones. But later eruptions were even more destructive. The one in 1660 broke down the sparsely inhabited western side of the volcano, creating a gaping hole, which the citizens hope is a safety valve. The volcano displayed its most malevolent disposition when it vomited tons of black smoke and sand upon citizens already terrified by an earthquake— the great quake of August 1967. Even its offspring, a lower summit called Aguagua Pichincha, or "Baby Pichincha," erupted in 1982.

In 1742, the peripatetic La Condamine, when not occupied with measuring distances between meridians at the equator, was the first European to peer into the original crater, which is in the most westerly of Pichincha's three summits. In the nineteenth century other climbers recorded that the temperature in its vents was 184 degrees Fahrenheit and at the same time they got water to boil at 189 degrees.

The highway loops up the slopes of Mt. Pichincha to an amphitheater summit with a ringside view of Quito in the bowl below. To the south were the white domes of numerous churches and, rising above them, the gray steeple of the old church of San Francisco aspiring to heaven. To the north we saw a casual arrangement of low- and high-rise buildings. Across the bowl shimmered Mt. Cotopaxi, an icy fan dancer whose teasing, drifting clouds were one minute hidden, the next minute exposed.

Senor Godoy, whose pride in the mountains of his country was nothing less than paternal, beamed as I climbed above the road to get a better view.

"It pleases you, Senora?" he asked. Only heart and eyes hard and blind as stones could not be moved by the views in the Ecuadorian Sierra, either from the top looking down or from the bottom looking up. Yes, I was pleased.

It is a memorable spot. Field Marshal Antonio Jose de Sucre must have been too busy to admire the view on May 24, 1822 when he and his army had marched in from the coast, stealthily climbed the mountains northwest of Quito and, on the slopes of Pichincha, fought the decisive battle that defeated the Spaniards and won independence for Ecuador. The victory was long overdue. In 1534 the Spanish conquistador Sebastian Benalcazar had wrested Quito from the Incas and founded the city upon the ashes left by Chief Ruminahui, who had burned the city ahead of the plundering Spanish. Nearly three centuries later, on August 10, 1809, thirty well-known and respected patriots signed a revolutionary document, the *Manifesto al Publico*, terminating the authority of the local royal magistrates and "leaving the sovereignty by necessity in the authority of the people." The Spanish President of the Audiencia was effectively restrained at home and his followers were deposited in jail. So peaceful had the takeover been that on August 16, 1809, in a grand ceremony at the Monastery of St. Augustine, all citizens—Indian and Spaniard, priest and soldier, rich and poor—pledged allegiance to the new government. August 10 is a holiday in the land celebrating the *Primero Grito de Independencia*, the "First Cry of Independence." When Quito schoolchildren, who know the date by heart, look out on the mountains ringing their city they must imagine their forefathers, not signing a document in great dignity, but standing on the peaks, waving arms and shouting independence to the heavens.

"The road does not go down yet," Senor Godoy informed me when I returned to the car and looked longingly at the bike in the trunk. He had promised me a long coast away to the west from Pichincha and I had imagined myself sailing down from the heights kissed by clouds to lush green canyons below. Instead we went up and down, passing little buildings where a few people made bricks, farmhouses with tilled acres hugging the rolling hillsides, and decrepit huts managing to remain upright despite their improvised construction.

"There are poor like that in my country, too." I pointed to the mere skeleton of a hut on the side of the road, remembering the tarpaper shacks I had seen beside railroad tracks in the United States. He was incredulous.

"Ah si? Here we think everyone in the United States is rich."

"No, we have poor, too." At one time I had tried to tell him that I was not rich, that I merely saved my money; but he regarded me with polite disbelief. No wonder. Anyone who can take a plane to his country or travel at all has to be rich in his estimation. And he is right.

We finally stopped at the top of a hill and Senor Godoy extracted the bike from the trunk.

"Now begin the battles, Senora," he grinned. I looked at the unpaved road, cut through with ruts as large as ditches, strewn rocks and slithering gravel. I would have battles all right. To make it worse, the black pants I had bought in Quito never seemed to fit no matter how I twisted them. They wanted to creep off my waist and escape me. Giving them one last hitch, I pulled myself onto my bike and started off.

The road went down but it would not be correct to say that I coasted down it. Grabbing the brakes, I bumped through the ruts and skidded on the gravel as I steered from one side to the other to get to smoother places. The bike and I shook like an old Ford with-

out springs going down a huge washboard. I clamped my mouth
shut. If I had opened it, my teeth would have fallen out. A truck
driven by a policeman passed me and the passengers piled in the
back yelled out, "He follows! He follows!" I found out later that the
policeman had been in a huff because Senor Godoy was going too
slowly on that narrow road. He pacified the officer by explaining

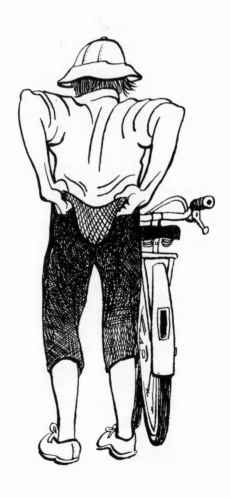

that he was only caring for the senora. As I rounded a corner, a small scruffy dog bristled toward me, barking fiercely. Nothing arouses a dog's warfare instincts more than moving bicycle wheels. Within seconds Senor Godoy had pulled up beside me, jumped out and ordered the dog off the road. Vanquished, it sulked away with a rumbling growl to the small boy who owned it.

The dog was not the only creature who was vanquished. "This road is too difficult," I admitted. "I am going to lose my teeth."

"The road does not serve for a bicycle?" Senor Godoy seemed surprised, but soon he was laughing happily and piling the bike and me back into the taxi, a lifting and stuffing operation that had become routine by now. He handled the bike as if it were a toy. After a few miles the road leveled off and we reversed the routine—he pulled out the bike and set it down. I twisted my new pants around my waist again and started riding.

We entered the gorge of the Pichan river, which tumbled down the mountainside beside us. A few houses were plastered against the hills on the left while others perched above the river on the right. The mountains closed in upon the road and soon we were burrowing into the shadows of a canyon. Green vegetation blanketing the canyon walls dropped into the dark river—a dramatic picture. I dismounted to take one. I screwed the waistband of my pants around until what I thought what was the front was in front, and started to twist myself back onto the bicycle seat. Senor Godoy smiled gently.

"Senora, I think you have the *pantalones* on in reverse." That must be the explanation, I thought, but I also concluded that there was no place in sight where I could change them without climbing the mountainside or lowering myself into the river. I gave a final twist and rode away.

We wound our way through the gorge, I on my bike, he following, to a small village, the name of which Senor Godoy had to ask of a passerby because it was not honored by being on the map. The road continued many miles beyond the village to the coast. Its state of disrepair would challenge the nuts and bolts of an army truck. We decided to go no farther.

We wandered around the village, which was easy because it consisted of just one street. The street was at right angles to a bridge, which crossed the river. A store of casual construction had a brazier in front of an open door and was offering for sale already cold *llapingachos*, mixed cheese and potato patties with fried pork bits.

"Who buys the *llapingachos*?" I whispered. This village seemed like the last place in Ecuador where a tourist or a truck driver would make a fast food stop. "No one," he laughed.

Small villages in Ecuador are the most optimistic places on earth.

The only other store, which was on stilts above the riverbank, seemed to sell nothing in particular or everything in general, but the three laughing and gossiping women in front appeared to be quite cheerful about having no customers.

A scrawny mother dog, who had more food for her babies than for herself, was taking a sunbath at the feet of the gossiping ladies. It seemed to me that most female dogs I had seen so far in the country were either pregnant or had just recently given birth. I asked to see the puppies and a woman, who smiled like a grandmother, showed me eight squirming creatures under the store.

After admiring the puppies, I walked to the middle of the bridge and stood for a while watching a woman and her daughter scrubbing clothes against the stones on the bank of the river. They waved gaily in my direction. The already scrubbed white clothes spread out on the bank to dry looked spotless. Senora Godoy, I learned, also achieved snow-white results without a washing machine.

It did not take us long to exhaust the village scenery and after a half hour we decided to return to Quito. The most interesting reading material in the cab were our two maps. After studying mine, I felt that there might be a road that would curl back northeast to Quito by way of the monument to the Middle of the World. Tucking the bicycle into the trunk, we bounced off, relishing the adventure of discovering a new road. But there was no new road to discover. The road leading off to the northeast passed through a half-awake village, bumped over ruts, dipped under running streams, and finally offered two choices—a swamp or a pathless route through a forest. A pair on horseback, elegantly accoutred, pranced near us and we hailed them to ask directions. They waved haughtily in the direction of nowhere and trotted off. I now understood the cliche, "pranced off on a high horse."

"The rich are not amiable," sighed Senor Godoy as we turned back to bump over the same ruts, ford the same streams, and dodge the same rocks until we reached the same road on which we had started that morning.

Halfway up a hill we saw two distressed men hovering over a stalled car.

"I must help," Senor Godoy announced. If he did not, it seemed, the two would be stalled there forever, miles from a service station. He examined the engine with the critical eye of a surgeon, ran back to his own car and promptly returned with the correct op-

erating tools in hand. Soon all three were bent over the front of the car, heads swallowed up by the ailing engine. In the meantime, I had seen an empty animal shelter where I could change my reversed pants. After switching them around, I no longer hitched and twisted. By the time I ran back to the car, the bodies bent over the engine had straightened up and the machine was making hopeful chugging sounds.

"Ah si!" they all shouted and in moments the car was on its way back to Quito.

Senor Godoy was disgusted. "Imagine! The only tools they had were a razor, a nail cutter, and the stocking of a woman. All this is avoidable."

He showed me his array of tools in the trunk. "My car is new, but the day I bought the car I bought all these tools." I was impressed. There were more tools than I could identify.

Before getting back in the car I examined the front of my slacks, now in front of me where it belonged. I saw a loosely knit pouch which I had no hope of filling. "Senor! These are maternity trousers!"

A hurricane of howls! "Yes, Senora, I knew. The lady in the store said to me that the trousers would not be appropriate for the senora, but I told her that if the senora was happy and did not know the difference, it was well."

So the clerk and Senor Godoy were not whispering about the prowess of the seventy-year-old lady who was about to bicycle over the Andes, but about the sanity of the old lady who was considering buying a pair of maternity pants. At least the pants would give me a youthful feeling.

Senor Godoy scrubbed his oil-stained hands on the moist pads I always brought along for cleaning up, and we again were chugging up the hill. Within half an hour we saw another stalled vehicle—a truck loaded with bananas and packed with helpless passengers in the front cab. Senor Godoy secured the taxi from rolling backward down the hill and jumped out to diagnose the ailment. Again the deceased engine swallowed heads. Senor Godoy operated swiftly with his tools, the motor began throbbing happily, the truck was on its way, and we were loaded with bananas from the grateful patient.

By late afternoon, just as we were cresting Mt. Pichincha above Quito, I suddenly discovered that I did not have my purse. I let out a yell and we began to backtrack. It had been on the seat beside me, but I must have knocked it out of the car when I got out to take a picture. We searched all the places where I could have dropped it, but it was gone forever. I moaned to myself, "I don't understand it." For years I had traveled and had never lost anything more important than a map. I moaned all the louder each time I thought of another item now gone for good: keys to the hotel strongbox; about sixty dollars; my favorite pen; worst of all, my glasses.

Senor Godoy clenched his fist and hit the steering wheel. "I thought this day would turn out better," he wailed.

On the way to the hotel I recounted all the valuables I had stored in the hotel strongbox: all my traveler's checks; passport; the tickets and papers for the five-day trip to the Galapagos, which would be starting early the the next morning. Of course, the hotel manager would open the box, I assumed, and probably fine me one hundred dollars for losing the key. Both of us began plotting how we would extract my belongings from the box if the hotel manager were away. Senor Godoy was in favor of picking the lock, or if that failed, discharging a mild form of dynamite. I was resigned to paying the fine, or, in the best of circumstances, offering a bribe.

The less than cordial senorita whom we had left that morning was still at the desk of the hotel when we returned. She greeted the bicycle with anger and ordered it pushed into an out-of-sight hallway. I had lost the key to the strong box? She glared at me and I suspected that she had been praying for this moment all day. Now she had it. She took out the document I had signed when I first filled the little strongbox and thrust it toward me.

"Since you do not have your glasses," she hissed in English. "I will read it to you."

She read slowly, letting each word scald me as it landed. I was to assume responsibility for the key. If lost, I was to pay $50, etc.

"See. Here is your signature." She jabbed a finger at it. I had to confess that the signature was mine. I insisted speaking to the manager. Tomorrow I had to leave early for the Galapagos, I told her, and all the necessary documents for the trip were locked in the strongbox. The senorita picked up the phone and soon was talking in Spanish. Senor Godoy, ears like antennae, was concentrating on every word.

"The manager will be here after six o'clock," she announced when she put down the phone.

"Please, can I talk to the manager? I have to open it," I begged. "He is not at home," she snapped.

We went up to the room followed by the bellboy with an extra key. I had forgotten to leave mine at the desk in the morning so now it was lost with the purse. I sat down and decided that my once-a-decade bawl was overdue. Senor Godoy sat opposite me, hands folded, patiently waiting.

"Senora, what disturbs me is this," he said when the brief shower had blown over. "She was lying. The manager was home. I heard her talking to him. When you come back from the Galapagos, you should not stay here." He was too tactful to say that the girl also detested me.

"Senora, you should not be here alone. I want to take you to my house." He must have envisioned me leaping from the window.

Soon we were all packed into the car again, including the pariah bicycle, which was to stay at the house of Senor Godoy's father, out of the reach of the five boys. About ten miles north of Quito, we turned west off the Pan American Highway. After bumping along a dirt road that slanted across a empty field and then turned northward, we started down a wide unpaved street between scattered stucco houses, a small store or two, and several stretches of brick walls that hid everything behind them. Senor Godoy had told me once that his house was in the country—and I did see lanes meandering off into farm country and sloping westward to the mountains—but this was the town of Calderon, or at least the dusty, frayed edge of it. The houses, once painted in pastel blue, pink, yellow, or buff, were now so faded that they blended with the dirty yards in front. There were no sidewalks. We saw two or three small boys playing in the street, happily throwing stones at each other. We slowed down at a brick wall and pulled to a stop in front of a drive-way leading to a stucco house large enough to shelter six rooms.

"This is the house of my father," Senor Godoy explained as he got out of the car. A dark-haired young woman who was washing a car in the driveway, glanced at us, gave a hint of a smile, murmured *"Buenas tardes"* softly and went on scrubbing. Senor Godoy whis-pered that she was the youngest of his four sisters.

As if someone had signaled an event of importance, within min-utes the house spilled out its human contents. A woman, face alive with smiles, rushed out to give me a hug.

"This is my mother," explained Senor Godoy.

"Oh, how terrible to have lost a purse," she commiserated. "Did it have money? You lost money too?" The words babbled on. "You are going to go to the Galapagos? How beautiful. Happy journey!"

After a few more words with Senor Godoy, the first-born of all her six children, she ran back to the house. A young man, quite drunk, appeared next at my elbow and greeted me in hesitant En-glish. He was having difficulty maintaining his vertical stance. "This is my uncle," Senor Godoy said, and I remembered that he had told me about an uncle, his father's younger brother who was only two years older than he was. They had gone to school together as little boys.

"You speak English," I said to the uncle, hoping he would stay upright long enough to answer.

"My English poor," he answered, straining to translate. His speech sounded like mush. "I lived in San Francisco. I worked cook—restaurant there. Too hard in America. I am back. You work too hard in America. So hard get along." He tottered dangerously toward me. "You go on bicycle? Beautiful!"

"Senora, here she is! It is *la tia la monja*—my aunt the nun!" Se-nor Godoy cried out and I saw a nun climb out of a car behind us. He had mentioned her before and I hurried over to greet her. Speaking in clear English, she told me she had taught in a San Francisco convent for twenty years, and that now she taught English and religion to young girls in Guayaquil.

"You must come to Guayaquil," she insisted. "You must stay at my convent. It is much safer than the hotels; they are not safe." I nodded.

Guayaquil in Ecuador, a large, dangerous port city, is preferably visited under military escort, provided the military happens to be in power at the time. She wrote her address on a small piece of paper.

"Your nephew is an excllent driver and guide," I remarked as I took her address. She brightened.

"I am glad to hear it," she said, as if she were a parent whose child I had just complimented. "But he does not speak English. I guess he does not know a single word."

Just then the uncle managed to totter over to greet her, but was scolded away. "You are not my brother if you are drunk," she reminded him. He slipped away like a whipped puppy. Senor Godoy informed me later that his uncle's wife had left him for another man.

The bicycle was stowed somewhere away from the hands of Senor Godoy's "five *bandidos*," as he often called them, and we again bumped up the street for a short distance. I looked at the brick walls, wondering which concealed his house.

Soon we turned into a lane where there was no brick wall and I stifled my surprise. I had expected a house large and strong enough to protect itself against five boys. Instead, we stopped at a blue stucco house so small that I could have gone from one side to the other in less than twenty ladylike paces. Off to the side of the house was a tiny detached building and through its open door I saw a toilet. It was a privy with plumbing and a shower. In front of the house a few undersized chickens pecked at the dirt without results. The house had two front doors that stood a few feet apart, and I followed Senor Godoy through one and came into a room that was no more than eight feet square. The wooden floor did not always meet the walls, leaving gaps, as if an amateur carpenter had not measured accurately.

Senor Godoy brushed imaginary dust off the room's one chair that stood tight against the wall.

"Please sit down, Senora," he said and then rushed off.

Two double beds, neatly made up, were at right angles to each other against adjacent walls. It would be just possible to squeeze between the end of one and the side of the other. From my chair I could have stretched out my feet and rested them on the bed pressed against the opposite wall. A narrow chest of drawers, with a few articles arranged on top, was tucked in between the side of that bed and the door.

Senora Godoy, wrapped in a brown poncho and holding the most recently arrived baby, came into the room and nodded to me with shy confusion. Her brown hair, curling softly around her face, hung in a ponytail down her back. The gentleness of her delicately formed face and the daintiness of her figure made her look like a young woman of twenty-one, ten years younger than she was. I stretched out my arms to hold and cuddle the baby, but when I took him he looked at me with alarm and soon set up a howl. He was as powerful as his howl and could have fought himself out of my grasp. I returned him to his mother. Still not having said a word, she left me. For some awkward moments I sat there alone, listening to the voices in the next room. After a few minutes, I got up, walked through a narrow door next to my chair, and entered a room only slightly larger. The one double bed in this room took up half the space. Above it hung a knotted twine hammock for the baby. A picture of the Sacred Heart of Jesus hung above the dresser against a wall opposite the second front door. Everything in the room was established in its appointed place—on the dresser was a TV with an eight-inch screen, a votive candle, a school book. On a small oblong table was an electric iron.

Now I saw the narrowness of the house. It was no wider from front to back than these two rooms; and except for a small alcove off one end of this combination bedroom-living room, these two tiny rooms made up the only space in which this family of seven could live. I ventured to smile at the senora, who took up a broom and started to sweep the wooden floor, which seemed quite unnecessary because it looked as if it had just been swept. Almost blushing she smiled at me and, trying to keep the wool poncho on her shoulders out of the way of the broom, she continued sweeping, as if she should be doing something but did not know what. She still had not spoken, she only smiled.

One by one the little boys who were ambulatory and not in school came in and, prompted by their mother, shook hands with formal courtesy. They looked as if they were about to enter an American jogging course, sweat shirts and pants still clean from the washtub, tennis shoes unsoiled, all scrubbed in a manner to which boys usually do not like to accustom themselves.

"The senora would like some coffee," my host said to his wife and she moved about softly as a mouse, putting a white tablecloth on a table that nearly filled the alcove off the bedroom-living room.

After she covered the cloth with a plastic sheet, she tiptoed into a narrow space off the dining area where she worked noiselessly around the small sink and gas burner. She soon poured me a cup of coffee.

Senor Godoy and I had just sat down alone with our cups when an audience drifted in the door and gathered around—members of the family whom I had not met. Senor Godoy was the oldest of six, and only he and a married sister no longer lived at home. Two of the sisters remained standing beside the door and regarded me with dark-eyed solemnity.

"She is going to the university," he said of one and I congratulated her.

"What are you studying?" I asked.

"*Ingles,*" she murmured, too embarrassed to say a word in that language. In a muffled undertone, she told me what else she was studying, but her Spanish was difficult to understand. The other one was teaching school at a remote village in the country, and she only opened her mouth when I told her I knew what a hard job she had.

"Yes, very difficult," she agreed. "We have seventy pupils. There are two of us teaching in the school. Seventy pupils!" She sighed and looked up at the ceiling, shaking her head.

Senora Godoy tiptoed up with a plate of two biscuits and put them on the table. "*Colada morada,*" Senor Godoy explained chuckling, but the "*morada,*" or juice, was missing. We were to dip the biscuits in our coffee.

We heard half-running steps outside the door, and Senor Godoy, the father of the family, bustled in, creating a breeze that stirred the room. He shook my hand vigorously. How did I like his country, he wondered, and why did I not move here if I thought it was so beautiful? While I was thinking of a polite way to explain that these two situations, liking Ecuador and moving here, were not necessarily compatible, a young man, unnoticed, had sat down in a chair near our table. Silent as a ghost, he must have mesmerized himself into the crowd. I thought he only came in to stare at the floor. The elder Godoy laughed jovially.

"This is my other son," I thought he said. "He wants to marry you."

"Me?" I cried out. There was a roar of laughter. He must have said that he wants to get married. I was having trouble understanding anybody but my host. At this, the Silent One wished himself out the same way he had wished himself in, still not having uttered a syllable. Having uttered quite a few, father Godoy left the same way he had come—like a sudden wind.

"Do not touch the iron! You will scratch it," warned Senor Godoy as a small child, just three, brushed too close to the electric iron on the small table. Hair black and face square, the child must have been the perfect copy of what his father looked like about thirty-three years earlier.

"He is a *bandido*," teased his father, sipping the last drops of his coffee.

"No, he isn't a bandit," I said soothingly in the tone one uses with the very young. I tried to pull him closer, but he slipped away from my arms like a wiggling puppy.

The stars of the equatorial sky were out by the time I had finished my biscuit and coffee, thanked all the family, and we started back to the hotel to face the guardian of the strongbox. The senorita was still watching over it like a bulldog when I returned, but the manager had materialized by this time.

"What am I going to do with you people here in the hotel?" he scolded, in too easily understood English. "Every day someone loses a key. Look at all the boxes that are missing!" He pointed to an array of empty slots. I went limp with misery. "I suppose you lost your passport too?" I shook my head and pointed to the locked box where the passport lay, at that moment beyond my grasp. "Where did you lose the key?" he went on.

"On a road far from Quito," Senor Godoy told him. "A very bad road on the way to Nono." His description made the place sound beyond the edge of civilization. The manager looked pleased.

"Since it is so far from Quito, no one will try to use the key. Otherwise we would have to charge you." Quite cheerfully he opened the strongbox with his extra key while the senorita at the desk continued glaring at me like a watchdog forbidden to bite. I had gotten more than I deserved.

I sat down in the lobby with Senor Godoy and he told me that early next morning he would take me to the airport for the five-day trip to the Galapagos. When I returned, we would plan the details of the bicycle trip. We planned to go north to *la frontera* first.

"One good thing, Senor," I said before he left. "Because of this I got to meet your family. Many thanks."

He smiled in embarrassment. "The house is very small, Senora. But I have more land. I am going to build a bigger house. When? Whenever it comes." He smiled again and shrugged his shoulders. In a moment the smile vanished like the turning out of a light. "Senora, will you be tranquil here tonight? You are tranquil now?" He poured an anxious look over me as if I were going into life-threatening surgery in the morning.

"Yes, of course I am tranquil," I assured him.

Not quite convinced, he hurried out to his car.

Unconvinced myself, I sank heavily into bed that night. When I closed my eyes, I saw a truck ramming into Senor Godoy's little taxi and my house in America filled with five orphan boys and a grieving widow. I saw the clumsy bike from Brazil coming apart as I sailed down a mountain road. I imagined myself flying into bits, hurtling into an abyss, and breaking into a hundred pieces. If I didn't close my eyes, I sat up and groaned. "This is all a mistake. This bike trip is going to be a disaster."

8

ZERO CENTIGRADE, ZERO LATITUDE

LIKE THE HORNS of an impaled elk, the bicycle handlebars stuck out beneath the lid of the taxi trunk as we bounced down the road into Calderon to take leave of Senor Godoy's family. I had just returned from admiring iguanas, turtles, blue-footed boobies, red crabs and frigate birds on the Galapagos and had come back to Quito convinced that I had seen enough iguanas, turtles, boobies, crabs and frigate birds for the time being. I was restless to start bicycling. As promised, Senor Godoy had "proportioned" my trip so that I would not have to pedal at 10,000 feet after rising abruptly from the sea level of the Galapagos.

We spent a day touring Quito, pushing our way through the crowded old streets, winding among the hills, loitering among the sidewalk vendors hawking fruits and ice cream from their pushcarts, creeping softly into old churches with altars sheeted with gold leaf, photographing the secluded courtyard of the presidential palace watched over by costumed guards who appeared to have no other existence beyond that spot to which they were glued.

Having spent the day readjusting to the altitude, I was now ready to travel north to the frontier with Colombia. Why north? Because the Andes generally slope slightly downhill in that direction, and the heights are less formidable than to the south. When Senor Godoy said he would proportion my cycling, he meant what he said. We would tackle the south later.

Only three *hombres* were home when we pulled up in front of his little house. The baby was snoozing in his hammock above his parents' bed. The three-year-old, whose face was an exact copy of his father's, followed his mother about the house. The oldest, still a thin-bodied twelve-year old, gentle in manner, shook my hand with the propriety of a foreign diplomat.

"You will go to *la escuela* in the afternoon," I commented. He straightened up proudly.

"To *colegio*," he corrected. "To *colegio!*"

To say one goes to *escuela*, or primary school, when one goes to *colegio*, or junior high or high school, is as much of a mistake as accusing a Ph.D. candidate of working toward his B.A. I bowed with exaggerated respect and we both grinned.

Senor Godoy soon appeared with the trim canvas overnight bag his wife had packed for him. Later, on the trip, out of the bag would come white handkerchiefs ironed and folded into exact rectangles, jersey shirts with collars pressed to a sharp point, trousers with knife-edge creases, all accomplished by the iron that must not be touched or scratched. After putting the bag into the cab, he pulled out from the back seat a fistful of long candles for his wife to light day and night to safeguard us for the five-days trip. With the enthusiasm of a papa bear he hugged his small three-year-old and exchanged respectful nods with his oldest, *hombre* to *hombre*. With a wistful look, he asked his wife to kiss him good-bye and then, moving like mercury, bounced into the driver's seat. We all waved continually as the cab backed away. On the way north we planned to spend a day visiting the Indian market at Otavalo so we would take three days to reach *la frontera* and two days to return.

I waited until the Quito traffic had thinned out and the road gave signs of going downhill before I asked Senor Godoy to lift the bike from the trunk. Ominously, we stopped beside a little roadside cross that marked the spot where a luckless traveler had plunged to his death in the abyss below. Fresh flowers ringed the base of the tiny memorial, probably left by the family on the Day of the Dead in sorrow or in supplication.

"Begin the battles," Senor Godoy chuckled as I hitched up my *pantalones maternales*, as he called them, and flew off; at least I was soon convinced that I was flying. Far below on the right, the Guylla-bamba River cut through the mountains. As trucks snorted past me, my hands soon began to ache from holding the brakes. Fortunately, the bicycle seemed to have conservative notions about going down-hill. Instead of swooping down like an eagle, I circled down the mile-long hill like a deliberating buzzard. This was good. I have learned not to trust steep hills. I was shaking and rubbing my aching hands at the bottom near the bridge over the river when Senor Godoy whisked in beside me and got out of the cab.

"*Esta bien*, Senora?" He grinned as I continued shaking out my hands. "The problem, Senora, is that in the Andes the road goes up as well as down."

We looked north to the road ahead. It was definitely going up and, according to Senor Godoy, would do so for some way until it reached the height of 10,650 feet, only the top of that particular hill, and quite a modest height for these parts. We stuffed the bike into the trunk and purred upward past brown and tan mountains, scrambled mud pies piled together. In places, acres of sheer rock poured down from the summits, flowing into patches of scrubby brown, yellow, orange and dying green vegetation, waiting for the rainy season next month. But colors change rapidly in the Ecuadorian Sierra. When we reached the top, we saw deep in a valley a river snaking a thin course through now green mountains, broken up by interlocking ridges. The ridges sheltered fields, orchards, and a few villages that eased up the mountainside above and hung like embroidery on the hem of a skirt.

"Begin the battles," the custodian of the bike called out again with his usual cheerfulness and I began the gentle forty-mile descent to the hacienda where we would spend the night. To Senor Godoy life was a continual succession of "battles," as he said, which he fought with his unfailing weapons of humor and persistence. He fought battles helping his boys achieve in school, stopping their pummeling and scuffling before the house collapsed, bartering for food to give them strength for more pummeling, and now watching me pump away on a bicycle. Like a charging warrior, he called out "Begin the battles!" each time I charged off on the bike. I felt like Don Quixote galloping off to find a windmill.

Before I had left home, a friend to whom I confided my intentions for an Ecuadorian bicycle trip said she could see it already—Senor Godoy creeping along beside me in his taxi, protecting me from even a breath of hostile wind. We had laughed. It was quite ridiculous. But that was just what was happening. The little yellow Peugeot crept behind me, seldom more than fifty yards away. Each time I stopped to take a picture, faithful as Sancho Panza, he would jump out of the cab, run up crying *"Esta bien?"*—Are you okay?—and then help me unzip the camera case. If I started to push the bike up a small hill, he would whip past me, park the cab at the top and run back crying out quite happily, "I help you." He pushed the bike up the hill himself while I, who had been pushing bikes up hills for years, walked up with my hands clasped behind my back as if taking a meditative stroll. Occasionally he rode the bike up the hills just to "test it," protesting meanwhile that he did not have experience with bicycles. Did I need suntan lotion? He would snatch it from wherever we had dropped it last and squirt it on my arms and hands, laughing merrily if it squirted on the ground instead. Did I need a drink? He would bring forth the Boy Scout canteen, brightly covered in red nylon. Ridiculous? Far more touching than ridiculous; I had not been so well cared for since infancy.

The two maps we had of Ecuador were forever contradicting each other. The villages permanently engraved on one did not exist on the other, which had its own set of villages. While one map apparently paid its respects to clusters of huts far off the road, which it recorded as being on the road, the other proclaimed that I was just now passing through Santa Rosa, a town ignored on the rival map. Santa Rosa was, in fact, a small village with shops fronting the highway. On the opposite side of the highway was a plaza filled with shade trees, flowers and little girls in snowy white dresses coming home from school.

Most of the towns I passed through were all alike with white, cream or brown stucco buildings; a church with exterior paint peeling away like leprosy; a central plaza, the heartbeat of the town, throbbing with vendors, strollers, and children dawdling homeward from school.

For me, all villages had one thing in common. As I pedaled past, a line of eyes, like black beads on a string, stared at me. At times children skipped along beside me; men held tools in mid-air as they watched; some women smiled as I waved. But Indian women, faces shadowed by large black hats, lowered their heads and pretended they had not seen me.

Always, though, other people stared.

The two maps were in perfect agreement about one thing—I was again about to pass over the equator.

On the Pan American Highway running north to Colombia, this unseen coordinate is marked by an unassuming monument—a cement globe of the earth about three feet in diameter, with the continents in bas-relief. Underneath a tall tree nearby, a bronze plaque, put there by Rotary International, says, "*Este arbol se nutre con la paz y la amistad de los dos hemisferios* 4-11-1983." (This tree is nourished with the peace and friendship of the two hemispheres.) The tree obviously predates the plaque. Long branches from its twenty-five foot height flow gracefully earthward.

As we lost altitude, the heaps of brown land edged into green

fields and large groves of pine trees cupped by the mountains, as if a giant hand had abruptly dropped an emerald veil. A few miles from the equator, the cultivated mountainsides wore patchwork aprons of green, dark olive and rich brown, hemmed at the bottom by fields and orchards, brown adobe huts and tiny white villages. It was dairy country, and in the meadows herds of cattle grazed. But their hind legs did not straddle huge bags of milk. They were thin creatures, tranquilly giving their best at that altitude. Wooden plows were not a novelty in Ecuador, but tractors were. I stopped to watch one circling a field, bumping along slowly over the rough ground, dragging enormous truck tires behind. The purpose for the extra tires must have been to level the ground and so far the farmer must have been only able to afford the tractor. Machinery to pull behind it would come later.

On my right I caught teasing glimpses of icy white 19,160 foot Mt. Cayambe. Its summit is the only spot on earth having both zero latitude and zero centigrade—although Mt. Kenya in Africa, at 0.10 degrees south latitude, might compete for the distinction. White clouds puffed over it, swelling up, rising, following each other as if they were having a pillow fight in slow motion.

In his book, *Travels Amongst the Great Andes of the Equator*, Edward Whymper, the pioneer British alpinist who was the first to climb the Matterhorn, describes his ascent of Cayambe around 1880. His climb was all the more remarkable because he accomplished the feat after a night of trying to rest on a sack of potatoes. He said he regretted they were not mashed instead of raw. His host, who claimed to own the mountain, inhospitably had offered him such a bed. During the ascent he was startled by an enormous shadow that suddenly blacked out the sun, as if it were announcing the end of the world. It was not the millenium, but a huge condor, hovering hungrily over the climbing party. They had to shout frantically to drive it away. The largest condors were said to be found on Cayambe, but unabated slaughter here and in other Andean countries has made them rare. Unlike Whymper and his climbers, I would have taken a fascinated look first before shouting, if the shadow of one suddenly blackened my path as I pedaled along.

Whymper climbed many mountains in Ecuador, including Chimborazo, the highest; but he did not dare tell the truth that he climbed them because "they were there." During his ascent of the Matterhorn four of his party were killed. Queen Victoria was so shocked that she threatened to outlaw mountain climbing. Whymper then claimed that he was climbing mountains to make scientific observations: why did the body suffer so at high altitudes? He theorized that it was because the internal organs were pushed somehow out of balance. He missed the point entirely that less oxygen causes the suffering.

We wheeled into a small dairy by the side of the road that sold crisp rolls called *biscoches*, and *manjar de leche*, a coffee-colored condensed milk as thick as butter. Senor Godoy also recommended Ecuadorian-style coffee, a variation of the French *cafe au lait*. The plump *patrona* first brought us foaming hot cups of milk. She then served us powdered coffee to stir into the milk.

"Is the milk pure?" Senor Godoy asked her before drinking the coffee.

"Si," she nodded. "Very pure."

"Here," he explained to me, "we drink the milk direct from the cow; in Quito it is sterilized and homogenized."

The drink was delicious. The milk diluted the Ecuadorian coffee, which often is potent enough to produce an overnight beard even on the stoutest drinker.

I prayed that the milk was indeed pure, and apparently I did not pick up any bovine diseases.

Instead, I got enough energy to pump along for the rest of the afternoon. Crossing bridges over streams that raced along tossing icy white ripples, I noticed, in the distance, slits in the mountains that held clusters of huts like toys in giant green fingers. The air was filled with a springlike warmth in that land cut by the equator, a land which has only two seasons—wet and dry.

I stopped to visit with a small boy trudging home from school, books in a satchel on his back.

"Where are you going, Senora?" he asked. "You are going all over Ecuador!" He whistled and came over to admire the bicycle. "Good journey, Senora. Good journey!" he called as I continued down the hill.

Lago San Pablo had become dark under the late afternoon shadows of the mountains as I wheeled down to it on the bumpy side road that led to the Hacienda Parador Cusin, where we would rest that night. The lake, 8,848 feet above sea level and 500 feet below Quito, is the largest in Ecuador. As Senor Godoy had said, the roads in the Andes go up and down, but the one to Lago San Pablo had been more down than up. The lake lies in an immense bowl surrounded by green-robed mountains glowering over it—Mojanda (14,088 feet), Imbabura (15,033 feet), and Cotacachi on the north (16,301 feet). The sides of the bowl have been cracked out of shape by the lesser mountains pushing down upon the lake. The surrounding land was as fertile as a greenhouse.

At a fork in the road, Senor Godoy sped around me to lead me in the right direction. I followed him, down and up, over cobblestones and dirt ruts to the walled-in Hacienda Cusin, tucked, as expected, beneath a green mountain. Alarmed at seeing two moving wheels instead of four, several dogs bristled and barked as I pedaled up. While I tried to pacify the beasts, Senor Godoy bounded up the steps to the door of the office.

He emerged laughing. "Si, there are two rooms for us," he announced. "You can come into the hotel, but the bicycle is not welcome." When I entered, I understood why. The hacienda was a museum of antiques. The small office opened into a dining room and parlor filled with Spanish colonial furniture of massive carved oak. Huge paintings of saints covered the walls, probably the same saints who attempted to save the souls of worshipers in the chapels of the conquistadores. All this made me feel like the twentieth century would not arrive for another 350 years. When I went into my bedroom, I was relieved to note that the twentieth century had arrived in the form of modern plumbing, clean white sheets, and scrubbed floors. The accounts that travelers have written about Ecuador's hotels in the last century have been filled with so many tales of fleas that it made me scratch just to read them. The modern flea had been banished from the tourist hotels we stayed in, because Senor Godoy seemed to know how to avoid the ones where the resident fleas had not yet been forced into exile.

I wandered about the grounds, finding my way along paths that wound lazily to nooks with benches and flowers, hidden trysting places for the daughters of conquistadores. After a while I came upon an open road that led to a fenced-in barnyard. The groom there was just letting out a corral-full of riding ponies and pet llamas onto a nearby meadow for the evening. I leaned over the fence and admired the beauty of the sleek, groomed ponies and the sauciness of the llamas.

"You take good care of them, Senor," I said.

He smiled. "Thank you, Senora. The daughter of *la patrona* goes for a ride in the afternoon after school. Every day I take her and we ride up into the hills. Yes, I care for her. She is seven."

I saw him hovering over every trot to make sure the child did not fall off.

Meandering back down the road we had just come over, I saw that the twentieth century had not yet come to the Indian lady who was washing clothes by herself in the small stream below the hacienda. Either she was getting an early start on her neighbors, who would be scrubbing clothes on the stones in the morning, or else she was just getting around to her daily tasks.

The *patrona* of the hacienda was tensely solemn when I registered, not even allowing a flicker of a smile to cross her lips when I complimented her on the decor. Soon the reason was apparent. She did not enjoy being an innkeeper, I decided; and too many guests worried her.

Just before supper a busload of tourists swarmed about the place. I gathered from overhearing their conversation that they were Americans who had just returned from the Galapagos. They were taking the customary hasty tour of the highlands of Ecuador and the Otavalo market before leaving the country. Cautiously they walled themselves from us at dinner, glancing over to our small table in the corner from time to time, puzzling over my nationality and the relationship between the two of us, as we kept laughing so crazily.

Senor Godoy did not need to go on a drinking binge to relax. Fortified with nothing stronger than a soft drink or mineral water, he could abandon himself to high spirits as we laughed over everything and nothing. We would be considered daft by anybody who asked us what was funny, especially when they did not see anything funny at all. All the simple adventures of the day amused us; and for Senor Godoy, laughing expressed relief that we had arrived safely, that I had not been lost or bumped off the road.

9

SEEKING THE LOWEST—OR HIGHEST

FOR YEARS THE INDIAN MARKET in Otavalo has been held on Saturdays. It is a most efficient arrangement for business. The Indian housewife can calculate her shopping needs for a week; the seller can pack up his goods on the burro and trot from one market to the next, knowing that as sure as sunrise the market will be held on the appointed day.

The guidebooks all advise arriving at the marketplace at the brutal hour of five in the morning, but Senor Godoy said there was no sense to it. You see no more at five than you do at eight, he said, and I had been pedaling past people with loaded burros for a day already.

Before we left the Hacienda Parador Cusin Saturday morning for the short ride to Otavalo, Senor Godoy suggested that I put on my *pantalones maternales* because there would be beautiful places to bike after we saw the market. He put the bike on top of the cab, safely out of the reach of wandering marketeers, and locked his tools in the trunk, which now could be closed. It was a morning with all the countryside sun-glinted, sparkling in true color. Lago San Pablo reflected deep blue with wisps of fog rising at its far edges. Quilts of morning-fresh clouds softened the intense blue of the sky. Within minutes we were pulling into the animal market just south of Otavalo, where sellers and buyers were still just arriving. The sun lit up faces, making them glow like amber. The little square was a cacophony of barnyard noises and we stepped carefully around, lifting our feet over weaner pigs restrained by ropes, giving wide space to cows tethered to the side of a shed, admiring sheep, sows or hens tied to stakes or held in arms, according to their size.

The Ecuadorian words for bargaining translate as "seeking the lowest" if you are a buyer and "seeking the highest" if you are a seller. It is an intense game of wits and poker faces. The two principals in a drama we watched had a pig at their feet.

A small audience surrounded them listening closely, ready to take part if one of the actors dropped out.

"Four hundred," said the buyer in a low voice that was scarcely heard. The seller inclined his head toward the customer and almost whispered, "Six hundred" in a lower tone. This went on for a minute, voices getting softer and softer, faces keener. But they could not make a deal. The buyer moved away, face like stone, while the seller began extolling the merits of his animal again, reminding the departing customer that he was a fool not to take advantage of such a bargain. "No better anywhere. Best in the country!" he called after him. But each knew that there was a point above or below which he could not go.

We left the animals, most of which had now become silent, as if cackling, grunting, bleating, squeaking or mooing would only make their fate worse than it was. We got into the car and inched our way through the narrow, packed streets of Otavalo. We eventually found a parking lot where a caretaker was charged to keep his eye on the bicycle roosting on top of the taxi. We hurried off to the market square a few blocks away.

Wandering through the market of Otavalo was like wandering through an art gallery. The Indians were portraits not framed in gilt, but in the reds, browns, blacks, blues, whites of ponchos or rugs for sale behind them in the open stalls. The face of each young Indian woman shone with a proud beauty, as proud as any Spanish senorita in a mantilla flirting behind the flutter of a fan. A white kerchief folded softly upon each lady's head, somewhat in the style of a Renaissance cap, would have been as hard for me to fold without instructions as an Indian sari. It enchantingly framed the black hair, black eyes, and ivory-clear skin. She wore strands of gold-colored beads like a collar upon her white embroidered blouse, and let fall upon her shoulders a solid-color hand-woven scarf of deep blue, maroon, red or black. In her long dark skirt, white petticoat peeping through in front, she moved with the grace of a princess. Coming upon one

suddenly, I gasped at her beauty, grabbed my camera to catch the glow of that face, but the harsh, late morning sun straight above played tricks with unexpected shadows.

The film never captured her beauty.

In Bolivia I had also seen such beauty. The proud senorita who used to stroll about the plaza in La Paz on Sunday mornings had been replaced by the gorgeously dressed Aymara Indian senorita. Her silk shawl lay draped over her shoulders, her brocaded and fine wool skirts swirled coquettishly. Her tiny shoes were like ballet slippers, her bowler hat was perched just so. She strolled along with head held high, holding the arm of a boyfriend, or covertly eyed one if she was with another girl. The Bolivian guidebook spoke of these women as "the rising middle class."

Just as impressive in Ecuador is the Otavalo man. Willow-slim, he has not stepped from anything as prosaic as a bandbox, but from the miracle of his wife's primitive ironing table. She has creased his white trousers to knife-sharpness; he has put on his broad-brimmed black felt hat, tipping it at a slight, saucy angle. He has crossed his poncho over his chest and let the two ends sweep over his back. Stepping forth, head held high, he never disturbs the absolute symmetry of his costume. To be so accoutred without the aid of modern appliances requires a skill that amazes the foreigner dependent upon automatic washers and electric irons—or dry cleaners.

On the trip the year before I had visited the one-room house of an Otavalo woman to buy a bag, or *bolso*. The hard dirt floor was swept clean; the unmade bed was a mattress on the floor. The baby was sleeping contentedly in a wooden box hung by ropes from the ceiling; pots and pans were hidden in the darkness in back. Important as a household god, the large and efficient loom filled one corner of the tiny room. From such a place comes the immaculately tailored Otavalo man and the Otavalo woman, a rival to a flower. If Gauguin had discovered the Otavalo Indians, he never would have reached Tahiti, and would have softened his glaring oranges and reds to blend with the olive green and rusty brown of the Andean landscape.

The huge market square, larger than a city block, flashed like a kaleidoscope with the movement and color of things being worn and things being sold. Booths bulged with *bolsos*, ponchos, rugs, jewelry, and reed baskets dyed red, green and blue. Hanging from wooden rods above the booths were embroidered blouses, long wool dresses with cross-stitch embroidery, one-size-fits-all short dresses with round, peasant neck lines, multi-colored belts, and heavy wool sweaters of many complexions and designs. Tourists bargained tentatively for such handmade articles never seen at home—at least not at that price. Natives bargained skillfully for leather belts, jeans, and clothing, which tourists do not buy. There was a murmur of voices and quiet movement, but no harsh cries of hawkers, no shrill argument. Faces, intent upon each other, warily concealed all expression. Bargains were sealed almost in a whisper; onlookers often could not hear the final price.

Suddenly Senor Godoy grabbed a tiny girl, growled playfully like a bear, and picked her up. She took the teasing with sober resignation.

"This is my niece," he explained. "She is the little girl of my sister."

Just then his sister walked around from a nearby fruit stand. As sober as the child, she nodded to me as if she were thinking of something else.

"The husband is sick," she explained to her brother. "It is his kidneys." Intent upon her shopping, she soon left us. On the edge of the market square a small group idled around a man with a combination can opener and screwdriver in his hand. He waved it about as he orated excitedly about its merits.

"Demonstrating," whispered Senor Godoy beckoning me away. The poor man is desperate to make a sale, I thought, but I had no use for the odd tool.

After seeing displays and demonstrations of many other things for which I had no use, I wandered into the nearby central plaza. It was like other Ecuadorian plazas: benches; flowers beds surrounding a fountain; bandstand, gazebo or heroic statue in the center; shade trees hovering over the benches; paved paths winding about; and flowers blooming extravagantly with no regard for conventional seasons.

I sat down on a bench. The occupant at the other end, a quiet gentleman dressed in a suit now dull black after years of wear, began a formal conversation, beginning with the weather, as one does everywhere.

"No, the weather is not always the same here in Ecuador, Senora. We have the wet winter from December to June and the dry summer from June to December."

I expressed suitable appreciation for this information and we were without words for a few moments.

"Are you from the United States, Senora? I have two sons there. One is an architect. One is an engineer. Very important jobs. But I do not see them frequently," he sighed. I commiserated with him properly.

"Are you traveling in our country?" he continued after a long pause. "What did you do in the United States?" I told him and then he sighed again.

"I cannot work now. I am not well. I do not have good health." I told him I was sorry. Ater he had exhausted the recital of all his problems, he rose and tipped his hat.

"I am at your command, Senora," he vowed and went sadly on his way.

An essential feature of a plaza is a church on one side. And across the street was the expected church, a bulky white building with steps leading to the wide porch in front. What was missing here was a crowd of beggars sprawled on the steps. Senor Godoy had just found me and we stepped inside. There was the quiet rustle of a few worshipers and the warmth and fragrance of candles burning.

"Look!" I whispered happily, pointing out the statue of a saint. Standing serenely in his niche, he was brightly adorned in a baby blue cloth robe with an overall pattern of white and pink flowers. On his head, at a jaunty angle, was a black felt hat. I tiptoed to the little Indian lady intent upon her prayers in a nearby pew.

"Who is the saint?" I whispered.

"San Gregorio *taite*," she whispered back, smiling proudly as if he were a relative.

Taite is the word for pope, or chief, in the Quechua language of the Andean Indians. I imagined that St. Gregory, seeing himself decked out so elegantly, had not had so much fun since he entered heaven in the year 604, after organizing numerous monasteries, writing a biography of St. Benedict, and in general, conducting himself with enough vigor to become a saint.

We left him in his niche, but only after first taking a photograph, and wandered into a side chapel where a young priest was energetically instructing a dozen or so Indians. Not a word could I understand. "He is teaching them the catechism in Quechua," explained Senor Godoy. But I wondered how much *they* were understanding. Some had the unmistakable look of those whose minds are on what they were going to eat for lunch.

We had the entire afternoon left to reach the hotel at Ibarra, only a few miles distant, but first Senor Godoy wanted to show me a mountain lake about fifteen miles northwest above Otavalo. You expect a mountain lake to be a turquoise gem in a concave setting and Lago Cuicocha is just that. The green peaks above extend fingers to hold the gem in place.

The lake is 10,200 feet above the sea, but the bike and I had risen up to it in comfort inside the taxi. This meant, of course, that when we had to return on the dead-end road, I spun down outside the taxi. But I was not going so fast that I did not notice the sky-reaching green mountains on all sides and the tilled farm fields with their tiny, thatch-topped houses. As usual the little yellow taxi inched along behind me.

Soon we had rolled along on two wheels and inched along on four until we reached the town of Cotacachi, where the specialty was leather. It was so filled with leather articles to sell that we could smell them as we wheeled down the central street. Open doors let us see leather purses hanging behind the counters, leather suitcases piled along the walls, leather belts suspended from the ceilings, and leather-colored faces looking out at me as I looked in on them. They beckoned me with smiles to come in and buy. Yes, a purse I had lost, but other leather purses I had at home.

Sudden cries made me stop pedaling. An old lady dressed in black had collapsed upon the sidewalk. Passersby had crowded around her, crying loudly, begging a car to stop, gesturing hopefully in the direction of Senor Godoy, who was creeping behind me. I plotted quickly that I would let Senor Godoy take her to the hospital while I found my way to Ibarra, but it was not necessary. Before Senor Godoy could reach her, another driver was already helping her into his car.

Senor Godoy frequently took tourists to the Hosteria Chorlavi in Ibarra, where we intended to have rooms for the night. He was well known there. When we had started out that morning, he commanded, "Senora, I want you to bicycle right up to the door of the hosteria." "Why?" I wondered. "Is it because you are proud that I have come on the bicycle?" He chuckled and nodded.

After I had lost my glasses, I had great difficulty trying to write. Senor Godoy had been helping me by recording the number of kilometers I had bicycled each day, and the elevations of all the high spots as registered on the altimeter stuck to his windshield. He also took brief scribbled notes about what we were seeing. I had purchased a pair of glasses from a Quito street vendor for three dollars, which magnified print enough so that I could at least decipher a menu, briefly read the newspaper and with agony trace our route on my map. The "glasses of emergency," as Senor Godoy called them, had immediately lost one bow, which refused to stay stuck back on with adhesive tape. After this misfortune, the glasses tumbled off my nose unless I held them in place with one hand. This did not leave any extra hands for holding a pen and paper. I had to be content with a trip diary that was a patchwork of numerals and comments in Spanish written by Senor Godoy in his peculiar scribbling, interspersed with childlike scrawls attempted by me without glasses.

So far for the day he had noted *"mercado de Otavalo indigeno, Cotacachi articulos de cuero, Lago de Cuicocha 3100 m."* I could never forget the "indigenous market of Otavalo" and the "articles of leather at Cotacachi," but altitudes and distances on the bike I would easily forget. I was grateful for his help. When we were near the entrance of the hosteria, he stopped, looked at the speedometer, made a mental calculation, and wrote: *"Hosteria Chorlavi 31 km bicicleta."* A scant twenty miles did not seem important to me, but he seemed to feel it was quite significant. I soon found out why.

He might have wanted me to pedal triumphantly to the front steps of the hosteria, but I was not to pedal in the same triumphant manner *alone* across the Pan American Highway to reach the long lane that led to the front steps. I stopped across from the lane on the right side of the highway and got off the bike to look carefully for traffic. Senor Godoy, who had been following me, whipped quickly past me, made a left turn into the lane, jumped out of the cab, and held up his hand in a gesture that said, "Halt!" I did.

Looking both directions, he crossed the road, took hold of the handlebars, and carefully looked both directions again. *"Esta bien,"* he cried and I meekly followed, never suggesting that crossing the Pan American Highway at this point was not to be compared with alternately leading and riding a bike through the traffic of London or even attempting the crowded ramp in Quito on my first day on the bike. After arriving safely on the other side, I remounted and started jiggling over the cobblestones to the hosteria to produce the effect desired by Senor Godoy. He was not disappointed. Before I had reached the front steps, a small group of hotel employees had already gathered, duly given advance notice by Senor Godoy of my prowess and the kilometers achieved that day. They stared at me with wonder, and said that after thirty-one kilometers on the bicycle they would be in the hospital. I basked in the undeserved praise. Even at that altitude the trip was nothing compared with my solitary struggle three years before for sixty-four miles over the brutal pitches of the Para Para on the North Island of New Zealand.

Travelers to Ecuador one hundred, or even sixty, years ago described the accommodations here as if they were the most primitive on the earth. But the modern tourist can find not only comfort but charm. The rooms of the Hosteria Chorlavi opened off a central garden court and featured Spanish colonial decor. The plumbing included everything I would need and worked perfectly. Outside the hotel, paths wander among the orchid and hibiscus bushes and duck ponds, where the occupants paddled about lazily. That evening the cook devised the best Ecuadorian dishes for our meal: an antipasto of steamed rice layered with slightly spiced chorizo, stews with crisp vegetables, fruit compotes for dessert, served by gracious waiters, all apparently friends of Senor Godoy.

Being around his friends seemed to have a restraining effect on Senor Godoy. We did not abandon ourselves to the usual gales of laughter at dinner. Among these people who saw him frequently he felt observed and obliged to maintain the proper attitude of employee with *patrona*. Instead of chuckles rising to guffaws, there were stiff smiles, nods, a proper bow of the head, just a hint of clicking of the heels when I announced that I was off to bed. He did not want his friends to think that the senora, prone to hilarity, was crazy, or that her relationship with her chauffeur was anything but impeccable. How they could think otherwise was beyond me. I was old enough to be his mother, or even his grandmother. In spite of his efforts, there was a repressed twinkle threatening to erupt at any moment. He was like a playful puppy that you attempt to restrain under the palm of your hand.

10
JUST SOUTH OF THE BORDER

THE SAME RECEPTION COMMITTEE that had met me when I wheeled up to the hosteria gathered in front of the veranda in the morning to give advice about the departure.

"Are you going to *la frontera?*" one asked.

"It weighs too much, the bicycle," suggested another.

"You need a bicycle that weighs very little. The tires are too *grandes*. Very delicate tires are better." To prove the point, the chief sidewalk superintendent lifted the bicycle and shook his head.

I smiled and emphasized that the bicycle was very stable. It did not fall over easily. He continued to shake his head as I mounted the machine whose qualifications were in dispute, waved to the grandstand of advisers and pedaled off, either with too much weight or with great stability, according to whose opinion I chose.

The green hulk of Mt. Imbabura glistened behind me as I pedaled down to nearby Ibarra. I found the city in a leisurely Sunday mood. This was the first Sunday of our trip.

"Do you want to go to church, Senor Godoy?" I asked.

He smiled and shook his head. "It is not necessary. The wife and the sons are lighting candles and praying for me," he answered. I agreed that it was a most pleasant way for him to fulfill any Sunday obligations. With divine protection thus arranged, I wheeled through the quiet streets of Ibarra and out of town toward the peaks rising beyond it. Suddenly a view stopped me. We had come to an opening in the rim of green mountains and a snow-glowing peak, proud, electrifying, had appeared like a Sarah Bernhardt making a stage entrance. "Cayambe!" Senor Godoy cried, his face aglow. We stood for some time in admiration.

"The Avenue of the Volcanoes" is what Ecuadorians call the

Eastern and Western cordilleras of the Andes and the corridor between them. Twenty-two peaks, almost all over 14,000 feet, rise out of the cordilleras within sight of each other. They form a line of volcanoes on the left and on the right. Some slumber and some still threaten. Like Cayambe, they are snow-topped if they are above the official snow line of 15,570 feet.

Leaving the view of Cayambe reluctantly, I pedaled and Senor Godoy chugged away. Within a mile or so I passed Lago de Yaguarcocha, the "lake of blood," only a mile and a half in circumference but more filled with legend than water. According to the legend, Huayna Capac, the great conqueror of the Inca dynasty, battled the rebellious tribe of Carranquis on its shores, and threw the bleeding corpses into the lake until it was blood red. The lake looked so insignificant that you would have to sit down and imagine bloody corpses being hurled through the air before you became excited about it or even took a second look. Now it is only an oversized, muddy brown pond.

To say that the scenery of the Ecuadorian Sierra has variety is prosaic. It is more than varied—it is unpredictable. Around bends in the road I saw mountains themselves change colors with chameleonic swiftness and impudent whimsy. The Sierra of Ecuador makes compromises with seaborn winds, lines of latitude, reaches of altitude, a noonday sun boring down at right angles, jungle steam from the east, the sea and Humboldt current from the west. Here occurs cosmic consultation between all the forces of weather.

As we climbed the hill above the northern Quito basin and rounded a bend at the top, I saw polychrome mountains streaked with brown and patched with green plantations. Huge washes of brown on the mountainside were ominous. Signs warned of *derrumbes*, or landslides; and in rain, drivers fear such forces—overpowering and lethal. I sighed happily that the day was warm and sunny. Over distant high valleys I got occasional glimpses of 16,299 foot-high Mt. Cotacachi to the northwest. The wisp of snow at its round top made it look like a white-haired old man going bald.

Below me now lay a valley, which the flooding of El Nino rains had left as brown as if it were covered with a dirty old rug. I rolled down the gentle slope, gripping the brakes only slightly. I stopped at the bottom to look through a row of trees at a crowd of black youngsters having a Sunday game of soccer on the dirt field below the highway. They ran for yards at a time as the action changed randomly from one end of the field to the other. One boy, obviously in charge, shouted instructions and strategies. Suddenly he yelled, "Rest!" Quicker than an eyeblink, the whole field of little boys rested by running up to the road and surrounding me.

"Please, do me a favor!" begged the leader, all but grabbing the handlebars of the bike. What he clearly meant was that I let him try out this two-wheeled marvel.

"No," I replied with the firmness of one who has taught school for years. Senor Godoy had a warning look on his face.

"Please, a little ride." He was quite insistent. I was equally adamant. "Then all of you will want to. It is not possible."

"They do not know how. I know how." I understood how he had become the leader.

"I would like a photograph," I suggested.

He straightened. "If you give me a ride first."

This promptly ended all bargaining. I pedaled off without a picture, the boys ran back to the field without testing the bike, and Senor Godoy, who had been grunting his disapproval all the time and exerting silent control over the mob of youngsters, hopped into the cab.

A mile of so beyond the soccer field the road forks. One road goes to Carpuela, the village of black former slaves who had been numerous in this area around Otavalo but were freed in the 1840s. They number the just-encountered soccer team among their descendants. The other road leads upward into the mountains to the west. Senor Godoy, whose favorite literature is a map, spread one out on the hood of the cab. He fished my makeshift glasses from the dashboard and handed them to me.

"Here, Senora, put on your 'glasses of emergency'." While I forced the glasses to perch on my nose, he showed me how we could take a looping detour to the top of the mountain to the west and then join the main road to *la frontera*. "There are more vistas there, Senora," he said.

I welcomed any detour that would open more vistas, so we put the bike in the trunk until we reached the little village of El Angel, appropriately floating among the heavens. Everyone seemed asleep except for stragglers who issued forth from the church on the plaza and a few others who stopped to gawk at us as we unleashed the bike for the trip back to the main road to Tulcan on the frontier.

Spinning down from the cloud-high town of El Angel, I saw that vistas, as promised, were abundant. When the road was steep, I could only grab the brakes and look hastily at the mountains rolling slowly along with me. When the road flowed in horizontal waves, I could stop for photos of such trivial things as sheep tethered to bushes or of monumentally glorious things like mountains and valleys. In the meantime the little yellow Peugeot was creeping behind me, its faithful driver jumping out repeatedly to attend to my various needs, both real and imagined.

"I need a bathroom," I finally told him. "Ah, a bathroom very private," he said. "The bathroom of the Indians."

His concern seemed out of all proportion to the task. Immediately he scurried off to investigate the bushes on a low bank above the road, beside which I had stopped purposely in the first place, and ran up and down on the bank, which sloped to the valley below. Finally he jumped down on the road again to announce that he thought it was all right. Whether he was worried about snakes, about my breaking my neck as I stumbled over the rough ground or that I would be spied upon, I didn't know. But when I returned to the road, unbitten, unbroken and unseen, I found him discreetly riding the bicycle yards away. Upon another occasion he had suggested that no, I was not to go on the right side of the road but rather on the left, for there were more trees there. Since I did not want to inflict the burden of selecting appropriate spots for such occasions upon him, I determined to avoid it at all costs.

By noon I was pumping my way due north on the main road.

Suddenly I felt that I was alone and stopped to look in back of me. No yellow cab was in sight. I had become so used to the closeness that I was alarmed. It was like pulling the string on a kite and discovering that the kite, unnoticed, had broken away and disappeared. I must have been alone all of ten minutes when the yellow Peugeot reappeared and swooshed to a stop behind me. Senor Godoy jumped out, flourishing a newspaper-wrapped package.

"Senora! We have *llapingachos*! Very typical!" He beamed.

He spread the newspaper out on the ground, extracted from the cab food we had bought earlier: the sacks of buns, guava jelly and *manjar de leche*. We stretched out our legs on the ground beside the

road and regarded the picnic with admiration before assaulting it.

Typical, indeed, are the *llapingachos*, especially for holidays. These round, mashed potato cakes before us were festive, especially livened up with cheese and *achiote*, a pulverized seed that gives them a delicate flavor and pale yellow color. Often they are fried with crisp pork bits on a griddle by a perspiring cook standing in front of a small store that is so dark and cluttered that you are not tempted to enter. Had I seen these fried by a similarly perspiring cook, I might not have been tempted to eat them, but I had faith that what I did not know would not hurt me. We both devoured the picnic savagely, slapping gobs of guava jelly on the crumbling buns, and gobbling *manjar de leche* by the spoonful.

"In good hunger there is no bad bread," chuckled Senor Godoy, opening his mouth wide over a stale bun piled with jelly.

Shortly the *llapingachos* were gone, the leftover buns were stored in the back seat of the cab to dry out further, and the tops were tightened over the jelly jars. Senor Godoy organized our belongings and waved me off with cries of encouragement. The cries varied from a chirping "Bye-bye", to a laughing *"Otra vez las batallas,"*—"Once again the battles"—to a rousing *"Nieque!"*—untranslatable slang used by Ecuadorian army sergeants to urge their rookies to chop their way through the jungle at top speed. "Get going!" it meant, with the "or else" clearly understood.

So I got going . . . on a road that slipped comfortably toward the border. I peeked at flirting Mt. Cotacachi for a few seconds before white clouds, like a toupee, hid the nearly snow-bald summit. Like huge quilts of brown and green pushed into folds on a lumpy sagging bed, the valleys below rolled toward the mountains on the west. Shortly I saw a gathering of people and cars ahead of me. I had at last reached *la frontera*, the border with Colombia. Our hotel, where we had stayed last year, was only a short distance away. The afternoon sun had dropped behind the mountains, leaving the little hotel in a chilly shadow. Just to mention *la frontera* to an Ecuadorian makes him shiver and brings about long conversations about the cold. But I had not yet begun to shiver as I turned and pumped up the road that leads to the hotel.

Two little girls ran after me, shouting, "Where are you from, Senora? Are you all alone, Senora?" Suddenly I realized I was. I looked back to the main road and saw Senor Godoy among a mixed crowd of Ecuadorians and Colombians. Obviously distressed, he was turning his head in all directions, straining to find me in the mob, looking fearfully in the direction of Colombia, where I had no intention of going.

His distress was justified. A rough-looking crowd hung around the sentry posts, some drunk, some jostling with each other and shouting loudly. After a few minutes he saw me, waved happily, jumped into the cab and soon led me down the cobbled road to the frontier hotel, a white stucco building clutching the steep hillside above a rushing river. It was a clammy place in a gap between the mountains where the sun is slow to get to in the morning and eager to leave early in the afternoon.

We had arrived a little before five o'clock so we easily got two rooms. Last year at this hotel, after Senor Godoy and I had settled down for the night in our two rooms, a flood of Colombians had overflowed into the place and taken all the remaining rooms. Someone even tried to take one that was not available. In the middle of the night Senor Godoy, awakened by someone unlocking his door and boldly walking over to his bed, thought that he was being robbed. He started to scream.

"Please, *amigo*," said the intruder. "Help me. I am cold. I have no room. Let me come in. *Amigo,* I am very cold." He was a tour bus driver whose agent had failed to see that his accommodations were reserved. While his tourists went on to Colombia, he returned to the hotel, only to discover that it was not expecting him. "There is another driver from Quito here," the clerk at the desk had said. "Perhaps you know him. He is all alone up there. There is another bed in the room. Go on up." The obliging clerk handed him the extra room key.

After he calmed down, Senor Godoy recognized the intruder and, also obliging, offered him the extra bed. With dramatic gestures, Senor Godoy described the encounter to me next morning and laughed about it for days.

Dinner was served late at this frontier hotel, and it was hard to amuse ourselves while we waited. We walked up a road beyond the hotel that got steeper and rockier with each step. The river roared below us on one side, and on the other, the bank shot straight up. On a rare flat place at the top, a little old lady, enveloped in black dress and shawl, watched over a pig. I wondered how she had gotten there. The pig was safely tied to a rough open shed into which he could fit quite snugly at night. But it was so small that he could not root around much in his sleep.

"Good evening," she called down to us.

"You have a beautiful pig," I called back.

"Yes," she answered. "He is a very good animal." She chattered on happily, I assume telling us more about the pig, but I could not understand it all. We were obviously a diversion. Visitors on that cliff would be rare.

We made our way back down the rough road to the hotel, where there was still not a sniff of dinner. Zigzagging down precipitous flights of cement stairs, which turned right and left several times before reaching the bottom, we came to the "game room," built on stilts on a cliff hanging above the river. The game was bowling.

"Boneheads," whispered Senor Godoy as we watched several teenagers play. They were not doing well, unless the object of the game was to roll the ball down the shorter than conventional alley toward the pins, and have it slip off harmlessly to the edge without toppling a single pin. A strike would have truly bowled them over with astonishment. Tired of the bowlers, we climbed one flight of stairs and crossed a cement walk to the dining room, a separate building below the hotel.

"Dinner is ready now," said the waiter who saw us as we were coming through the door. We went in and sat down at one of the dozen tables in the dining room. We were the first guests.

Soon a few others trickled in. "Cold! We are cold here!" each exclaimed as he nodded to us.

When Senor Godoy and I were halfway through our dinner, I looked with surprise at six gentlemen who came in to sit at a nearby table. They all wore their hair just below the ears. Their long waxed mustaches curled downward. The flashy colors of their silk shirts made me think of macaws I had seen in the jungle.

"They are Colombians," Senor Godoy whispered to me.

Even on the streets of Quito, I noticed later, most men from Colombia are distinguishable a block away. Wearing broad-brimmed floppy hats and outlandish colors, they look conspicuous against the clipped hairstyles and dark suits of most Ecuadorians.

One dinner guest from Colombia dared to be different. He wore a brown suit and was busy reprimanding four small sons. He would have no spare time to deck himself out in the flashy costumes of his countrymen. "Colombians like to come to Ecuador," Senor Godoy explained as we left the dining room. "Things are cheaper here and the police are so polite. In Colombia the police are very bad."

The next morning I got up early and went into my bathroom to take a shower. But when I turned on the faucet there was nothing but a satirical hiss. I tried the washbowl faucets, but they had also run dry. I dressed quickly and rushed down to the lobby to protest to the clerk at the desk. He only shrugged and rolled his eyes heavenward.

Soon the six gentlemen from Colombia I had seen in the dining room last night swarmed into the lobby and protested to the clerk even more loudly than I did. They were still in their bathrobes and held toothbrushes loaded with paste. The helpless clerk again shrugged.

Resigned to being unwashed, I sat down on a davenport to wait for Senor Godoy. The Colombians, who were not resigned, wandered aimlessly around the lobby with their loaded toothbrushes and looked imploringly to heaven. They seemed to expect God to turn on divine spigots.

Senor Godoy trotted down the stairs after a few minutes and joined me on the davenport.

"Those *locos* from Colombia," he chuckled, as he watched them.

But this would be one of our long-lasting jokes.

"Water for the Colombians!" Senor Godoy called out the next few days whenever we passed a waterfall or saw a stream. And we laughed crazily.

But that morning at the frontier hotel we soon stopped laughing as we sat on the davenport waiting for breakfast. The hotel was as slow getting breakfast ready as it had been getting dinner ready the night before. By the time we finally sat down in the dining room we were starved.

As we were waiting for the waiter to serve us, I noticed that Senor Godoy was not only unwashed but unrested. Every morning it was our custom to ask each other how we had slept. Usually he answered that he had slept like a *tronco,* or tree trunk. This morning his reply was different.

"No, Senora. I did not sleep well. I did not get to sleep until four this morning."

I was concerned. He seemed worried about something, but he did not explain to me what it was.

11

STATUES LIVING AND OTHERWISE

IF MY TRIP DIARY ever should fall into the hands of a future archaeologist, he would be as perplexed as if he were the first one to tackle the Rosetta stone. He would find, for example, the following note scribbled by Senor Godoy: "Nov. 13 *En bicicleta hasta entrada a el Angel 35 km. Llego a Tulcan frontera con Colombia total km 76 a las 4:15. Salio de Ibarra a las 8 a.m.*" He would have little difficulty translating: "Nov. 13. On bicycle to the entrance of El Angel, 35 km. She arrived at Tulcan, frontier with Colombia, total 76 km. at 4:15. She left Ibarra at 8 a.m." If he were a ten-speed bicyclist with muscles like steel ropes, he might not be impressed with the total distance of forty-five miles.

Next he would see a huge scrawl, written by me: *"pastuzo*—bonehead. Imbabura; *imperdible*—safety pin; Rumicoca—*rio de la froisbra.*" The last word was as close as I could get to *frontera* without my glasses. At this point the archaeologist would give up.

Pastuzo, as Senor Godoy explained, is the vernacular for someone who wears an overcoat when the weather is hot, and shorts when it is freezing. It was the word he whispered to me when we were watching the young fellows bowling clumsily at the frontier hotel alley. Anxious to pick up some Spanish slang, I had faithfully recorded it. Imbabura is the name of the mountain I could never recall. Although I had difficulty remembering the mountain, I had no difficulty remembering the slang, because the translation was always made instantly clear by Senor Godoy. He would begin with "For example, Senora," and then give me just the right example by way of illustration, as if he were helping one of his boys with homework. *Imperdible* referred to the safety pins, which I had to use to hold up the hems of my maternity pants when the stitches I had basted in them failed me. If the archaeologist has a map, he might figure out that "Rumicoca" was the river that circled and tumbled around the hotel. This all got jumbled together because I had to keep my ideas in mind for hours when I was on the bicycle. I wrote them down later when I got back in the taxi. I could be sure, too, that before we started our trip back south to Quito this morning, Senor Godoy would take up the diary lying beside him on the cab seat and write down the kilometers registered as I started to cycle.

The morning departure ritual was just as predictable. I would change into my *pantalones maternales*, pack my tiny suitcase, scan the room for forgotten items, and call out "Yes!" when Senor Godoy knocked on the door and asked "Ready?" To be on the safe side, he might add, "And the head, Senora?" To which I would reply, chuckling, "Ah, that is what is missing!" Ever since I had dropped my purse the first days of the trip, he felt it was necessary to make sure my head was still placed firmly on my neck. His own head, obviously well-established in its appointed place, was constantly taking inventory of our possessions, anticipating problems, solving them before they occurred, or figuring out exactly how long it would take for me

to pedal from point to point, the ups and downs being what they were. When I picked up my feather-light suitcase, he would exclaim, "Now the Mercedes Benz!" and pick up the lead heavy bike and carry it down a flight or two of stairs. The "Mercedes Benz" always stayed beside my bed except when the hotel provided locked storage for it.

Not far south of Colombia's border is the town of Tulcan. At its edge is a cemetery Senor Godoy said we must see. "My father says it is so pretty," he said.

Within minutes of leaving the hotel at *la frontera*, we turned through an open wrought-iron gate into what at first appeared to be like all other cemeteries in Ecuador, or in Europe. The dead reposed under monuments bedecked with flowers or in crypts stacked one on top of the other like sepulchral condominiums, to save space. Each crypt had a small front window revealing plastic flowers or holy cards inside.

Whoever designed this cemetery, however, wanted to cheer and amuse anyone who entered it. Enclosed within the grounds we found a large topiary garden of figures and animals carefully carved with pruning shears from cypress bushes: a huge Galapagos tortoise with his head drooping over the cypress base; another tortoise standing on its hind legs; a scowling Inca chief; an Indian woman going to market; an Indian mother carrying a baby on her back; a pious woman praying; fishes with flopping tails; birds with bulging fluffs of feathers; bowls of many shapes; a host of creatures, persons, and objects seen all over Ecuador and bigger than life. There must be no merriment in heaven greater than that in the part directly above Ecuador, where the assembled canonized saints can chuckle over the brightly patterned clothes and saucy hats decorating their statues; or where the larger assemblage of uncanonized saints, without statues, can smile over the topiary garden lovingly grown to decorate the place where their humble bones rest.

I pedaled away from the cemetery, and from the chill of the hills imprisoning Tulcan, up into the sunshine of the highlands. Here the fields were green with legumes and grain growing in regular rows. Cows grazed placidly on the sloping meadows, or wandered just as peacefully into the middle of the highway, making trucks crawl around them.

Bare sticks that had been driven into the ground beside the road puzzled me at first. Then I noticed that they were really saplings that must take root easily. Some had already leafed out and were forming hedges. The farmer had a cheap and ingenious way to improvise a fence.

Around mid-morning we turned off to the east at a tiny village lying on a flat area above a deep valley. Hidden in a cave far below us in a corner of the twisting valley, we would find *La Gruta de la Paz*, the Grotto of the Peace, a shrine to "The Virgin of the Peace," where pilgrims gather from all over Ecuador to pray. We decided at once to go down to the shrine. Senor Godoy must visit it to leave candles and I must photograph.

We put the bike in the trunk and started bumping down the cobbled road, wriggling and spilling into a valley so narrow in places that it seemed to have been formed by splitting a mountain in two. After a couple of miles the road dropped onto a short bridge over a roaring river and then climbed up quickly to a parking lot in front of a stuccoed, whitewashed store selling cold drinks, biscuits, rosaries and holy cards. Two buses from Cuenca, over 450 miles away, had managed to squeeze down the road before us and were emptying their loads of Indian pilgrims. The women tumbled out of the bus like spilled baskets of flowers. Each wore an orange, magenta or red skirt of fine wool with rows of embroidered flowers and tiny metal mirrors at the hem. Their blouses, snowy white, newly washed and pressed, were almost hidden under bright-colored triangular woolen scarves they wore over them. These scarves might also serve as a sling for a baby. They wore white Panama hats as proudly as crowns.

Senor Godoy stored the bicycle in the little shop, where he bought some candles. I clutched my camera and we climbed down the curving flight of stairs to enter the enormous grotto, many meters directly below the parking lot. The wet walls of the cavern dripped constantly. Stalactites, just as wet, hung like so many icy, runny noses. All this moisture seeped into a dark pool which flowed outside to join the river we had crossed over. Deep in the grotto, the statue of the Virgin, with a constellation of candles twinkling at the base, glowed in the dimness. The Virgin's blue wool robe, covered with a pattern of pink flowers, fell softly from her shoulders to the pedestal below her feet. She held the baby Jesus in her arms and her expression was not saccharine, like so many cheap statues of the Virgin, but compassionate. The Indian pilgrims climbed up the few stairs to reach the platform on which her statue rested, looked up at her face, and beseeched her with prayers not heard but seen by the soft movement of lips. Occasionally one would pin a paper sucre to the hem of her robe.

I found an empty place to sit in the rows of benches in front of the statue and watched the brilliance of colors and softness of movement. Skirts of red and of all derivatives of red, brushed like whispers against brown legs as the barefoot Indian women tiptoed about. Jet-black braids fell freely because all hats had been removed. Hands touched the Virgin as gently as if she were alive. One man near me crawled under a bench trying to find the money he had dropped— perhaps months of savings for this trip. A circle of friends above him whispered suggestions and helped him search the dark stone floor for his coins. Some young girls, smiling playfully, dipped their hands in the springs of water at the sides of the cave and splashed it on their faces.

I set up my camera upon a small tripod, attracting two boys who tiptoed wordlessly up to me, only their dark eyes questioning. I let them look through the reflex lens of the camera. In it the statue floated ethereally. Shortly, I was helping a dozen boys have a look, lifting up the smaller ones, guiding the heads of the taller ones, watching eyes glow with wonder at the miracle of modern photography equipment.

His candles lit, the Virgin venerated, Senor Godoy sat down beside me. I shook my head as I watched the faces of the devout; their trust and anxiety blended, as they looked up at the serene face of the Virgin.

"Oh, that they might have health and wealth," I whispered. He nodded in sympathy. Scorn for such devotion was only possible for the comfortable, well-shod and well-fed, who feel no need for supplication or entreaties for their own well-being. Still I felt alien. I smiled at some, admired the babies of others; but I could not reach across the distance of pride, shyness and dignity. Few smiled in return.

"Tell me about the Virgin," I whispered again. "Are there miracles?"

He shook his head. "I don't know. I think she appeared one time, but that is all I know."

We climbed up the wearying flight of stairs back to the taxi and I reminded Senor Godoy that this was his second round trip here. He had forgotten matches to light the candles the first time and had bounded up the steps two at a time to buy some at the little store.

"You should get absolution for climbing these stairs twice," I panted, stopping halfway up to catch my breath. He chuckled, having plenty of wind for the rest of the climb.

When we reached the parking lot, we saw a man in tattered clothes crooning over his burro, whose coat was also tattered. "Poor little thing! Poor little thing," he kept saying, rubbing its bushy neck. The burro pressed his head on the man's shoulder, no doubt thinking that stumbling down the long cobbled road to the shrine was more than an animal should bear.

I hoped that there would be absolution, or at least heavenly rest, for farm animals.

The Indians from Cuenca had also climbed up to the road and had spread themselves out over the grassy area under the trees beside the parking lot to eat a picnic lunch. The "Panama" straw hats, actually woven in Cuenca, were back on the women's heads, and their wool skirts of many colors lay fanned out around them. Indian women wear wool all year round in the cool Andes, wet season or dry. Children sat obediently near their parents and, like them, chewed on chicken bones and sipped soft drinks.

Soon we were back on the high road, sitting on a grassy plot ourselves. Beside us was a large shrine inhabited by the Virgin—a different one this time. Her benign statue, towering above us on a high pedestal, protected the valley below us. We would shortly drop down to this very valley after we finished our standard lunch of gooey *manjar de leche*, guava jelly and aged buns. Somehow we had also managed to pick up bananas at the village.

"It will be very downhill," Senor Godoy remarked as he trotted back from the village faucet with water to wash the goo from our hands. The road could not be anything but downhill. We had to be on the top of the world; nothing higher was in sight from that spot. He hauled the bike out of the trunk, and I started off on what I assumed would be a spectacular ride.

At first it was. I could stop to photograph a man plowing black earth into patterns. His field was all but sliding off into the valley depths. I could look off to the west to the high mountains, folded, pleated, and tangled together. I could admire the black rolls of plowed land close at hand. But only for a few miles. The highway, with ruthless disregard for the strain on the brakes of either machines of two or four wheels, started to dive into the valley, the bottom of which could not be imagined or seen as I turned and twisted downward. Cliffs and mountains were on one side, unfathomable emptiness on the other. I squeezed the brakes with throbbing hands, forcing the bike to drift down as slowly as possible, and did not dare to turn my head for fear the steepness would throw me off balance. I would see a curve ahead and for a moment hoped that the road would level off enough for me to shake out my hands. False hope. The road merely hurled itself downward in a different direction. The only way to stop would have been to skid off the road and be thrown sky-high off the bike. The agony lasted for eighteen kilometers, or eleven and one-quarter miles, until at last I swung around a giant turn and saw the straggling houses of a village below. Unless the inhabitants were mountain goats, the village had to be at least partially on flat ground. It was. Still sailing along, I whipped over a bridge crossing a wide river and was surprised to see two ebony women balanc-

ing huge baskets on their heads as they walked along the riverbank. Their posture and grace would be the envy of queens. More women, kerchiefs and baskets on their heads also, walked ahead of me in a symphony of graceful movement.

I had reached the village of Carpuela, where the boy soccer players I had watched the day before lived. By now I could release the brakes a little, shake the paralysis out of my hands, and continue unrestrained. Equally unrestrained were the spectators beside the road who yelled, waved, called out congratulations, and smiled. Their enthusiastic welcome made me feel as if I were the heroine of a ticker-tape parade. Accustomed to the shyness and reserve of the Indians, I welcomed their contagious exuberance and yelled, greeted, and waved back. I really wanted to linger, but black clouds were churning up beyond the mountains to the west, and I began to pedal wildly to get ahead of the rain.

Meanwhile, in the taxi Senor Godoy had observed the menacing clouds and preliminary raindrops. He whisked around in front of me, jumped out and waved me down. "Senora, it is going to rain. I do not want that you should catch cold."

That I would catch cold was unlikely. I had stuffed galoshes (of the obsolete variety) and a huge rain poncho into an extra handbag and was prepared for a deluge. However, I got into the car meekly, he put the bike into the trunk and we splashed off into the downpour. I felt lucky. This was the only rain that fell on me while I was biking. The official rainy season would not start until December, a month later, and would continue until June. Except in Quito, where the sky seems obliged to maintain a moist reputation by pouring down rain every afternoon no matter what month it is, the weather behaved beautifully, as if it knew there was a time and a season for all things. Now, season or not, the rain was beating against the cab and running across the road in rivulets. I did not mind letting the rain gear go to waste in the back seat and admitted to myself that the cab felt cozy. Senor Godoy looked over at me with concern.

"Senora, when you went down the mountain, my heart was a bell!" He pounded his chest in a ding-dong rhythm.

12

MONDAY BLUES

THE CLOUDBURST WAS OVER by the time we had driven the few miles to Ibarra and had checked back in at the Hotel Chorlavi. I quickly put my things in my room, changed into a wool suit, and went out to sit on the hotel veranda. The gray clouds still sulked beyond the hills in the east, but the air refreshed me.

Senor Godoy did not take long to come to the veranda. Shoulders tensed together, he pushed himself stiffly into a chair beside me. I noticed that his customary bubbles of merriment were missing. I remembered how worried he seemed before we had left *la frontera* that morning.

"You said you did not sleep well last night," I ventured. "What is the matter?" This loosened the first olive from the bottle.

"Oh, Senora, it is the sons." He was almost moaning. "They are males. They are very strong."

I could not imagine what insurrection could have come to pass in his household. I begged him to tell me what was wrong.

"Oh, Senora, this is Monday and it is very bad. The oldest must go to school at 6:30 on Mondays. He must study for school also. The problem is the wife. She plays with them."

I could see his pretty young wife romping with the boys while the homework lay about unworked; the public bus that took them to school waited unmet; schoolbooks, pencils and notebooks were unbought; and the *particular*, or private school, for which he paid at least 300 sucres for each child, or about $3.70 a month, was unattended. He described the schedule they had to keep to get the boys to school for an elementary education: the second son, ten, had to leave every morning at 6:30; the oldest, twelve, had to leave that early only on Mondays, and all the other days he had to be in *colegio* at one. On those days he did not get home until past 6:45 at night, when it was dark. The five-year-old in *jardin*, or kindergarten, had to leave at 7:30 in the morning and got home at noon. It was a schedule that would challenge any mother. His wife needed a computer to keep track of all the comings and goings. While papa was away, he was sure, all schedules would be tossed aside while the mother played with the sons.

I began to have doubts about our trip. "Senor, is it good or bad that you have to travel with me?" "Oh, Senora, it is very good!" The words exploded forth as he looked at me with the gratitude of a man who has just been pulled out of a whirlpool. I had once asked him if his country was safe enough for a woman to bicycle alone, and he looked so alarmed at the thought that I might dispense with his services that I had to immediately assure him that I had no intention of doing so. The importance of my tourist dollar now jolted me.

In an instant his face sobered and he shook his head again. "The wife was very angry with me. She wanted me to teach the oldest to drive the taxi. Imagine! He is twelve. She was angry. She would not speak to me for a week." His laugh was a nervous twitter as he recollected the misery. I wondered privately if the solution might have been to take his wife for a ride in Quito traffic. She would soon be convinced of the folly in trusting a twelve-year-old with the source of the family income in that game of wits requiring skillful dashing and dodging.

For a while we were quiet as other guests came up the steps of the veranda and exchanged polite pleasantries with us.

"Senor," I began when we could no longer be overheard, "when you were young did you have the same opportunities that you are giving your sons?"

He shook his head slowly. "No, Senora, we were very poor. I worked when I was fourteen as a mechanic. I was the oldest. I had to help the parents. My brother, I helped him, too, and my four sisters. I was the oldest," he repeated.

"Life is sad, Senora. I also help my niece. She is the daughter of my wife's brother. He died and they have five children. She could not care for all of them. My wife cried and cried so now the niece lives with us. She is eighteen."

"Does she have a sweetheart?" I asked, hoping that if she married he would have relief from part of his burdens. He shook his head.

"But she helps my wife, who needs help." He moved around in his chair and half-laughed as he remembered something else. "My wife has a brother and she wanted him to come too. She cried and cried, but I said I could not," he explained, shaking his head vigorously—as if an explanation were necessary.

"Your heart is bigger than your house, Senor. Your father named you well when he called you 'angel.' "

He only sighed again. "Life is sad, Senora." He paused to consider the sorrow of it all. When he could earn a steady income for several weeks, as he now could because of me, he could not supervise his family properly. When he could supervise his family properly, he did not have time to earn a steady income. Without his supervision, school and study would be skipped and the boys would roughhouse. "I castigate them. I control them," he told me once when he described how his boys loved to wrestle. He had been thinking of a karate class for them so that their energies could explode safely without reducing the small habitation to shards and splinters.

"Si, Senora, life is sad," he repeated yet one more time, pulling his chair closer so that he couldn't be overheard by some guests who had just come onto the veranda. "You see all I have to buy for the family." I thought of the bushel sack of potatoes stored on the back seat of the cab, the bicycle having preempted the trunk.

"Generally, Senora, I earn 1000 sucres a day. It has to cover all my expenses—for the sons, the car, the house. My wife is very good, very good with the money." But no matter how skillful she might be at handling the household expenses, twelve dollars a day would be hard to stretch over all those mouths needing food, all those bodies needing clothes, all those good minds needing schooling. And the taxi needing upkeep. If I had felt guilty for the luxury of Senor Godoy trailing me in a taxi, I could now convince myself to feel virtuous. We had agreed on a daily rate, which he had asked me not to reveal since it was special for me. It was far more than his daily take. Normally, he waited outside the hotel in his taxi to take tourists out to dinner, or less frequently, on city tours. Perhaps once a week there would be someone who wanted to go to the markets outside of Quito. Thus, both of us now could luxuriate in our companionable arrangement.

"I am going to go to English classes next year. English is necessary." His shoulders straightened. "Then I can get more tourists." He was silent for a while, perhaps thinking of the tourists who would swarm to his cab once he had learned English.

I remembered last year how he would pause at dinner, fork in hand, and stare straight ahead, completely preoccupied with worry. I reminded him of it. "Did you worry because the wife was going to have a baby?" I asked.

"Si, Senora, always she has a hard time. Each time. And oh! Would God grant that we would have a baby girl." He smiled tenuously, thinking of the persistent arrival of boys. He told me that he had hired someone to help his wife right after the babies had arrived, but such help was only temporary. Too soon she must face all the tasks alone again.

"Perhaps it is good that she is alone for a while, Senor," I suggested. "Every woman should know how to manage things by herself." He replied with a doubtful "Si." How could he expect her to manage alone when he did not expect me to cross the Pan American Highway alone?

It was nearing the sociable hour of six, and other guests were gathering on the veranda. Senor Godoy pulled his chair away and smiled again as the tension partially dissolved. "But, Senora, why does one work? It is all for the sons that one works."

That night he disappeared after supper without the formal good-night nod. It was shameful, perhaps, to have confessed so many problems. At any rate, we would find out about his family when we reached Quito the next day.

We started out in the morning back on the Pan American Highway going south to Quito. White-peaked Cayambe, now seen from a different direction, flirted with us through a heavy veil of trees and between the green masses of other mountains. Whether or not Senor Godoy's sons made it to school, other children whom I saw along the road had. They stopped the ball game they were playing on the school playground to watch me bicycle past. Farther on, some ran to the top of a dirt bank to stare down at me. I waved and photographed. The black-eyed, short-haired little boys, wearing t-shirts and cotton pants, could have passed for American boys in the 1940s. The little girls could have stepped from an artist's canvas. Long black braids fell over bright shawls, which they held in place with the air of grand ladies. Their skirts were of many colors and had been scrubbed so painstakingly over rocks in streams that the wearers were obliged to be ladies all day long, and to return to their mothers just as clean and pressed as they were when they started out in the morning. For a long time the children watched me without a hint of movement, somber-eyed, as much in wonder over a lady on a bicycle as I was over their beauty. I waved good-bye finally and they ran off, laughing with each other.

I pedaled on for several miles, occasionally passing men on horseback—brown and orange ponchos swept across their shoulders; dark hats not plopped on casually, but placed on with a deliberation that demanded respect; backs straight; their whole bodies moving rhythmically as their horses stepped along. The men had never walked; they had been born riding.

I stopped abruptly when I saw a little girl, barefoot, not more than seven years old, walking toward me. She looked as somber as an El Greco painting. Her drab shawl was folded across her shoulders to hold her baby brother or sister. Her face, melancholy as an old woman's, hid in the shadow of her brown felt hat. Senor Godoy gave her a few coins and she let me take a photograph. Then the baby started to wail. Half-whimpering herself, she turned away.

After I pedaled for a few more miles through the bucolic valley I had come through four days ago on the way to the frontier, I stopped at a fork in the road. Senor Godoy jumped out of the cab and ran up to me. "Senora, we will take the road to the right. We will see different vistas." He showed me on the map that the road made a twenty-mile loop and then rejoined the Pan American Highway.

I turned onto the new road and shortly pedaled through Tabacundo, a village that fades into anonymity as soon as you pass through it. It was past one in the afternoon and children were dawdling home from school, their books in little satchels slung over their backs. After a few miles on the westbound road, the green of field and hill bled into the harsh brown of mountains churning together toward the blue sky. The road fell down like a wildly twisting snake,

burrowing unseen into the lower folds of the mountains ahead.

I stopped to study the situation. Senor Godoy hopped out of the cab, chuckled happily and gave the brakes a final test. They would stop, if not on a dime, at least on a dollar bill.

"Bye-bye," he called out as always. "Again the battles!"

The "battles" did not begin at once. The pavement was smooth, the traffic was light, and only a truck or two snorted beside me. Senor Godoy's little yellow taxi crept behind me like a concerned snail. Soon the hill became steeper and I squeezed the brakes with increasing ferocity. I began to think pleasantly about how I could fly off the earth if my brakes failed. The bike strained beneath me like a fettered racehorse. I was not having any fun at all, and I wondered when I would reach bottom.

After fifteen miles, I did. The road branched in two: one way turned ninety degrees to cross a bridge; the other went straight to start up a hill. A grim-faced Senor Godoy shot past me and turned to go across the bridge. By now I was able to stop. Inwardly I was shaking. I would have enjoyed sitting down in the middle of the road and indulging myself in a fit of hysterics.

"Senor, never again!" I panted as he came running back to me. "Never again will I mount the bicycle for a hill like this." He smiled with relief.

"My heart was a bell, Senora," he said, just as he had said at the bottom of the last long steep hill.

He put the bike in the trunk with emphasis. I was through for the day. Besides, we were nearly back to Quito, which meant climbing out of what we had been plunging into.

After a few miles we stopped at an immaculate little cafe, which had a large sign in front advertising *locro,* another specialty of the country. Starved, we went in. The waitress brought each of us a bowlful of *locro*, a potato and cheese soup, steaming hot with a large avocado floating around in it. Still starved after the first bowlful, we ordered more. It soon stabilized my trembling interior.

For once not missing the bike at all, I crawled into the cab, and we sped toward Quito. "I must see my family, Senora," Senor Godoy explained anxiously, and by late afternoon we were bouncing over the street leading to the little house of his family in Calderon, north of Quito. We found it still standing. Apparently no rampaging boys had razed it to the ground. School had been attended on time; homework had been done; floors had been swept; domestic machinery had spun around with the efficiency of a good Swiss watch—all the more remarkable because the machinery was all hand-run.

For just a few moments I rested on a chair in the boys' bedroom, which I now realized had to accommodate the orphan niece and two small boys in one bed and the two older boys in the other. A telepathic signal of our arrival had aroused the neighborhood, and soon all the women relatives from up and down the street came to welcome us, shaking hands, hugging, laughing, jamming themselves into the tiny bedroom of the boys and orphan niece. They sat down where they could find space on the edge of the beds, and stood when the last square inch was occupied, trying to keep off the small boy who was in one bed sick with a fever. Outside the bedroom door Senor Godoy greeted his wife soberly and they whispered together for a few moments. I presumed he was asking her how it all went.

Continually interrupting me with exclamations of delight, the women listened to my recital of all the places we had visited. I felt like Marco Polo returned from Cathay. But I could not understand all their questions or excited responses to what I was telling them. "They are not accustomed to talking to tourists," Senor Godoy explained to me later.

In the midst of this babbling hubbub, the orphan niece, black eyes and round face solemn, came in carrying the Godoy baby. Without a word, she took the plump infant into the next room and handed him to his mother, who put her hand under his back and held him out straight in front of her while the niece deftly changed his diapers in mid-air—a practical solution to limited space.

After we had visited an hour, Senor Godoy, relieved that his household had not disintegrated during his absence, drove me back to my Quito hotel. At the edge of the city I became alarmed. On the road just ahead of us a crowd of shouting men had set fire to a pile of tires.

"Demonstration!" explained Senor Godoy, without further comment. He did not consider the commotion alarming or explain the cause of the demonstration. A few days before, the newspaper had reported a student uprising against inflation or low wages. The grievance was not clear.

"Last year the taxi cooperatives went on strike," Senor Godoy said. "I had to stay home. It was dangerous on the streets. They threw stones at taxis."

Such obstacles as tire-burning demonstrations or a mountain we could overcome. You merely went over one and around the other.

13

LAND OF CAVES AND HOMEWORK

"SENORA, WE MUST GO to your room and plan our journey to Cuenca," said Senor Godoy when we got to my hotel, a newly remodeled one he had found for me after my trip to the Galapagos. He was eager to continue our tour of Ecuador. He had assured himself that his family was well and had deposited, for their continued well-being, sacks of produce he had bartered for to and from the border. He was relaxed.

The prospect was exciting. I had written him before I left home that I wanted to visit Cuenca, 295 miles south of Quito. Most of the road I biked over this year I remembered from last year. Spots where I had paused to take photos were spots where I might have paused previously. "You took that picture last year," Senor Godoy would remind me.

Now we were to head south, past Ambato, where I had been to the market last year, on to higher places and unknown roads. We had been fluttering up to mere heights of 8,000 to 10,000 feet so far, but south of Quito we would soar to 14,000 feet. Senor Godoy, as promised, had conditioned me for the gradually increasing altitudes as carefully as if we intended to tackle Mt. Everest.

We sat down at a table in the room and drew up a schedule for the trip to Cuenca. I had spurned the idea of taking a day of rest in Quito. I could feel the bike wheels spinning beneath me and wanted to set out in the morning. We planned to make long looping side-trips over both the Eastern and Western cordilleras, and chose to stay at places where at least passable hotels existed. We needed no advance hotel reservations because tourists would dwindle the farther south we went. No, we did not want to go down to Guayaquil on the coast, but we would visit other cities on the coastal plain instead.

The trip would stretch over two weeks so the only preparation for me was to be sure I cashed enough traveler's checks, which we would do when the banks opened early next day. That night I slept well. By now I was confident that I could get up and down all hills without accident, that no trucks would attack me, that the sun would shine, and that all the mountains would come out from behind the clouds to greet us.

Next morning the sun did shine; and at the second it turned 8:30 A.M. Senor Godoy bounced into the hotel, called out a cheerful, *"Com' esta, Senora?"*, grabbed the bike, placed it upright in the elevator, and wheeled it through the lobby past the approving staff. The manager himself, who had informed everyone quite erroneously that I had biked all over the world, wished me a good journey and begged me to return.

In jovial spirits we spun off on the well-paved Pan American Highway to the south. In one-half hour, after we were safely out of the heavy traffic near Quito, Senor Godoy turned to me sitting beside him in the front seat and smiled. "Is this good for the bicycle, Senora?"

It was. The sweeping valleys, towering green hills, and tilled fields covering the earth like corduroy cloth were irresistible. Senor Godoy parked beside the road, extracted the bike from the trunk, fastened the camera case to the handlebars, and set me on my way.

I rolled along easily. Curious Indian women looked up from their huts beside the road, then quickly covered up their nursing babies as I pedaled past. A few were too preoccupied with cleaning lice from a child's scalp to notice me. Other Indian women were hoeing the fields or punching holes in the ground with digging sticks. A string of children followed to push plants into the holes. Still smaller girls acted as nursemaids, carrying babies in shawls slung over their backs. I never saw an Indian child of the Sierra playing.

After a few miles, I slowed down for a crowd gathered at the edge of the road. They were standing helplessly beside a cow that had been hit by a car. It lay dumbly in the ditch, its big eyes rolling up beseechingly. A policeman who stood amidst the mute and disconsolate cluster was sympathetic but ineffective. The driver who had hit the cow had vanished.

We reached the highest point for the day, a pass a little over 10,000 feet, and chose a spot beside the road where we could lunch and admire Mt. Cotopaxi off to the east. Whymper, who had climbed the peak around 1880 to pitch his tent above the hot ground at the top, called it the highest volcano in the world "in good working order." According to his careful measurements, his tent floor was 110 degrees Fahrenheit, while outside, on the windward side, the temperature was a chilly 13 degrees Fahrenheit.

Officially listed now as a "steaming" volcano, Mt. Cotopaxi was neither puffing nor steaming as we watched it; but living near Mt. St. Helens in Washington state has taught me never to trust a sleeping volcano. The height of Mt. Cotopaxi, 19,347 feet, is only 973 feet less than that of Mt. McKinley. Framed in a dazzling blue sky, Cotopaxi is like an icy princess with white robes flowing from her shoulders in a perfect isosceles triangle. Today, however, the mountain was like Medea in a frenzy, tearing smoky gray garments away as scowling clouds scudded past to hide her.

We spread out our lunch and watched. With the excitement of a parent trying to take pictures of his first child, Senor Godoy exclaimed every time a cloudy veil passed away from the sharp peak, "There it is! Now! A photograph!" Obediently I alternately jumped up to snap pictures and sat down to smear guava jelly on a bun. After lunch I cruised along in a valley with surpassing views; but in Ecuador each new view seems to surpass all the others. The little yellow taxi crept faithfully behind, whizzing past me each time we came to an inconsequential hill. Out jumped Senor Godoy at the top, announcing cheerfully, "I help you!" He pushed the bike up the hill, or rode it if he wanted to make sure it was in good working order. Once I caught up, I had a swig of mineral water and a squirt of suntan lotion, and pedaled off serenely.

An army camp spread over several acres south of where I entered the valley. A high fence enclosed it, and signs warned people

away. As I wheeled by, I caught sight of a tiny blue daisy-like flower outside the fence that was struggling to be beautiful in this grim setting. I took out my camera and started to focus when Senor Godoy stopped me. "Senora. I do not understand your camera. I see the picture and then a blur in the middle."

"Here, let me show you how to make it clear," and I started to give him a demonstration of the single lens reflex system. "Halt!" shouted a rough voice and I looked up to see a soldier with a gun.

"No Senor, no Senor!" I cried, expecting to be hauled off.

"She is just a tourist, Senor. She only wanted to take a picture of the flower." Senor Godoy's smile would have placated Attila the

Hun. The soldier could see no sense in someone taking a picture of something that could be found beside any road, grunted in disgust, and ambled back to his post. For the rest of the day, Senor Godoy would imitate my frantic pleas for mercy: " 'No, no, no, Senor' you said," and he would blow away in a storm of laughing.

After a few miles we neared Latacunga, a city of 21,000 inhabitants. In the past it was the starting point for a treasure hunt; or at least it was until they lost the map. When the Spanish conquistadores imprisoned Atahualpa, the last Inca chief, his Indian subjects throughout his Andean empire amassed gold for his ransom. The Spanish kept the gold, but strangled Atahualpa in Cuzco, Peru. According to the legend, the Indians in what is now Ecuador buried the gold they collected for the ransom in a secret cave near Latacunga and hid the map of its location in the city.

Eventually men obtained the presumed map and followed its directions, rock by rock and tree by tree. But as it has been for many treasure seekers throughout the years, the map became vague just when the treasure was within grabbing distance. Neither cave nor gold was ever found. The tale has persisted, but not the map, which has mysteriously disappeared.

Geologists have found marine fossils in the Andes, evidence that the continent lay beneath the sea countless eons ago. Limestone, formed from the sediments of the sea when the continent was submerged, is also found high in the Andes. Many caves, such as the *Gruta de La Paz* we visited, riddle this soft rock.

There is something about caves that arouses curiosity and imagination. Another legend tells about a witch priestess whose temple was a mammoth cave near Latacunga. One day she changed herself and all her worshipers into stones to keep them from being slaughtered by an enemy prince and his army who had burst through the opening of the cave. The true part of the story is that in 1882 three men fleeing the police stumbled into a cave where they saw stone statues and an altar. An enraged bull in the cave frightened them away before they could investigate the mystery. The men eventually returned to their homes with the amazing story of what they had discovered. But could they ever again find the cave, immense as a cathedral and filled with strange stones? No, not among the honeycomb of caves and tumble of cataracts, high mountains and deep gulleys in that region.

No caves with treasure or bewitching priestesses were near enough to beguile me when I finally reached Latacunga. The road swinging down into the town was just right for freewheeling but just wrong for traffic. Cars and trucks politely avoided me, but there was not much room for both of us. With relief I pedaled into Latacunga and stopped at the intersection of the Pan American Highway where a road led off to the left into the town center. A young, amiable policeman, waving traffic to and fro in the middle of the intersection, regarded me with amazement. He began a barrage of questions: "Where are you from, Senora? Did you buy the bicycle here? Where are you going? Are you an American citizen? Do you like Ecuador?"

I was impaled to the spot answering him while traffic brushed past me on all sides. In the meantime, Senor Godoy, who had already zipped out of the intersection, had gotten out of the cab and was looking for me with some consternation. He soon spotted me and waved energetically. This made the policeman happy. "You have a friend in Ecuador?" he asked, starting another volley of questions. Since the truth would have involved explaining to him that I did not have an *amigo* but a *chofer-guia* at so much per diem, I nodded "Si" politely and escaped.

The selection of hotels in the town was limited to one, but it was clean and very cheap—two dinners and two rooms, each with plumbing both private and functioning, all for $7.50. The kindest thing that could be said about the dinner in the hotel was that it was anonymous. This meant that I never remembered what I ate but suffered no ill effects. The dining room was large, as undecorated as a barn, and almost unoccupied except for a family sitting at a long table at one end. The three adults were hovering over two small children bent over their notebooks, noses only a few inches from pencil and paper. I walked over to see what they were doing. The little girl must have just started school because she was writing line after line of letters of the alphabet, frowning over each one as she formed it. The boy was doing simple arithmetic, devotedly and without frowns. I patted the little girl on the shoulder and praised her beautiful letters. She wiggled in her chair and then went on practicing her alphabet. The three adults continued to assist from time to time, clucking like so many banty hens all charged with the care of two chicks. The mother stopped long enough to look up and ask me if I were touring the country.

"The economy is bad here," she sighed. "We cannot travel in our country."

I nodded sympathetically and asked about the children. "What do they study in the school?" Sighing heavily, almost as if it were her responsibility to learn the same things all over again, she recited the list: arithmetic, reading, spelling, history, grammar. She shook her head when she came to the problem of grammar. "Look, Senora."

She picked up the newspaper. "Look here. It says 'House White.' Your language is in reverse, Senora. You say 'White House'.."

She looked at me accusingly. Not wishing to go into the history of language, I thought it best to compliment her. "Your language is very complicated, Senora. The grammar is more complicated than English."

She smiled, believing that this was an attribute of language that was desirable, providing one knew how to speak it already.

"Ah, si, Senora. The verbs! We have the imperfect, the preterite, conditional, future, present subjunctive, imperfect subjunctive!" She groaned, seeing future sessions of homework when she would have to name them all over again to her children.

"I am impressed," I said to Senor Godoy later. "You also spend many hours with your sons over their homework."

"Si, Senora, I know the grammar and I scold the sons if they do not have the grammar. The little one, he cries." He demonstrated by wiping imaginary tears from his eyes. "If I am not acquainted with the subject, there is someone in the family who is."

I could see devoted aunts, a grandfather, grandmother, orphan niece, mother, father all coming to rescue the victims of the homework session.

After supper I explored the town alone to find a can of oil for the bike, which had creaked rheumatically ever since the day of purchase. Sewing machine oil would do, and I found some in a small shop, scarcely ten feet wide, that sold a sewing machine or two and assorted tools. Clutching my can of oil, I walked out into the street for a stroll. The temperature was just right, if you had a wool jacket; and after a few minutes, I sat down to rest on a park bench in front of the hotel. The park, a block square, was a pleasant place with flowering trees and shrubs, comfortable benches, and walks for strolling. Soon Senor Godoy bounced up. He had also been hunting for sewing machine oil.

"Senora, I lack experience with the bicycle, but there is a shop that will take the bicycle apart and check it. It costs 1500 sucre. It takes a day."

I thought for a moment. I doubted that the small bicycle shop had much experience with bikes either, and I could see the poor "Mercedes Benz" returning with some of its vital parts missing. "No," I said finally. "It is too much money. Too much time."

For a while longer we rested on the bench and watched the strollers as the lamps flickered on, casting a pale watery light over the walks. We got up to stroll about ourselves.

"This is so nice to take a walk after dinner, Senor," I said. "At home I don't enjoy walking after dark alone."

From then on, he always suggested to the senora in need of protection that we should take a stroll after supper. The only difficulty was that he only had a light jacket and was shivering and ready to come in long before I was.

If we thought the two rooms in the hotel were cheap, the breakfast was a giveaway. We ate in a little cafe with six bare tables, spartan as a monk's cell, where one little man was rushed around trying to feed people on their way to work. Our choices were the usual: how did we want our eggs and what juice? For the equivalent of fifty cents each we had toast, eggs, coffee and mora berry juice. The man brought a tiny glass pitcher of *esencial*, a concentrated distillation of coffee beans, to add to hot foaming milk in the amount we wished. The mora berry juice had a different tang from that into which I had dipped my dry biscuit at Mama Clorinda's restaurant in Quito. This juice was as tart as loganberry and would have glorified the driest of biscuits.

A man sat hunched over a notebook at a table below the cash register. Standing restlessly behind him was his young son, who looked anxiously out into the street. It was getting late for school. His father was carefully drawing in his son's notebook, reversing the usual homework routine. He looked up at us, smiled briefly, then went on drawing, earning an undeserved grade for his son.

After breakfast, we stepped out of the cafe into the Spanish colonial streets of Latacunga. The early morning light softened the arcaded lanes, best seen before the harsh glare of the noon-climbing sun exposed the dirt and debris, the potholes and rubble. The old street lamps hung from wrought iron fixtures that curved gracefully above the walks. Sun-glinted, Mt. Cotopaxi shone taffy-white above the buildings at the eastern edge of town. Down one street a crowd of girls in red uniforms hurried to school. Flowing along like a river, they filled the narrow street from side to side.

Down a different street in the opposite direction, a flood of boys in brown jackets raced along on their way to school. Their chatter and the pounding of running feet on the cobblestones echoed in the town until silence came abruptly at seven-thirty, when they all reached school.

We peeked through the fence at one school playground where an elderly priest, white robes flapping at his ankles, tried to shake the hand of each small boy who ran onto the grounds. As he reached out in all directions for quicksilver youngsters, he rotated uneasily about like a wobbling top.

After our walk, we stuffed the bike into the trunk and fought our way out of the traffic of Latacunga, bumping over cobblestones until we reached the highway. There Senor Godoy lifted out the bike, set it firmly on its wheels and took out the oil can. Shortly a small group of men sauntered over to see what was happening. They stared at both of us, speaking to each other in whispers. Senor Godoy oiled away with the dedicated fervor of an engineer attacking a train locomotive. The men kept staring and whispering and Senor Godoy kept squeezing and tapping the can over the bike's various orifices. Soon the bike began to drip oil in protest. He then tested the brakes, was satisfied, and at last announced happily, "The Mercedes Benz is ready, Senora."

The hushed audience stared solemnly. Just as solemnly I mounted the bike, but with more than the usual flourish, like a performer on a stage. I could feel their stares until I rounded the next curve and pedaled out of their sight.

14

KING OF THE ANDES

WHEN IT LEAVES LATACUNGA, the Pan American Highway winds between the Eastern and Western cordilleras through what is called the "Ambato Basin." It might be described as a valley, except that the bottom of the basin itself has hills, canyons, and even other small mountains.

Flowers and blossoming trees abound in Ambato, rightly called "The City of Gardens." But lawyers are even more in bloom than flowers. As we drove down one street in the business section we lost track of the number of placards proclaiming their services from the second-story windows. *"Abogado"* signs were more plentiful than the fruit on the trees. I concluded that the citizens must spend most of their time suing each other.

The Villa Hilda, where we stayed, was a cluster of low buildings surrounded by flowers of all kinds.

Roses, hibiscus, mimosa, bougainvillea, delphinium and daisies flourished in well-tended beds. Iridescent hummingbirds spun from blossom to blossom, pausing a moment inside, and then shooting to the next in a whir of wings.

Rural life pressed close to the villa. Below the balcony of my second-story room were several sheep munching and bleating, staring up at me with stupefaction from time to time. Out of sight somewhere, but not out of sound, was a sty full of pigs. They protested their ultimate fate in the roasting pan by squealing and grunting by the hour. Eucalyptus trees towered so high above the balcony that I could not see the sky.

"Let us walk," Senor Godoy suggested after supper. We strolled out into the warm evening air, scented with roses all up and down the street.

"Let us look at the houses of the rich," he suggested mischievously. We were indeed in a rich neighborhood. We looked at their houses, not large but sumptuously appointed, protected by high walls all around. Through ornate metal gates we saw masses of flowers, and through large picture windows we saw elegant furnishings. One home was so imposing that it looked like an office building, an embassy, or at least an exclusive clinic. A guard stood in front of it.

"What is this building?" Senor Godoy asked, after I had first given him a nudge. The man stiffened, suspicious of us. "It is all right," Senor Godoy assured him. "The senora is from the United States and she is very curious."

The guard not only relaxed, he expanded. "It is just a private home," he began. "The people are very rich. There are three daughters who are coming home this night. Each of them has a Mercedes Benz. Yes, Senor, they are very, very rich!"

"Ah, how marvelous!" we exclaimed, expressing the required admiration. The guard, with this confirmation of his importance, expanded further—he grew inches in height. If you must guard something, it must be most gratifying to have it be three Mercedes Benzes.

Down the street we strolled until, with the suddenness of an exploding bomb, a dog rushed toward us, barking in a terrifying manner. I screamed and jumped. I soon saw that the monster was safely penned inside the fence and couldn't chew us to bits unless we jumped inside—or he vaulted the wall. Senor Godoy and I sat down on the curb to laugh at ourselves.

"I have great fear of dogs, Senora," he said, between gasps. "One time I was walking home in the dark and a dog jumped out at me. The dog ran after me with terrible barking! I ran home very rapidly." He gasped again. "I had much fear." Dogs in Ecuador mean business, and most of them—unless they are too starved to raise their heads—consider their business to be scaring intruders and innocent pedestrians.

Next morning I started pedaling south on a road that climbed gently toward the higher Andes. As I left the fringes of Ambato I could look off into the distance and find scenery that helped me ignore the clutter beside me—debris in the streets, the drab houses with peeling layers of stucco, the dingy little stores with wind-deposited refuse in front. But the outskirts of most cities in the world show dirty petticoats.

In the Ecuadorian Sierra every road is scenically worth the energy to pedal over it. No eye-wearying flat expanses of land stretch endlessly into the horizon. No begrimed factories sully the sky. No orderly industrial parks impose efficiency upon the landscape. The traveler can look beyond the villages to the glory that frames them. In no other country had I found such continuous beauty and variety as here. Even in Norway, enchantingly beautiful, I could always predict what the fjord or lake at the bottom of the downward twisting road would look like. I had to stop in rapture at every curve of the Amalfi Drive, but the drive was only thirty miles long. In the Ecuadorian Sierra the scenic roads rolled on for miles and I could not predict what was around the next mountain.

A little south of Ambato I stopped to watch a brickmaker at work. He was scooping up thick gobs of brown mud, sloshing and slapping it into a wooden rectangular form, smoothing the top surface and then running with it over to a neat stack of already formed bricks. There he eased it into place on top. After lifting off the wooden form with care he ran back to do it all over again with another brick. Warming up to an admiring audience, he began working faster and faster, slapping the brown goo vigorously, smoothing it, hurrying with it over to the mounting stack of drying bricks. Glancing at me out of the corner of his eye, he ran back and forth like an actor in a Keystone Cop movie jerking along at double speed. I took picture after picture and he formed brick after brick. After several minutes he stopped long enough to look toward Senor Godoy.

"Is it possible to have a picture, Senor?"

"No, it is not possible. The pictures are not Polaroid," he explained. "They are just transparencies. Perhaps we will return this way when the pictures are ready." Partially comforted by this improbability, the man went back to work.

I pedaled off, leaving the man to slap his bricks together. He made 260 in one day, he told us, and left them to dry for fifteen days. The next day he would make another 260 bricks, stack them up to dry—each day the same as the next, until he would be too old to run back and forth. By then, perhaps, his sons could take care of him.

We passed by many little industries making bricks, in the same brown color, of the same size. All would appear eventually in the construction of the houses and stores along the road. After I had pedaled a few miles farther, I saw no more people making bricks; instead they were planting seed in the fields of rich black soil. "*La tierra negra da buenas semateras,*" Senor Godoy wrote in the diary later that day. The old Ecuadorian proverb means "black earth gives good

yields." I never could find *semeteras* in the dictionary under any conceivable spelling, but it was obvious that that rich, almost juicy-looking soil would make anything sprout and grow that consented to grow at that altitude to begin with. In this case the products were potatoes, beans, wheat, and corn.

The black soil was something the wealthy landowner could hand down to his sons. But I wondered how much would be passed down to the sons of the Indians who were tilling the soil, planting the seeds, living in the one-room huts with walls of brown bricks and roofs of straw.

Unexpectedly, Senor Godoy yanked his cab to a stop behind me. "Beans!" he cried out and ran over to a small roadside table covered with plastic. On one end was a large steaming pot. A plump woman ran out to meet him, he pointed to the pot, and she ladled out large spoonsful of beans onto a piece of newspaper.

He offered me some when he got back to the cab. They were flat like lima beans and had been simmered gently so that the outside skin was hard and the inside soft. He put a bean in his mouth and spit out the tough skin as we do when we eat sunflower seeds.

"Very good, Senora." He put another bean in his mouth and spit out the skin. "Last winter I drove some engineers to Cuenca. They wanted to go all in one day. They did not want to stop for lunch—for nothing. It takes seven hours to go to Cuenca. This is all I ate—these beans."

I was dismayed at the stern stomachs and sterner souls of his passengers. "Did they not stop even to see the vistas?"

"No, Senora. They slept all the way."

I hoped they were not as stern with their purse strings, and asked him.

"Oh, yes, they paid me very well." He chuckled happily and went on chewing the beans and spitting out the skins as I pedaled off again.

The road was now starting to rise, and as I saw the long hill ahead, I knew that my trusty guardian would whip the taxi past me in a second, jump out, and there would be tacit agreement that I would ride in the cab up to the top. I got off the bike, and in seconds all had happened as I expected. The "Mercedes Benz" was stowed in the trunk and I was in the front seat. I sighed happily. If hotels in the Sierra had been at intervals of twenty-five miles I would not have minded trudging alone up the hills, leaning on the bike, taking countless pictures of the mountains and of the billowing brown and green fields skirting them. Even so, I was able to pedal most of the forty miles from Ambato to Riobamba.

Soon we reached a leveling place at the top of the hill.

"Is it good for the bike?" Senor Godoy asked.

Soon, I sailed off. It was impossible to do anything else but sail—like a bird drifting on air currents. We were not going over a pass but on a high road 12,000 feet above the sea that waved for miles ahead like a wind-caught banner, gently drifting downward toward Riobamba. On either side of the road, brown fields soared off to east and west. Distant huts, like bumps on a coarse wool weave, stuck out here and there. Now and then an Indian farmer in dark poncho, long stick-of-a-tool over his shoulder, climbed a steep slope beside the road. He would stare, and then wave.

"It is rare to see Chimborazo, Senora," Senor Godoy had told me repeatedly. Apparently, the highest mountain in Ecuador is only to be imagined, never to be seen. Somewhere west of our road, be-. hind piles of white clouds, the mountain was hiding. I looked in that direction often but with no hope. By noon I was starting the long final hill down to Riobamba. I looked toward the west again but saw only the base of the mountain tucked away under the clouds. Disappointed, I went on. Soon I was in the midst of small pine trees growing in scattered patches close to the road. All at once I looked over to where Chimborazo was supposed to be. Not only was it supposed to be there, it *was* there. I hailed Senor Godoy, still trailing close behind. He stopped, leaped from the car in a flash and looked up at the mountain, by now brilliantly exposed.

"Chimborazo, Senora! I have only seen it once completely. Only once, completely." His face was radiant. I wondered if his face could have burst with more radiance when he looked upon his first-born son twelve years ago. He seemed to feel a paternal joy at seeing the mountain.

"We see it completely," I echoed, just as elated.

"Chimborazo, king of the Andes!" he went on. "It is the second highest in the Andes."

I did not have the heart to correct him. All South Americans know that 22,834 foot Mt. Aconcagua in Argentina is the highest. According to the 1987 World Almanac, Chimborazo with a mere 20,561 feet tags along below it in thirtieth place among the great Andean peaks. In Bolivia the guide had told me that their highest peak, Sajama, was the second highest in the Andes. It is only fourteenth. As I looked at Chimborazo, I would have believed it if someone told me that it was the highest peak of all. It thrust itself above the green mountains below like a monstrous giant, shaking snowy white fists, defying all the peaks in the Andean range. It was not a cool and symmetrical peak like Cotopaxi, but an enormously lumpy one. It looked like a prize fighter rolling his muscles.

We ran all around, dancing from one side of the road to the other, trying to find the best spot to take photographs. After a few minutes white clouds swept across it again. Like a haughty monarch, the mountain had closed the curtain, scorning its humble subjects. Just then I happened to look at my camera. The film had not been advancing. The "King of the Andes" had vanished into emptiness inside my camera.

"Damn!" I exploded, as Senor Godoy ran up to see why I was distressed. I hoped that he would not pick up my language, although I felt like giving him even better examples. He was fascinated when I explained how I had not checked to see that a certain knob was turning to tell me that the film had been loaded properly. "Ha, it did not give turn," he said. Whenever I took a picture after that he reminded me to make sure it "gives turn." I never missed a picture again.

I mounted my bike and slipped into Riobamba, a city of 28,000 people, creeping and stretching up the mountainsides to make room for itself.

"Sultan of the Andes," Senor Godoy called the city as he took me on a tour of it later. Magnificent as a sultan it was, surrounded by a crescent of peaks to the east, and Chimborazo as sentinel to the west.

Its people could act as proud as sultans, too.

At lunch in our hotel, the other guests, dropping in from downtown, picked at their food with sour dignity and glanced at us disapprovingly as we kept bursting into ripples of laughter. The more solemn we were expected to be, the more rebellious we felt, and the more we laughed. Proudly insistent, too, was the store clerk who was determined that I buy her favorite brand of shampoo instead of mine.

"Look at my hair," she said, fluffing it with her hands. "Isn't it beautiful? Your shampoo is for babies. Mine is much better." She scowled as I walked out with my shampoo, the same brand I used back home.

The air was gentle and warm when Senor Godoy escorted me on our evening stroll. We walked slowly past the windows of the hotel banquet hall where elegantly dressed guests were at a reception, moving about with stiff restraint, having no fun at all. We continued down the hill past a large school where the lights were still on and we could see a man in one room, writing on a blackboard.

"It is the night school, Senora," Senor Godoy explained. I assumed that there were unseen hands taking notes and unseen adult heads trying to absorb it all after a day of work.

I wanted to know more about the education of Senor Godoy's children. "How long will your sons go to school?" I asked. The reply was complicated and I had to balance the "glasses of emergency" on my nose in order to write it all in my diary as he dictated in Spanish. The weekly schedule of schools and classes, with many daily variations for five boys growing up in succession, would go on for years. The five-year-old would be in kindergarten for a year. After this, his mother hopes, he would not pummel his little companions because they "molested" him. His father, I observed, chuckled when he described his feisty behavior.

Next there would be *escuela primaria* for six years. By that time, the child would be eleven or twelve. He will then enter *colegio*, which corresponds to the American junior and senior high school.

For the first three years of *colegio*, all students take the same basic courses. For the next three years the curriculum is diversified. A student may take the most suitable course to prepare himself for the university or for a trade. Senor Godoy said he wanted his eldest to study mechanical skills and, after six years of *colegio*, to specialize at the university in a *curso mecanico*.

The state schools, which families avoid if they can afford something better, charge no tuition, but pupils must buy all books and supplies. The *particular*, or private, schools charge a minimum of 300 sucres a month, or about four dollars a month at the current rate. All Senor Godoy's children went to these *particular* schools, which happened to be Catholic and taught by *curas*, or priests.

"Did you teach in a private school, Senora?" he asked me.

"No, Senor, in a public school." He could not have looked more shocked if I had told him I had been imprisoned for murder. The excellence of the public schools of Washington state would have been beyond his comprehension. I did not try to explain.

15

THE TRAIN THAT DOES NOT EXIST

"BAD NOTICES!" SENOR GODOY EXCLAIMED as he bounded out of the hotel into the cab for our afternoon tour of Riobamba. I wondered if the "bad notices" meant that the taxi had an expensive ailment difficult to cure. The taxi was in good shape. The road we were to take south to Cuenca the next day was not.

"It is because of the train that does not exist," he explained cryptically. The tracks and stations were there, but no trains ran over them. The workers of the one railroad of the country, which descended dizzily over the Andes from Quito to Guayaquil on the coast, were on strike. The workers wanted more money and fewer hours, but the railroad could only give them fewer hours. It had lost 417,000,000 sucres the past year—about $5,200,000, a crippling amount for even the best of railroads. In December of 1982, during the murderous storms of El Nino, the train had derailed, plunging down the Andes and killing several people. After the damage had been repaired somewhat, the trains had been hauling freight only. For months the strikers had been negotiating but getting no results, so they had decided to publicize their grievances by jolting the railroad company as well as the entire country into action—or more correctly, into inaction. How they were trying to accomplish this paradoxical situation we were soon to see.

We drove off to inspect the road we were to take next morning. It was rumored that it was blocked. Senor Godoy looked ahead grimly. We could be stuck in Riobamba until the strike was settled—unless we could escape on an unblocked road.

After driving a few miles, we slowed down when we saw several police flanking the road.

"They are protecting the right of the strikers to strike," Senor

Godoy assured me. But I was apprehensive.

We looked ahead and saw that they were also protecting the right of the strikers to block the road. They had pushed four freight cars across the highway and shoved huge boulders from a nearby steep hill down upon it. An earthquake could not have done a better job.

Ignoring the police, I snatched up my camera and jumped out of the cab.

"She is just a tourist," Senor Godoy hastily explained to the alarmed constabulary. "She does not harm. She only wants a photograph."

For a minute Senor Godoy surveyed the enormous obstacles across the road. "We need to go south," Senor Godoy asked a policeman. "Is it possible?"

The policeman explained that there was another road several miles to the east that paralleled the main highway and went around the blockade. This brought the twinkle back to Senor Godoy's eyes. Escape tomorrow might be possible. We turned around to drive back to the city, which we had begun to consider a prison.

Our spirits soared when we saw Chimborazo, looming to the northwest as we drove into the city, unsullied by a cloud or a wisp of mist, waiting to be recorded on now properly-loaded film. And, if we believed in signs, our good spirits could soar sky-high at the sight of a large sentinel-like billboard standing at the outskirts of Riobamba. In its center was a large heart, into which black lines were traveling from all directions. Disregarding the likelihood that at that moment all of the routes to the city were blocked off, or soon would be, it proudly proclaimed: "All the roads lead to Riobamba from the Fatherland."

"Look!" Senor Godoy exclaimed as we reached the city and were passing the railroad station. The strikers, not wishing to waste their forced vacation, were having a rousing game of volleyball on an improvised dirt court beside the train tracks. "The strikers exist," he laughed. "The stations exist. The tracks exist. But the train does not exist."

Early the next morning we took the detour the policeman had described to us, passing through wooded country south of Riobamba, winding up and down between furrowed fields scratched out on the brown soil of the hills. It was a hard-pounded dirt road, respectably free from ruts and bumps. It hardly deserved detour classification.

Within half an hour we were climbing out of the wooded area to the sunny heights where the ten-mile detour joined the Pan American Highway. At the top of the hill we stopped abruptly. Ahead was a string of freight cars almost across the road. With just enough room to slip through, we drove to the other side of the unfinished blockade and got out to look. On the road in front of the cars was a scatter of broken glass over a pool of dried blood. In the dark, a hapless driver came upon that freight car wall and crashed against it. Senor Godoy's face had hard lines of grimness. Sobered, we continued south.

Once safe on the main highway beyond the blockade, Senor Godoy pulled the bike from the trunk and I pedaled off. But grimness trudged ahead of me on the road. I passed a trickle of Indians, padding softly on bare feet, coming from or going to what place I could not see in that wilderness of brown dry mountains.

As I bicycled along I waved at a woman who was switching a burro ahead of her. She turned away. She was bundled up in the universal costume of that remote part of the Andes—an old brown felt hat, ragged brown skirt, worn shawl over her shoulders, tough bare brown feet—somber hues of destitution. Climbing up the steep hillsides on my left were a few farmers in ponchos with brown felt hats pulled down over their foreheads. One of them, followed by a small boy also in a poncho and brown felt hat, was carrying a long wooden hoe over his shoulder. Both man and boy were camouflaged against the brown earth. I waved at them from my bicycle, and more at ease than the woman, they waved back.

"The Indians here are different than those in Otavalo, Senor," I commented when I stopped for suntan lotion. "Their faces are sad. Most do not like to look at us."

He nodded slowly. "Si, Senora, pride is lacking to them." I admitted that a stance of erect confidence would be difficult to maintain when faced with such barrenness, when beaten finally into lifelong resignation. Pride—the last luxury relinquished to poverty!

In a basin-shaped valley below the road we saw scattered huts pressed tightly against the hillsides, each at the back of a small rectangle of cultivated land. When I stopped the next time for water, Senor Godoy told me each was owned and tilled by a large family.

"Is it possible that one family lives on such a small field?" I asked. "How do they eat?"

"Ah, Senora, it is because of the agrarian reform. It was not well-programmed."

I had read of the Agrarian Reform Law of 1964 in Ecuador. The land was distributed to the tenant farmers who were then responsible for tilling and cultivating it. I had been heartened by what I had presumed to be the improved lot of the tenant, actually the serf farmer who had worked for the landowner. Pride of ownership would be a great incentive, the Indian would prosper—at least those were the expectations.

"No, Senora, it was not well-programmed," he repeated.

"What do you think is the solution?" I asked. I started to write his "solution" in my diary but my "glasses of emergency" kept falling off my nose. Patiently he took over pen and notebook.

"*Huasipongo*," he wrote, "was the land the Indians lived on when they worked for the landlord. Living on the *huasipongo* was better than what happened after the Agrarian Reform Law, because Indians (after the reform) had not sufficient land for making a living. They immigrated to the principal cities, leaving the fields and agriculture abandoned. It would have been better if the landowner had helped the sons of the Indians to get an education and if they had been given social security, medicines, etc. What they received after the Agrarian Reform Law was not sufficient."

Such a solution, I had read, had been tried about thirty years ago by a progressive landlord north of Quito. The Indians had been encouraged to develop their skills in weaving, embroidery, rug making, and basketry—native arts which had market value.

There, Indians were proud and educated. Here, we were seeing nothing but barefooted dejection: Indians toiling in the fields with tools used for hundreds of years; children not in school but following their parents and dropping seeds in the holes made with digging sticks. Education was compulsory by law—but only in theory.

Pedaling south, I discovered that riding the bike was going to be limited. The country must have given up the idea of keeping the Pan American Highway paved, and I had to dodge ruts, bumps, ditches and rocks. Still, for Ecuador, it might be considered a "good road." In *Travels Amongst the Great Andes of the Equator,* Edward Whymper quotes a native's description of a really bad road: "A road is bad when beasts tumble into a mud hole and vanish right out of sight."

I saw that I would be in danger of vanishing right out of sight if I did not crawl onto a safe seat in the cab. Senor Godoy, skillfully avoiding the many obstacles, drove on cheerfully without dropping out of the sight of anybody.

"This is not good for the bicycle, Senora?" he asked as we twisted about on a downhill run. I agreed.

We both remembered the rough road where we had tested the bike, west of Quito.

Here the road snaked above precipices, terrifying in their depth. High ridges and peaks, brown and rust-colored, were jumbled together as if they had exploded from a boiling caldron and had been left to dry. The mountains were awesome heaps of earth in the agonies of birth, like the rampaging land I had seen a year after the eruption of Mt. St. Helens back home—land which nature was reconstructing after a brutal assault. Off to the west, the peaks were piercing thick mattresses of fog lying over valleys without number. It was landscape which excited, not pacified.

Senor Godoy wrote later in the diary: "She did not mount much the bicycle for the difficulties of the road—only 32 kms. Already it is very difficult in this sector of the Andes. The height of passing over the road was 3500 meters over the level of the sea. (11,483 feet)." Still it was a comfortable height. By first going north, he had conditioned me well.

Nature can be ruthless in the Andes, but the people have learned to live with her savagery, always deferring to her barbarous caprices, settling down after a flood or landslide, resigning themselves to the catastrophes occurring again and again. Shortly I would see how brutal nature could be here.

We looked off to the mountains beyond the abysses and saw where the side of a mountain had slid down, leaving bare, hugely scraped wounds behind. That mountain was so isolated that the landslide could not have buried anyone. Above a highway, however, a mountain attacked by the flooding tempest of El Nino was deadly. We were coming to Chunchi where a landslide had made worldwide news in the spring of 1983, just six months before. A line of cars had been waiting on the road for bulldozers to clear up a small landslide. Suddenly, with a terrifying noise, more of the mountain crashed down upon those waiting—buses, trucks, cars, several hundred people.

We drove up to where the tragedy had occurred and stopped at a spot on the road which had been cleared. We shuddered to look at the bare and clawed mountainside on our left, the tons of earth in heaps below us on our right. I got out of the car and looked at the churned up mud beneath my feet. I wondered if I were standing above the bodies of several hundred victims, buried alive, left under those tons of earth.

"They must leave them," Senor Godoy said. "It is the law." Of course, digging for bodies would only cause another landslide and bury those digging.

The torrents of rain brought about by El Nino in the winter of 1982–1983 had loosened the earth and caused floods all over Ecuador. Streets of Quito were still torn up by the deluge of water which had washed over them. Even in normal times, a flood of afternoon rain races toward you as you try to walk or motor up a hill. The water level beneath the ground was high, disrupting the efficiency of sewers. We were warned never to put toilet paper in the commode.

"Your face is sad, Senora. Is it the landslide?" Senor Godoy asked after we had driven away. I nodded. Senor Godoy was concerned if I were not in a constant state of elation over the trip around his country. Depressed I was, as we left the buried, yet unburied.

We continued driving south for about twenty-five miles to where you turn off for the "tourist attraction" of southern Ecuador—Inga Pirca, Inca ruins found five miles off the main road among the mountains of the Eastern Cordillera, and visited the way you visit all ruins, by climbing up and down and imagining what really existed beneath the ground or within the walls left standing.

A stone quadrangle several feet higher than a man's head, open to the clouds and sky above, loomed above the valley on a vast bare, wind-whipped hill. The taxi zipped up a long hill, and at the top we stopped before the rickety gate protecting the ruins. Soon a guide appeared, greeted us in clear, slow Spanish, motioned to four Argentine tourists who had been waiting, and slowly led us across a field

toward the huge stone structure at the top of the hill. With easy confidence, he pointed out significant configurations of stones as we went along. He described one circle of stones, about five feet in diameter, as a grave of women; at least, that's what I thought he said. It was improbable to me that the encircled ground could hold many bodies.

We kept trudging up the hill until we reached the principal ruins, walls of enormous stones marvelously fitted together with the same baffling precision as the stones in Machu Picchu in Peru—all without the use of mortar. Inga Pirca is called a fort, but some archaeologists argue that it was a temple. It commands a view that is open, airy and looks east and west up and down a long valley. If it were a fort, enemies could not approach unseen. Unlike Machu Picchu, it is not crowded in by peaks.

Senor Godoy, who had never seen the ruins before, had been so excited at the prospect of the visit that he had brought his little snapshot camera along. He scrutinized every inch of the ground, concentrated upon every word of the guide, hushing me politely when I interrupted to ask for an interpretation of the Spanish.

We climbed down a narrow path and then dizzily up again to a high mound on which was a circle of stones. The guide, with the same easy confidence, assured us that this was a bath. In heavy rain it might have been possible to bathe in the hollowed-out stone bowl, if someone felt sufficiently in need of ablutions to climb up the steep steps leading to the place. At best his explanation could only be conjecture. My guide at Machu Picchu had been more cautious. "We can only guess what all was used for," he had said repeatedly. Certainly the Spanish conquest of the Incas in the sixteenth century must have been one of the most cruel of history. Not only was a people destroyed or enslaved, but a history was silenced. Tongues alone could relate the story of the Inca civilization. The Incas had no writing. While it is true that Garcilaso de la Vega, half Indian, half Spanish, in 1619 wrote chronicles of the Inca history as told to him by his Inca princess mother, modern scholars claim many inaccuracies in his work. But inaccuracy itself serves a purpose by urging further research. The purpose of Machu Picchu and Inga Pirca is still a mystery. Those who could have told of their purpose, after defeat and subjection, closed their lips. As a means of preventing rebellion, the Incas themselves scattered abroad all conquered tribes, such as the Aymara in Bolivia, whom they could not assimilate within the already enslaved empire. Thus pre-Inca history was also silenced. Scholars believe the pre-Inca Quitu peoples made use of the location of Inga Pirca, but how? In Ecuador much remains to be excavated and studied—expensive projects.

"How does this seem to you, Senora?" Senor Godoy asked after we had been walking around for some time. "Is this as big as Machu Picchu?"

Machu Picchu had far more extensive ruins already excavated. It was hard to answer for what was still under the ground here at Inga Pirca and Senor Godoy, I knew, wanted these ruins to attract as many tourists as those in Peru. Set on a more dramatic stage, Machu

Picchu seemed like a petrified eyrie, surrounded by a fence of peaks which protected it like so many green pointed pickets. Inga Pirca had a spacious outlook, and a good road would make it quite accessible, despite its Andean location.

A cold wind whipped through us as we left the ruins and made our way back to the car. We rested for a while and munched our faithful buns that persisted in staying with us no matter how we tried to get rid of them.

"I love the history," Senor Godoy commented between munches. "Two places I want to see—Mexico and the Panama Canal. Why Mexico, Senora? In Mexico there is much history; there are many ruins. But first the house—a bigger house for the family."

We started down the mountain road from Inga Pirca in a cloudburst and soon were bumping onto the Pan American Highway again. For the rest of the afternoon we crawled over, climbed up and braked down the remaining twenty-five miles into Cuenca. No matter how hazardous the curves and mud were, it was a safer way to go than flying.

"It is very dangerous to fly to Cuenca," Senor Godoy explained as we finally hit pavement a few miles north of the city. "See that mountain over there? Last July an airplane hit that mountain when it neared the airport. Very bad fog."

The killer mountain to the left of us did not loom menacingly. But just like the ones that have buried cars and people, the Andean mountains attack stealthily. Fog, rainstorms, and clouds are their weapons.

16

THE SHOD AND THE UNSHOD

THE FRINGES OF CUENCA were like the fringes of most cities. Drab buildings lined the dusty streets leading into the city: a gas station or two, small shops selling tires and servicing cars, smaller grocery stores with dim and indistinct interiors—a hodgepodge of modern miscellany on the outside of the city that belied the history you see inside.

Cuenca is an outdoor museum of Spanish colonial architecture, the guidebook had declared, and as we drove slowly down the narrow cobblestone streets, squeezing among all the other cars, we saw that this was so. Balconies edged with wrought iron railings hung over the streets. A few wooden doors bore carved decorations—scrolls and flowers polished to the soft glow of old age. A miscellany of tiny shops hid behind unlit windows.

But here in the city, the tiny shops had the dignity of wise old men.

Ecuador itself considers Cuenca a showplace and we planned to stay there for four nights to explore the old buildings, visit villages in the nearby mountains, and bicycle south down the valley.

Like a bloodhound, Senor Godoy sniffed the presence of an excellent hotel as we inched down one street. He parked and ran in, only to run out again in a few minutes. He snorted with disgust.

"It is too expensive, Senora, but there is another hotel down the street." He had been equally disgusted when he had seen me pay the equivalent of a dollar for lipstick.

We drove to the next hotel and he zipped in while I waited in the car to protect the bicycle in the open trunk. He soon trotted out to announce that the prices of rooms in this hotel were more suitable for my pocketbook. Next he lifted the bike from the trunk and deposited both of us in the hotel lobby while he went off to find a protected parking lot for the car.

The bicycle, leaning against a wall at the foot of a flight of stairs, was a guest more puzzling than unwelcome. The senorita presiding at the desk opposite it stared in disbelief but said nothing. One man coming down the stairs looked at it, smiled, shook his head, and also said nothing as he hurried out the front door. Nobody paid any attention to the superannuated lady in maternity pants who was modestly sitting nearby.

After ten minutes Senor Godoy, chuckling, breezed into the lobby. "The car is safe, Senora. I found a good place only three blocks away."

It was more work to park the bicycle in the room than it had been to park the car down the street. The elevator was off a small hallway at the top of one flight of the stairs, but stairs do not defy Senor Godoy and heavy bicycles. He picked it up and carried it to the top in seconds. The elevator, however, defied him. It was the smallest space into which we had ever tried to squeeze the bicycle. Senor Godoy summoned the elevator, opened its glass door, and then examined its interior.

"Battles, Senora, we have battles!"

For moments he pondered. It seemed that the only thing to do was to stand the bicycle on its back wheel and send it up to the fourth floor on its own. We finally decided that I would precede the bicycle to the room, he would cram it in the elevator, and wrap himself around it like a contortionist. During all this calculating, he was laughing so hard that an uncontrollable attack of hysterics was threatening to burst like a storm, which would have prevented him doing anything about the problem at all.

"You go first, Senora, and I will come up the elevator later with the bike," he finally decided.

I ascended by myself and waited in my room. Scarcely recovered from laughing, he appeared in a minute or two escorting the bike and parked it at the foot of the bed. Saying he would see me at dinner, he bustled off to his room next door.

My room, like the elevator, was designed for a midget. Between the bottom of the bed and the bicycle now standing against the wall there was just passing space for one person walking with care. An armchair scarcely fitted between the bed and the windows. Almost touching the other side of the bed was a closet and small writing desk. To make use of either required deliberate movement. The bathroom, opening off the tiny entry inside the door, was adequate for one person.

A balcony stretched outside my windows. I pulled open the squeaky French doors and stepped out onto it. Looking at the roofs, I saw that the outdoor museum of colonial architecture we had admired from the street extended upward. Across the small plaza below the balcony was a church surmounted by a tall steeple. I discovered later that it had a bell that dutifully summoned worshipers in the early morning or at dusk. Prominent above the rick-rack aggregation of roofs were the round blue domes of the cathedral, which themselves dominated other rounded domes, sprouting among the roofs like so many mushrooms. Since 1517, when the Spanish founded the city on the site of the old Inca town of Tumibamba and renamed it Cuenca after a province in Spain, the same domes and spires have loomed above its roofs.

As if sheltered in the palm of a giant hand, Cuenca lies in a basin at a comfortable altitude of 8640 feet, almost a thousand feet lower than Quito. East and west of the city are the spines of the cordilleras, twisted arthritically, concealing villages that have found flat places to take root. Senor Godoy knew of three such villages that could be reached by a dirt road that snaked and burrowed through the deep canyon of the river Paute. We started early to visit them our first morning in Cuenca, going back north on the Quito-Cuenca Pan American Highway until we came to a road turning east. The road was gouged out of the grim rocky walls of the canyon, and ran a dark, wiggling course above the roily river. We chugged along for an hour, tunneling through the shadows of the immense cliffs on each side of the blackish river, until the road climbed up, and stretched out into sunny, open areas.

It was Sunday and life, which now appeared along the road, was happily aimless. Some men were lying beside the road, quite drunk. Their state of happiness was not so easily determined as their state of intoxication. We passed a group of boys having an energetic game of volleyball, slamming the ball back and forth over a net stretched across a small yard.

Senor Godoy nodded toward the game. "When I was in the army, I was very good. Every Sunday the officers wanted me on their team. All Sunday I played ball. Ah! The nights I went to bed. . . . " He finished his sentence by throwing back his head and arms, remembering how he could have slept forever after a day's bout with a volleyball.

By nine o'clock we had climbed up to the village of Gualaceo, alive with the bustle of the Sunday market. We parked the taxi nearby and wandered through tables piled with fruits from the coast—mangoes, maracuyas, chimoyas, bananas, oranges—guarded by women wearing Sunday-best Panama straw hats and bright wool skirts with a constellation of metal mirrors at the hems. The women ventured a few words in recommendation of their produce, but the sales pitch was aloof. They watched impassively while I went about admiring carrots and potatoes, sniffing mangoes, trying to find one that was fragrantly ripe. It was off-season for them. I selected the best-smelling one in the plaza, but it had no flavor. On one little cart were squares of candies called *bocadillos*, arranged in rows with the precision of a loving architect. They were concentrated cane sugar juice, looking like blocks of maple sugar candy, strong with molasses and so sweet that a bite-sized bit was enough at one time, if your jaws or hands were strong enough to reduce the block to a bite.

Roasted pigs, complete with hide, bristles, hooves, heads, and eyes staring bleakly at nothing, were stretched out on several tables. Beside one splayed and forlorn corpse a woman was vigorously peeling potatoes and tossing them into a huge stew pot at her elbow—creating the ubiquitous fast food of the Andean marketplace. The sun-soaked square was festive, jovial, relaxed, in a Sunday mood.

We started to wander away from the plaza but I soon saw that

Senor Godoy had no intention of wandering aimlessly. He began to trot down the street with determination, his eyes lighting up with the unmistakable glint of someone who is about to make an exciting purchase. I was breathless trying to keep up with him.

"There are many shoes for sale here, Senora," he explained, grinning. "Much cheaper than in Quito."

He showed me a piece of paper on which were neatly written

the shoe sizes of all the people in his family—five sons, an orphan niece, his wife, himself. As we bounced along the cobbled streets, the smell of leather overwhelmed us: the smarting smell of leather being tanned, the fresh clean smell of leather in new shoes, the smell of leather so strong that it saturated even the stones.

As methodically as a quartermaster shoeing a platoon of foot soldiers, he went into store after store, referring to his list, pulling shoes from piles or rows and examining tops, bottoms, sides; bargaining and pleading with a charm that would make a tap dancer willing to sell his own shoes and go barefoot the rest of his life. He frowned and walked out if the shoes didn't fit the foot or purse.

By the time we had reached store number six, he saw that I was only slowing down the expedition, so he deposited me there on a chair. With a hasty "One moment," he hurried back into the street. I was glad to sit down, and somehow soon found myself with a strange baby on my lap, which further anchored me to the chair. After many more moments than just one, he returned, grinning broadly and carrying a heavy plastic sack filled with shoes.

"Finished?" I asked hopefully, having finally gotten tired of sitting and having somehow managed to persuade the mother to take back her baby. No, finished he was not. He had forgotten his boy in kindergarten. So off we both trotted again, looking for shoes that would just fit his kindergartner. After a store or two he found a pair that was satisfactory, and with a great sigh, announced that all he had left to find were shoes for the littlest one.

"But, Senor, he does not yet walk," I protested, thinking that he could save a little money. He was unmoved, and stolidly ignored me when I described how I did not buy shoes for my little girl until she was reliably vertical and ready to step forth into the world. At last he found two tiny shoes for the little one of eight months. This time his sigh was prodigious. "Finished!" he chuckled on top of the sigh. There were ten pairs of shoes in all: one each for himself and the five sons, two apiece for his wife and the orphan niece—5,000 sucres in all, over sixty dollars and five days' wages, if he calculated his average daily take for the entire year. Would they all fit?

He grinned at the question. "If the shoes do not fit one, they will fit someone else who is bigger or smaller.''

I left Senor Godoy locking his shoes in the trunk, and strolled into the church across from the market square. Worshipers drifted in, stopped to pray and then tiptoed out. Some eased themselves into pews and settled themselves on their knees for prayers before mass. Their devotions competed with the twanging of a guitarist and the wheezing of an organist, who were practicing a swinging gospel hymn that I had heard in Protestant churches back home.

My intentions were less celestial. I had hoped to find a costumed saint to photograph and there, back in his special alcove, I found him—stylish in black wide-brimmed felt hat, fluffed out in a white wool robe as convoluted as that worn by Roman statues, cinched in by a gold belt, flourishing a red ribbon on his right wrist, and swinging a flower-embroidered black cape over his shoulders. His true residence might have been in heaven but I wondered who his worldly valet was. His clothes were immaculately pressed and freshly fluffed. Standing before the elegantly accoutered statue was a devout little old man in rags and bare feet, murmuring his prayers. He saw me, smiled, then shuffled near to whisper the credentials of the saint. He was Santiago, patron of Gualaceo and all the inhabitants therein, including the shod and unshod as well as all the shoemakers.

"The village saves the village," Senor Godoy had told me, quoting an old Ecuadorian proverb, which means the same as our "Heaven helps them who help themselves." Going to the next village we found it was true.

Leaving Gualaceo we went a few miles uphill on a good road south of the town and came to the village of Chordeleg, sitting on an airy flat place on top of the hill. Its clean, swept sidewalks surrounding the central plaza bordered shops that displayed a variety of handmade goods for sale—straw dolls, wood and stone carvings, embroidered shirts and blouses, a few leather goods. A guidebook I had read described the village as "touristy," but the enterprise of the people was encouraging to see after the sorrow on the roads south of Ambato, where brown-clad Indians trotted along in bare feet and in despair.

The village may have been considered touristy, but there were few tourists. I saw only two. One was a man who had the scornful sniff of someone passing by something malodorous. Some persons remind you of plants. He was a prickly cactus. A beggar brushed by him with outstretched hand. Startled, the cactus pulled away. The beggar was harmless enough, and Senor Godoy tossed her a coin or two.

We walked into a small museum on one side of the square. On a balcony above a jewel-like inner court the curator had displayed examples of local crafts—hand-woven shawls, simple carved creches, baskets woven from straw. In one corner photographs of the village spinner and weaver showed how he had prepared the wool from sheep's back to ours—shearing, washing, carding, dyeing, spinning, weaving. Placed beside the photographs, pieces of the wool itself illustrated the changes from rawness to a woven marvel.

At the museum shop, I bought a tiny creche woven from straw dyed in magenta, purple, green and yellow—all made by hand. It was the quintessence of simplicity, yet everything was there: black hair and halos for Joseph, Mary and the Baby; a cradle; ears and tail for the lamb. The creche was woven securely to a straw base, and on the bottom was the price—150 sucres, two dollars—so that I would never forget it.

All at once we heard a cry in the plaza. Immediately a crowd coalesced in front of the church like so many beads of mercury. I could hear a pair of angry voices.

"Please, Senor Godoy," I urged. "Go to see what has happened." He trotted off obediently.

After sorting out the confusion of voices all shouting simultaneously, he came back to report that it was alleged that one woman had snatched a gold chain from the throat of another, which action the accused was loudly denying. The victim then had shouted even louder that the gold chain had been slipped to the husband of the thief. This turned up the decibels of the shouts of the thief, who screamed that it was all not so. The only thing clear was that nothing was ever going to be clear. The crowd walked off, disappointed as children who have been spilled off someone's lap with the story half-told. Senor Godoy shrugged, chuckled over my curiosity, and we drove away.

Paute is about ten miles to the northeast, and we climbed over a twisting hard dirt road to reach it. What distinguishes the village is a hydroelectric plant high in the mountains above it, which Senor Godoy said furnished power to Ecuador and Peru. It is a mammoth installation, but the road leading to it is so primitive that few brave it to get there.

"Grande, grande!" he laughed, amused at the irony. "But imagine! Such a horrible road there." Up to that point I was all for driving up, but changed my mind. In the center of the village we found a market where I could bargain for woolen Indian skirts with embroidered flowers and tiny mirrors at the hems, for three granddaughters.

"No one in the United States will have skirts like these," Senor Godoy commented. This should please three teenage girls who scorn wearing anything that anybody else does, I thought. The mirrors, much loved by the Indians, are also significant historically. The colonial padres placed them alluringly around the churches and thus enticed the Indians inside to convert them.

Inebriation, not piety encouraged by mirrors, was the principal occupation of the village on that Sunday morning. Drunks were in abundance, in various states of needing support. Some, still upright but listing dangerously, were held up between two friends. For others, even a semblance of a vertical posture was impossible. They were stretched out quite horizontally beside the road, to be propped up later when conditions were more favorable.

"Understand, Senora," Senor Godoy explained patiently. "It was Saturday night. It was the end of the week." I did not belittle the blessings of Saturday night, but here it seemed to take on an exaggerated importance.

"Did you get drunk when young?" I asked him.

"Si." He looked solemn. I could not imagine him reeling, even when young. The most daring drink he usually had on our trip was mineral water laced with cola, although I would have been glad to buy him a cool beer. Was he setting an example for his sons even when out of their sight? He never explained.

17/

QUAKES MADE BY GOD AND MAN

OUTDOOR MUSEUMS MANY TIMES are not static. In the reconstructed buildings people are moving about, demonstrating spinning or weaving of wool, working with tools long since obsolete, wearing clothes that seem anachronistic and ill-suited to the modern wearer.

The people in the "outdoor museum" on the streets of Cuenca did not need to be costumed for display purposes. They were wearing what they had been wearing for ages, what belonged to the setting.

Sitting by the window in the coffee shop for early breakfast on the two weekday mornings we were at the hotel, we had a view as if we were looking through glass at a museum display case. The contents were not only alive, but changed rapidly. First, Indian women, in black felt-brimmed hats and with wide bright shawls slung like hammocks over their backs, were pattering along the street, half-running. A baby might be a bump in the shawl, tiny head bobbing over the mother's shoulder. Some had enormous baskets strapped to their backs. A few were gossiping with friends trotting along with them. The red or orange embroidered wool skirts were turned inside out to keep them from being soiled. If they were turned right side out, the tiny metal discs sparkled at the hems. Faces were bronzed by the slanting morning sunlight. Cheeks were red as polished apples. Bicycling at that altitude had also made my face brown and my cheeks unnaturally rosy.

The Indian women never strolled. Some trotted, some half-ran, others walked rapidly as they spun wool, holding the fleece under the right arm while the right hand pulled and twisted the wool onto the distaff held by the left. This maneuver slowed them down sufficiently to talk with a companion beside them, who also coordinated spinning hands and hurrying feet.

Soon the display case changed. Small boys in brown pants and jackets, all dressed uniformly, hurried along the street, turning into the old school building across from us. Some of the boys held onto their father's hands, others raced into the building alone. Crosses and sparse religious symbols decorated the windows, but the school was no longer under the tutelage of the church. Above the main door were the words *Escuela Fiscal de Ninos*—Fiscal School for Small Boys. "Fiscal" pertained to the state treasury, and the government now had assumed support of the school. Taxation only furnished tuition, but no books, pencils or other supplies.

The school saddened me. The leprous bricks, clinging tentatively to each other, bore the grime of ages. The windows, one story above the street, had cracked or missing panes. It looked like an inner-city school in America that had lost bond and levy elections to the point of hopelessness. Yet the boys, lovingly polished and brushed by their mothers, hurried to it, not like Shakespeare's "whining schoolboy . . . creeping like a snail, unwillingly to school," but excitedly, impressed with the importance of it all.

The boys did not have time to get out of the showcase before little girls in red jackets appeared, walking with dignity to a girls' school in the opposite direction, holding onto their mother's hands.

Within minutes all the little boys and girls were safely sequestered inside. They would emerge around one in the afternoon, walking slowly, books and homework in the satchels slung over their backs. I wanted to visit a school, but Senor Godoy protested.

"It is very complicated, Senora," he explained with obvious consternation. "It disturbs the teacher. It is necessary to get special permission."

I realized all this, so the thing to do was to greet the teacher at recess. I had done this in other countries, but even then, the eyes of the teacher always darted in the direction of the school building, looking for the headmaster who would not permit such a distraction. It is possible to visit a small country school if you happen to come upon it at recess time. The lone teacher there is king in his solitary castle.

By eight-thirty, the jeweler across the street pushed up the metallic shutters covering the windows of his shop, which was soon followed by a banging of shutters up and down the street. Men in business suits and women in print dresses and sweaters walked and talked their way down the street, mingling with the trotting Indians. Almost lost among them was a small, barefooted boy leading a milk goat. He carried a pail and looked beseechingly up at passersby as he slipped in and out among them. I ran out to take his picture, but he scooted away, deftly disappearing among legs and bodies.

"He is ashamed because he is not in school," I said to Senor Godoy as I walked back to the breakfast table. The humiliation of being outside school when the more fortunate are in, must be as painful as being without shoes.

After breakfast we started out to explore Cuenca, which seemed like walking through a picture gallery. It began as a pleasant day. The old colonial churches we visited had the expected beauty as well as the expected beggars draped on the steps, their heads hidden under old felt hats. At the bottom of the steps the beauty of the blind girl who sold devotional candles made me stop to admire her. Her black braids glistened. Unlike the beggars around her, she wore sandals. The large plaza across from the cathedral was crowded with trees, benches, boys hawking newspapers, grandfathers watching babies, a child or two playing with a ball. On one side of the plaza was a flower market drenched in sunshine; on another side, under a shaded arcade, was a long row of shoe polishers, who were either vigorously rubbing the shoes of customers sitting on stools above them or were looking critically at the shoes of the passersby and suggesting that they needed a shine for twenty sucres.

We had wandered through the covered market, sprawled over two blocks, where the smells of dried spices, roasting pig, gunnysacks of dusty potatoes, freshly dug carrots, sliced pineapples dripping with juice, filled the place with an invisible steam. Plump women, skin glowing like oiled walnuts, children clustered tightly near them, entreated us with smiles, not voices; but we were only looking. More appealing was something not for sale—a tiny boy,

black eyes peering over a potato sack, skin as brown as the potatoes.

We made our way back to the crowded street lined with booths of clothes, shoes, paste jewelry, and gewgaws defying enumeration. Something made me look down at my little camera bag.

"Someone robbed me!" I gasped. The zipper had been opened, too furtively for me to have felt it. My close-up lens for my camera was missing.

Senor Godoy stared, unbelieving. "It is not possible. It is difficult to open." He knew because he often struggled with the zipper as he helped me extricate my camera from the bag. I had to admire the professional skill of the thief. "Perhaps it is at the hotel," Senor Godoy added hopefully. I knew it was not. I could see my lens lying in a gutter, a child's abandoned plaything, useless to anybody who did not have my model of a Leicaflex, now obsolete. I had never been robbed in my years of traveling and I was not taking the loss philosophically. Later we searched my hotel room, but the lens was nowhere. Senor Godoy, downcast, returned to his room without a word. Months later he would write me to say how distressed he was that I had lost anything; but I answered that the lens was insured, and to my surprise, I had been able to replace it.

Late in the afternoon Senor Godoy knocked on my door. I opened it to find him bubbling with smiles. "Senora, Pancho is here! Do you wish to see Pancho?"

Of course I wished to see Pancho, one of the seventeen presidential candidates to be voted upon two months later. For miles I had passed his campaign exhortations: black letters painted on white-washed rocks, his picture shouting from the white sides of buildings on the roadside. Campaign expenses must have consisted mostly of whitewash, black paint, and brushes, wielded by a host of volunteers who would cover every available space throughout the country not already used by the sixteen other candidates.

We ran out into the street and headed down to where we could hear the most noise. We soon arrived at the uproarious center of the campaign hurricane.

Banners screaming "Pancho!" hung down from balconies, supporters waving more banners hung over the balcony railings, people stuffed into the street waved a windstorm of banners. The noise rose to a tempest when a band came tramping by, trying to outblow the uproar of the crowd with a thunderous Sousa march. Those in the street, waving and shouting, paraded along with it. A huge tractor, also splendid with banners, started growling its way through the mass. This roused the shouts of *"Pancho pueblo! Pancho pueblo!"*—Pancho for the common people—to a frenzy. Not a chicken in every pot promised for this crowd but a tractor in every field. The tractor rumbled along, the horns of the band blared, and suddenly the shouts rose a dozen decibels.

Now we caught sight of Pancho himself, waving, grinning, turning his head from one side of the street to the other as he walked along. By standing on our toes we could just get a glimpse of him.

"I want to hear the speeches," I shouted to Senor Godoy, who had read in the newspaper where they would take place. We ran from the parade and hurried up a back street toward a church square. We beat Pancho and his mob of supporters there, but still had to squeeze our way into the crowd in order to get a look at the banner-bedecked platform in front. The platform was bustling with people checking chairs and testing a mare's nest of mikes and lights scattered all over, under their feet and over their heads.

All at once the crowd began chanting wildly: "*Pancho Presidente! Pancho Presidente!*" There he was, moving across the platform, privileged attendants following. He shook his hands above his head, precipitating even wilder shouts: "*Pancho pueblo! Pancho pueblo!*" Infected with the massed enthusiasm, I began to believe that Pancho was really "for the people" and I wished him success. The shouting and chanting swelled, the banners waved, the lights on the platform went out and were relit—all taking up so much time that I doubted that Pancho would ever get a chance to open his mouth. He kept on waving, grasping his hands above his head, grinning in appreciation, nodding vigorously, ignoring moments of darkness when the lights became disconnected, ignoring other muffled moments when the microphones went silent as someone was trying to introduce him.

At last Pancho's campaign manager held up his arms to quiet the crowd and the shouting subsided to isolated outbursts. He spoke well but long, extolling the virtues of Pancho, promising changes if he were elected, decrying the needs of the country: "Money—Si!"; "Good roads!" (I waved discreetly); "Help for the poor!"

I looked back to a gentle man behind me who was listening with patient resignation, having heard it said and promised before.

On went the speaker, his voice dropping to a mumble when the mike failed and ringing clear again when the mike was revived; continuing undaunted when the lights failed and he was partially visible in the evening gloom. After fifteen minutes the speaker introduced Doctor Pancho, next president of Ecuador, he hoped. Immediately outcries of "*Pancho Presidente*" and "*Pancho pueblo*" started all

over again. The crowd was having more fun making noise than listening to Pancho, who had grown hoarse in the line of duty.

"He is from Guayaquil. It is difficult to understand," Senor Godoy whispered and the crowd must have felt the same. People, who had been silent during the long introductory speech, murmured restlessly. "Let's go," I whispered to Senor Godoy and we snaked and squeezed our way back to the street. Carefully we passed through a cordon of policemen, who appeared quite bored and neutral in the matter of political speeches.

"They are protecting Pancho," Senor Godoy laughed.

I did not realize how necessary protection was until I read in the paper the next day that a political rally in a city of northern Ecuador had left two supporters—or objectors—dead. Alarmed, I pointed out the article to Senor Godoy.

"Si, Senora, with Pancho I thought, 'What do I do with the Senora if there is a problem?' I thought, 'I must grab the Senora and run.' "

Pancho had promised many things, all requiring money. That night at supper I asked Senor Godoy, "With what? Where will Pancho get the money?"

"Oh, it is only a theory, Senora. There is tax for what you earn, but it is just a theory. It is not regulated. For example, I do not pay a tax."

Supporting eight persons on his earnings, he would hardly owe any. But what about roads? Yes, we had passed checkpoints where he had to pay a small toll in order to pass.

"In my country the employer keeps money from what you earn to pay your tax," I went on, trying to explain withholding tax. He understood quite well.

"Si, but here it is just a theory," he repeated.

A sympathetic employer, he told me, might not withhold part of your salary for taxes.

"I have to send in money for taxes," I said. "But if I send it too late I have to pay a fine." He commiserated with me over such a misfortune. "If I pay too much, the government will return the money," I went on. He was astonished, unbelieving. His fork had stopped halfway to his mouth.

"Si, Senor, there are cheats and liars in my country too, but most of us pay." This time my fork stopped in midair. I felt as if I had just attested to a miracle, a miracle I had not recognized before.

He stared at me and shook his head. "Very interesting."

I thought of the wistful face of the gentle little man who had been standing behind us at the rally. With all my heart I wished the next president well.

The next morning, when the campaign shouting had died and the citizens had forgotten all that was promised, I grew restless. We had shoed all the Godoys at the mountain village; we had explored Cuenca on foot. Meanwhile, the bike had been parked idly at the foot of my bed. I assumed that the "Mercedes Benz" from Brazil was getting as restless as I was.

"Is it possible to bicycle in Cuenca?" I asked Senor Godoy, almost piteously.

"Surely, Senora," he promised. So on this last day in Cuenca I stepped again into my *pantalones maternales,* put my sun hat on my head, hung my purse around my neck, and sat down in a chair to wait for Senor Godoy to knock on the door. Perching my "glasses of emergency" on my nose, I started to read; but after squinting over a few lines, my eyes hurt. A sudden trembling startled me. The chair beneath me quivered like jelly. "An earthquake!" I almost screamed. I knew the helpless terror of being shaken without warning and of having no way to escape the disaster. In a few seconds the jelly on which I was sitting stabilized itself, but I held my breath. I waited for the violence that might follow, that might knock the room asunder. It didn't come.

Soon Senor Godoy knocked on the door. He looked as cheerful as usual and quite unshaken. Earthquake? He had felt none. Instead, he chuckled and began taking inventory of the equipment needed so that I could emerge clothed and in my right mind: "*Pantalones maternales?* Camera? Purse?"; and as the usual final precaution, "The head?" Having made sure that I was gathered together, he laughed happily, picked up the bike, and assisted it on its tight, contorted trip down the elevator, past the astonished clerks at the desk, through the front door and out into the street.

The Peugeot also had been resting in a parking lot down the street, but its resting place did not resemble the paved lots of the U.S., filled with cars and guarded by an attendant in a white sentry box. Here it was a small area, dirt-covered, fenced in on three sides and protected by a dwelling on the other. Only four vehicles were parked there. A woman ran out to greet us and to collect the fee. All

expenses with the car were the responsibility of Senor Godoy, but hewas not sure that his cab was safe even in this guarded lot. Every night of our trip he had lifted the hood of the taxi, removed the distributor from the engine, and pocketed it, disabling the motor as well as any common thief. Now he lifted the hood, replaced the tiny distributor, and we drove off a half mile to a wide road where city traffic had thinned out and I could bicycle.

The paved road wound south, through a green valley, skirted farms and wooded hills, and crossed a bridge over a glass-clear river that kicked up white waves as it splashed along. Upstream a crowd of women were washing clothes, using elbow grease and rocks instead of soap, ringing out the clothes tightly and spreading a motley mosaic of whites, reds, greens, blues, blacks, browns on grass and rocks to dry. Several small children were having their clothes washed right off their backs. Naked as cherubs, they were playing quietly near their mothers. Farther upstream two women were washing out long strands of black hair, splashing water over each other's head. Standing on the bridge 500 feet away I could hear the women laughing and chattering, making washday the social event of the week. I was not going to trade my washing machine for rocks and a stream, but my basement laundry room now seemed a sterile place.

Before noon I pedaled through a scattering of houses and a store, which Ecuadorians would call a "population," rather than a village. Children were poking on their way home from school. Some smiled and said "Good day, Senora," when I spoke to them; others merely stared, too surprised at the bicycle to nod their heads.

Senor Godoy called it the best day on the bicycle yet. Not once did he have to stop and lift it into the trunk. What hills there were could all be pumped up. He relaxed in the taxi while I pedaled along as easily as at sea level. No wonder. The altitude of the valley was a mere 8640 feet.

Basking in the sunshine, we picnicked at noon beside the river which ran through the valley. Our fare, if not gourmet, had the virtue of being everlasting. There were always leftovers, and when one article of our diet was consumed it was immediately replaced by the same thing. We had no decisions to make when we shopped. All we could find in the stores was the same food we had just eaten.

Senor Godoy was listening to the news over the car radio when he thrust his head out the window. "An earthquake! There was an earthquake in Quito!" It had caused no deaths or damage, but had been strong enough to pass under several mountain ranges and shake my chair in Cuenca. The news report said that people in buildings had felt the quake, and rushed out into the street. The people on the street, however, had felt nothing, and wondered why the wild-eyed people were tumbling out of the buildings. Even the people at the radio station were not alarmed, and continued the political propaganda which had been saturating the airwaves for months. Later Senor Godoy would find out that the earthquake had caused his family considerable trouble.

The narrow valley where we were was a gentle place which made you forget earthquakes. The river which fed the lush meadows on either side of it ran along quietly, as if it were in no hurry to tumble through the Andes to reach the sea, as if it were reluctant to leave such secluded peace in a land where the mountains hurl rivers abruptly and savagely downward. Peace surrounded me as I pedaled farther south. Few cars, few trucks, few walkers were on the almost desolate highway, which my map showed could end up in Loja, the most southern city of the Sierra; in Machala on the coast; or even in Guayaquil by a long, roundabout route.

I reached a small village where the road forked and no road signs informed me whether to go left or right. Since we had no destination, the decision was not painful. I merely pedaled straight ahead on the road to the right, and looked across the valley to the left to see the rejected road hugging the hillsides.

Sitting up straight and surveying the benign countryside, I wheeled along for miles under a friendly sun. My bicycling uncle would have called it "an afternoon stroll." Now and again a tiny hut sat beside the road. In front of one, under the cover of a wide overhang of the thatched roof, a man bent over a large loom. Leaning against the side of the hut were two younger men—motionless, open-eyed sleepers. I stopped and greeted them. The weaver did not look up from his work; but, without moving his head, he had noticed my bicycle.

"Are you touring the country by bicycle, Senora?"

He did not lift his eyes or stop his fingers from pulling threads through the warp. "Where do you come from? The United States?"

Shortly Senor Godoy pulled up beside us. "Ah! Is he accompanying you? Good!" Without turning his head he had caught sight of the taxi and driver.

Two women soon appeared in the open doorway and smiled at us. The inside of the hut behind them was dark and windowless. The only light came from the low doorless entrance in front. The dirt floor was swept clean, and bare of clutter. Pigeons flew about restlessly, not satisfied with any place they could find to roost. Some ventured inside the hut and the women promptly shooed them out. Both shooers and shooed took the confrontation quite casually.

"Senor, how much did she pay for the airplane to get here? Would it be a thousand American dollars?" the weaver asked, still never lifting his head. The weaving on his horizontal loom was loose and resembled macrame.

"What are you making, Senor?" I asked. I had not seen anything in Ecuador like it.

"It is for a bed," he explained quite inadequately I thought, eyes and fingers still fixed on whatever it was going to be.

"Someone has ordered me to make it. They pay me for the work."

I asked his wife if she wove too; but she shook her head, and noisily shooed another pigeon from the doorway.

"Every man in this *pueblo* needs two women," he said, in an effort to explain the presence of the two females standing idly in the doorway. Both the women and Senor Godoy laughed at what was supposed to be a huge joke, or compliment to the man, I didn't know which. I rolled away, waving at the man who didn't look up, and at the women with cheerful smiles shooing away pigeons. The upright sleepers, still propped against the hut, had not stirred.

"Liar!" snorted Senor Godoy before I started down the road. "Two women! Every man in that pueblo does not need two women."

After a mile I pumped up a small hill and reached a promontory that overlooked a vast chaotic upheaval of high peaks and low clouds. The pavement ended in a kilometer, we learned from a passing motorist, and then the road tumbled downward for sixty-four miles, struggling to reach Loja not far from the southern border with Peru. It was an impassable road and Senor Godoy did not recommend it. I climbed up on a lookout and bored my eyes into the horizon. The boundary between Peru and Ecuador, still unsettled, strife always threatening, was a little over a hundred miles away. I had pedaled as far south in the Ecuadorian Sierra as I could.

Senor Godoy had been anxious to talk to his wife back home contending with the five boys, aided only by the orphan niece. This was not an easily accomplished project because his little house had no phone. The first night we were in Cuenca, he had managed to reach a friend who had a phone and could get a message to his wife. Senor Godoy told him the name of the hotel in Cuenca where we were staying and asked that his wife phone him there. The next night, carting along who knows how many children, she had succeeded in getting to a public phone and calling him at the hotel. Through the thin walls separating our two rooms, I had heard him talking to her, raising his voice to a pitch necessary to carry it across miles of Andean ranges.

"My children have been sick," he told me later. "My wife had to carry them to a doctor—an emergency."

Now he could not rest until she would call him that night at the hotel and let him know how the children were. Again she would walk down to the public phone and call him precisely at five o'clock.

I turned away from the mountains scrambling their way toward Peru and looked at my watch. It was two o'clock. If I pedaled furiously, we could get back to the hotel in time. I started out at once—pedaling furiously. We had discovered that the two unlabeled roads back at the village had separated, only to join later before flinging themselves down as one to Loja. I turned on to the beautifully paved road, quite new, which I had spurned before. I sailed along like an eagle, a steady twenty kilometers, or twelve and a half miles an hour, Senor Godoy informed me later. That was a fair clip for that heavy, unstreamlined bike, and Senor Godoy seemed impressed. At the beginning of the bike trip he told me that he had expected my legs to pump like two slow-moving pistons. Languidly, he moved his fists up and down to illustrate.

Soon I whirred into the wide place where the two roads rejoined, and Senor quickly hurried the bike into the trunk for the last five miles to the hotel—an uninteresting repetition of the beginning ride of the morning. I didn't object. I had biked fifty miles.

The hurrying was useless. He waited in his room for the telephone call, but I could hear no conversation.

"I do not understand," he kept saying at dinner time. "She did not phone."

"Perhaps it was the earthquake," I suggested. He shook his head. I didn't want to increase his worries by arguing about the devastating effects of earthquakes upon communications. He knew that she would have tried to reach him. Something must have happened.

18

FOUR-HUNDRED-MILE DETOUR

WE WERE CLIMBING out of the Cuenca basin, the fresh morning sky sparkling above us, and heading north to Riobamba, going back over the same road. By late afternoon we planned to be in the hotel where we had been a week before. It was important to be in that hotel by late afternoon. Before the earthquake, when Senor Godoy had shouted directions to his wife over the phone in Cuenca he had told her the name of the Riobamba hotel and asked her to phone the night we arrived. Sitting beside him in the cab, I could sense his tension. He was anxious to hear about his sick boys.

After an hour I saw that we passed a paved road that led westward to the coast. But we kept on north, still climbing and reaching for the clouds. We had chugged up several miles, when I noticed that no cars had been coming toward us. The tracks of the striking railroad crossed this highway and I remembered the freight cars that had been pushed partly across the road. I still saw the broken glass and blood shed on the pavement where a motorist had banged into the cars in the dark. By now the strikers could have pushed those heavy freight cars completely across the road, stopping all southbound traffic. Senor Godoy, whose face was now grim must have been thinking of the same thing.

After a while we saw a solitary truck braking downhill toward us. Senor Godoy hailed it.

"A question, please, Senor," he called out. "What has happened? Is the road blocked?"

"Do not go, Senor," the truck driver warned. "Turn around. The road is blocked completely. Turn around." Immediately we turned around.

"I understood him, Senor," I cried out. "No cars were coming. I was worried." We pulled off the road and Senor Godoy's hands fell from the steering wheel to his lap.

"Senora, I do not know what we do."

He drove slowly back to the junction, his hands drooping disconsolately over the steering wheel. We were dismayed to find a number of cars parked there. The drivers were all eddying about, as if lost and without compass. He jumped out and ran over to the driver of a truck which also had been heading north. Again I perched the "glasses of emergency" on the end of my nose and studied my map. On it existed, or the cartographers wished it existed, a road to the coast which started from the junction we had passed. I decided not to worry.

Soon Senor Godoy trotted back, grinning, his whole face aglow.

"Adventures, Senora! We have adventures."

The "adventure" was that the road at the junction which headed toward the coast actually did go to the coast, safely around all the treacherous tracks. It led to Guayaquil, where neither of us had any desire to go, but it was the only escape hatch. There was only moderate fog, he had been told, and it was a good paved road. We would have to reach Guayaquil before six o'clock darkness— only a distance of about 205 miles—but a super highway it would not be. It would squirm slowly over the Western Cordillera and no, there would be no time for the bicycle.

Senor Godoy jumped back into the car and we turned west down the road.

"This is a joke, Senora," he laughed. "We did not want to go to Guayaquil and here we go to Guayaquil."

The road started burrowing downward through gashes in the mountains, ducking under light carpets of fog which hid the peaks. Looking off to the south we could glimpse the barren *paramos*, as they call the cold, bleak plateaus of the Andes; but we soon dropped beneath them, twisting our way through dark canyons hidden from the sun.

"No, Guayaquil does not please me," Senor Godoy began again

as he cautiously rounded the curves of the serpentine highway. "I had to drive someone to Guayaquil one time, but I did not want to stay there overnight. It is hot and dangerous. I came back to Quito at night. There was a moon, but the trees made shadows on the road."

He relaxed when the road straightened and we passed a tiny village which was gripping the hillside so that it would not fall off. Señor Godoy started to laugh uproariously.

"A black cow was crossing the road. Think, Senora, a black cow." He doubled over the wheel and laughed with abandon. I was impatient.

"What happened? Hurry. Tell me." He only laughed harder.

"The black cow crossed the road," he gasped, "right in the shadow of the tree. I came along just then. There was the black cow in the black shadow."

I now saw nothing but destruction.

"I saw the cow." He could now speak above the subsiding gasps. "I turned just in time." He jerked the wheel so that I could see how he had avoided plowing into the black cow in the black shadow. I wished that the unfortunate driver who had failed to see the space between the two freight cars which the strikers had not yet pushed across the road near Riobamba had been as alert.

We had been twisting down for an hour or so and we now felt a subtle warmth. The gullies beside us were no longer brown and erosion-scarred, but were green with trees and shrubs. As we got lower, we brushed along orchids flourishing above the banks of a brook. Almost suddenly, surprising us, the road made one last turn and leveled out with a sigh as it dropped upon the wide plain of *La Costa*.

The world had changed—from cool sunshine to dripping heat, from peaks and *paramos* to endless flatness, from tailored fields of grain and potatoes to enormous plantations of pineapples, papayas, rice, rubber trees, bananas, and cacao. Grazing near the marshes beside the road were herds of cattle carrying on their scrawny backs numerous *garzas*, or cattle egrets, who paid for the ride by picking off ticks. Constantly the birds flapped back and forth between the accommodating cows and the nearby streams and pools.

On and on we went, straight without deviation, on flatness stretching to the horizon.

After some miles we began to pass through little towns and at one Senor Godoy abruptly turned away from the highway and picked his way through the cars, dogs, children and meandering pedestrians on a side street. He was seeking the telephone center office. He must somehow get in touch with his wife to let her know that he would not be as planned at the hotel in Riobamba, that he wouldn't know where we would be for the night, and that she would not be able to reach him. The logistics of two people trying to communicate by telephone when neither has a telephone involves difficulties as great as those which beset Stanley in his search for Livingston. Stanley at least had the benefit of native drum signals.

For miles Senor Godoy had been testing one plan after another: he would call the school his oldest son attended and the *cura* would

be sure the boy would get the message and deliver it to his mother; he thought of a friend whom he might reach by phone; he would call his younger brother at work. Suddenly his face fairly exploded with enthusiasm. That was it. He would call the younger brother.

We whipped into the parking spot in front of what was a combination of a telephone office and phone booths—a small, recessed area in front of a building, like a porch enclosed on three sides. The phone booths lined one wall.

"One moment," he said as he jumped out of the car and hurried up to the counter along the back wall. For a long time I could see him talking with the girl there who made the telephone connections. Getting through to the messenger seemed to be as difficult as deciding upon the messenger in the first place. After many moments he disappeared into a booth. Minutes later, happy, he bounced down the stairs and got back into the car.

"What battles, Senora! The senorita said that it was not possible to talk to Quito because of the earthquake. I said, 'I must talk.' She said, 'No, it is not possible.' I said, 'Look, Senorita. I have not been with my family for a month. I must talk to them.' "

A man longing for his family convinced the senorita that the impossible was possible, and quickly the wires were put in order so that he could talk to his brother. Yes, the children were well now. Yes, they had felt the earthquake and, yes, the brother would go to the senora and tell her not to phone him in Riobamba. I wondered if carrier pigeon might have been simpler. Later we learned that it would have been more effective.

As we neared Guayaquil, he stopped the taxi again to lift the bike from its vulnerable spot in the trunk to a less accessible location in the luggage carrier on top. He threaded and tightened the straps around the bike and slammed the trunk lid shut against intruders. Even by skipping our usual gourmet picnic, it was late afternoon before we were pushing our way through the traffic of Guayaquil.

"Is it possible to stay at the convent of your aunt the nun?" I pulled out her address from my pocket. His aunt the nun, or *la tia la monja,* as we always called her, had urged me to visit her in Guayaquil. Her convent certainly would be safer than a hotel, as she had said. He shook his head.

"Understand, Senora, I have the greatest respect for my aunt, but I cannot talk to nuns. They are different. With the *curas* at the school of the boys it is easy. I can talk to them. As you say, it would be better if we had written her first."

I agreed. I was really too tired to do anything but settle in a hotel. I would not want to disturb the evening peace of the convent by landing there unexpectedly and bedless.

The more tumultuous the traffic and crowds of Guyaquil became, the more I wished not for the peace of a convent, but for the solitude of a monk's retreat. We muscled into a side street where we saw a large hotel. There Senor Godoy knew one of the chauffeurs, who magically appeared at the same time that a policeman walked up, scowling at the bicycle roosting on top of the cab.

"I should fine you for carrying a bicycle up there," he growled.

Senor Godoy answered growl with grin. "Why, Senor? I have carried it this way all over Ecuador!" The policeman argued, Senor Godoy made conciliatory remarks, the policeman cited the alleged law, Senor Godoy spoke amiably but firmly, and at last the policeman withdrew with apologies.

"Hmph! He only wants money," I sniffed when he had safely disappeared. Senor Godoy laughed and nodded.

His chauffeur friend had directed us to a hotel on the Guayas River, which I envisioned as being in the midst of peace and space. It was. Across the street from it was a tree-shaded park with a promenade overlooking the wide river, swiftly sweeping its brown sediment and debris to the Pacific.

A watchman stood guard in front of the hotel all night long and Senor Godoy offered him money to be a nursemaid to the taxi. Thieves in this city might know how to contend with missing distributors. Senor Godoy, as usual, took the extra precaution of removing it from the engine.

Senor Godoy led the bike into the lobby, mollified the clerk at the desk by addressing him as *"caballero,"* or "gentleman." Without complaint, he assigned the bicycle and me to a room on the second floor overlooking an indoor court where a few shrubs were trying to grow in the confined air and obscure light.

The hotel restaurant was on the top floor with picture windows overlooking the river, now flowing darkly, occasional ripples catching sparks from the city lights. This port city was the place for fish, so we ordered *ceviche,* an appetizer of raw white fish marinated in lime juice and onions—a specialty of the country—and *corvina,* a white fish simmered gently so that its delicate flavor would not be lost.

After supper there was a soft warmth in the air and we strolled across the street to the park. A dozen couples were leaning against the low wall above the river, too wrapped around each other to notice anyone else. We passed by them discreetly, but avoided the knots of rowdy young men at the other end of the little park. "I have no confidence in them," Senor Godoy explained. "Thieves!"

Back in my hotel room I was the one who had no confidence. I started to chain my door shut, but the chain had been broken. I reached down to double-lock the door, but the lock had been yanked apart. One remaining lock still locked, but feebly. I pushed a large desk up against the door, tied my camera to my ankles, hung my purse around my neck, turned the noisy air conditioner low, crawled into bed and slept.

In the morning we found that thieves did not break in and steal, the all-night watchman had not let the taxi escape from the exposed parking place in front of the hotel, and the lively gang of visitors from Colombia who had come down to inexpensive Ecuador for Christmas shopping had stuffed themselves back into their tour bus and driven off. We hurried off too, untempted to go sightseeing, restless to run from the maelstrom of honking horns and shouting people, anxious to ascend to the coolness of the Sierra. Fearfully, I looked up the railroad tracks as we crossed them outside the city, but the strikers were pushing no cars across the highway. We were now taking a different highway back to the Sierra, one that was north of the unplanned one we had taken the day before.

For several miles out of the city we passed by villages that seemed awash in mud—mud in the streets, mud splashed on the walls of the houses, mud on the children, mud on ragged clothes. If the Sierra had brown silent poverty hiding within tiny mud-brick shacks or pattering barefoot behind donkeys, the coast had mud-brown poverty lived outdoors.

Babahoyo was the last large town we passed through before we climbed again to the Andes. Everyone seemed intent upon a variety of occupations: students clustered in front of a large technical school; ragged children filled the sides of the street; a few businessmen in cool slacks and sport shirts were strolling to offices and shops; housewives were plodding along carrying pails or plastic jugs.

"I believe they have a problem with water here," Senor Godoy remarked, nodding toward the women. The destructive floods of El Nino had also violated plumbing systems on *La Costa*.

Outside Babahoyo, due eastward, the road went past straggling houses on stilts, many open in front, destitution exposed, people free to stare out or stare in. Gradually the houses beside the road dwindled, and we were passing only plantations, pastures and swamps.

"How does it seem to you?" Senor Godoy asked.

"Very interesting, as always, Senor. But very dirty and there is much poverty."

"I think the same." He sighed heavily. As a man from *La Sierra*, he had little affection for those in *La Costa*. "We call them monkeys," he had said.

Ahead a colossal tree aglow with yellow blossoms towered skyward. Beyond it we could see not the mountains but mists shrouding the mountains, blending them into the watery gray sky above. Abruptly our road shot upward, and soon reached a village that threatened to tip off the side of a hill. The road was new to Senor Godoy. He stuck his head out of the window and hailed a passerby.

"A question, please, Senor. What is the name of this village?"

"Balzapamba," he answered.

Here at Balzapamba, then, was a problem. The road forked and neither of our maps would hazard guessing which road would be better or where they really went. Both go to San Jose, the man assured us. Both were good roads, but one was higher than the other. "Vistas are pleasing to you," Senor Godoy suggested. "We will go on the higher road. Hit me with a shout when you want a photograph."

We turned to the high road and started climbing. I did not have a chance to hit him with a shout. We hit something else instead—a wall of fog thick as skim milk. Only the hood of the car was visible. We pulled ourselves slowly around another curve just as a car dropped toward us. We crept around each other as cautiously as two prowling cats.

"I must go in front with a red light," I suggested, and we both laughed. I felt completely relaxed. Fog was merely another problem my driver could solve.

We inched up the mountain. At times it felt as if the car were

standing on its back wheels and reaching for the road ahead.

"Is it difficult to go up?" I asked.

"It is a good machine," was the terse reply.

No more cars dropped on top of us. I noticed that Senor Godoy was tensing as we rounded each curve; at least, I assume that it was a curve because the car was turning. I could only trust that the road was still beneath our wheels.

After an hour, without warning, we burst into sunlight. Only remnants of fog swept over us, and we gasped with relief. Shortly we found a clear spot where we could park, and we ventured to the edge of the road. Breathless with shock, we stared down. If the blinding white-out had been terrifying, even worse was the sight of the abyss. Blinded by the fog, we could have slipped off the road and hurtled downward for over a mile.

Far below, the fog was a white mattress thick enough to jump up and down on. Only a few peaks poked through. Above us the Andean air sparkled, so clear it seemed that it could shatter like crystal. We laughed with relief at still being alive, climbed back into the cab, and continued scratching our way up on the dirt road.

"Out of the fog, when we looked down, it was even worse," Senor Godoy kept saying. "I would not go over that road again for a million sucres."

We reached what could be considered the top, and joyfully I started out again on my bicycle. In this almost hidden part of the Andes, I skimmed along a road that hung above deep valleys, sometimes dipping toward them frighteningly. I passed few people. Little huts of mud blocks and straw roofs were open on one side and empty. Clinging to the last bit of earth below heaven, a village or two hung above me.

After fifteen miles of cycling I looked down into San Jose, a small town with buff stone buildings cuddled by hovering hills. From far above, the town looked as if it had been designed as a giant bracelet. Toy buildings ringed a spacious plaza, and on one side the tall, creamy white stone spire of a church was set like a gem. The town was inviting to anyone looking down from the road above.

Besides, it was time for lunch. I suggested to Senor Godoy, who had just pulled up behind me, that we should turn down to the village and eat at a restaurant. He wrinkled up his nose. It had been one of our jokes that I could be depended upon to select the worst restaurant in town. He had a nose that never failed to find a good one. On the other hand, I always knew when a church was open, despite his insistence that it was locked. I looked down again upon the bracelet of toy houses around the beautiful plaza, and was sure that my nose sniffed out a fine restaurant.

I bumped down the dirt road leading into the town and soon was in the plaza. The toy buildings ringing it were now cast-off blocks, worn out and needing paint. The plaza, no longer camouflaged by the charity of a distant view, was grimy and covered with jarring cobblestones which threatened to cast all my teeth asunder.

Children poured into the street and started calling after me, "It is too difficult for you to ride on the street, Senora. The street is bad. The street is very bad, Senora."

I bumped around to the far side of the plaza and, from all directions, a dozen men quickly clotted into a group around me, looking in wonder at my bicycle.

"What are you seeking, Senora? Where are you from?" There was concern in their questions. I had apparently dropped from another planet. Strollers around the plaza stopped to stare and then sauntered over. For a few seconds I looked around for the little yellow taxi. As if from nowhere it appeared, and I hailed Senor Godoy. Like black bugs who vanish from a dark room when you turn on the light, the men scurried off. Nobody took another look in my direction.

We surveyed the plaza, and on one side saw a besmirched building with an open area in front. A few people, sprawled around disarranged tables, were slopped over half-drunk glasses of beer. Inside, beyond a wide open door, I could see a jumble of a kitchen. I wheeled the bike away, convinced that the place only served dysentery and hepatitis. Senor Godoy chuckled. His unerring nose for a bad restaurant had been vindicated. We settled down in the cab, drove to the edge of the town, pulled out our sack of well-worn rolls and *manjar de leche*, and laughed as a flood of tropical rain crashed down upon our roof.

19

EQUATORIAL DEEP-FREEZE

As ABRUPTLY AS IT HAD STARTED, the rain stopped. The sun flashed through the retreating clouds above us as suddenly as the downpour had started. It made me eager to get back to my bicycle. We brushed away the scattered crumbs on the car seat, drove up to a level place at the top of the hill and repeated the ritual necessary to get the bike out and me on it. I pedaled away in excitement, for we were now approaching the highest point of our trip.

We planned to find a hotel that night in Guaranda, only ten miles north from San Jose. Guaranda was once the primitive village where mountaineers started the trek to climb Chimborazo, and staying there had been part of our original plan. The railroad strike had blocked our route to Guaranda north from Cuenca and Riobamba.

Excitement, not the dirt road, gave me the illusion of flight as I bumped along. I gloried in being two and one-half miles above the sea and close to Chimborazo, hiding somewhere behind the humps of mountains. Would I be lucky enough to see it next day?

By midafternoon I reached Guaranda or, more accurately, the foothills of Guaranda. I stopped on the road and looked up to the town sprawled over the mountainside. In seconds Senor Godoy zipped past, parked and then gathered the bicycle and me into the cab. After climbing up the short hill, we squirmed through the narrow, crowded streets of Guaranda to ferret out a hotel. We saw one with an inconspicuous HOTEL sign above a dirt-encrusted window. Senor Godoy trotted briskly through its doorway, but trotted back just as briskly. It had no private bath for the senora.

Not more than a few turns away we found a hotel on an airy corner. Its amenities appeared complete—restaurant, private bath, and spacious lobby on the second floor with TV and davenports.

Woven mats and rush screens sheltered the reception desk and warmed the walls of the lobby. I walked down a hall to my room and passed doors identified not by numerals but by names like Chilanes, Huanujo, or Santiago. Whoever owned or designed the hotel was determined to be original.

I went into the room named Huanujo and rejoiced to see a comfortable bed and bottle of mineral water on the nightstand beside it. At that point the amenities ended. If the designer had been original in the decor of the hotel, he had been adventurous in the design of the plumbing. I turned on the faucet in the washbowl and at once water splashed all over my feet. I explored beneath the bowl and found that the pipe that was supposed to be attached to the bowl was detached instead. I tried to shove it back into place, but my efforts at reconciliation were rebuffed with a loud splash as the pipe only separated itself again, and the water from the bowl splattered all over the floor. I ended up washing my teeth in a trickle of water from the shower head.

When I emerged, half-cleansed from my room, Senor Godoy already was in the lobby ready to explore the town. We walked downstairs to the street and picked our way over rocks and around holes in the badly fractured sidewalks. We climbed up hills and braked down, stopping for breath in the depleted air. Mists covered the distant mountains, hiding Chimborazo if it *was* visible from Guaranda.

So far we observed nothing that enabled it to exist. The high Andean town gave us such an illusion of isolation that it was hard to imagine how the inhabitants got established there in the first place, to say nothing of how they might earn a living. Farms, with Indians planting rows of grain and potatoes, hung on nearby hillsides. Two hotels existed, but it was not obvious for whom. I was conspicuous as the solitary tourist.

"This little town exists because God is great," chuckled Senor Godoy.

A small child skipped up beside us. She was as wispy as an elf. Clinging to her hand was her tiny sister. Afraid of us, she snuggled

close to her older sister when we tried to talk to her.

"Are you American? I study English," the older girl announced in Spanish.

"You are in school?" She stopped me before I could ask what year in *escuela*, and pulled herself up to an extra foot in height. "No *escuela*, Senora, *colegio*!" she answered emphatically. Again I had made the mistake of merely using the general term "school." It seemed impossible that this tiny creature could be twelve years of age, old enough to have advanced to *colegio*. Black eyes sparkling, she danced along, pointing out all the important buildings and then asking for their names in English: her *colegio*, the convent, the shoe store, the house of her family hidden within a walled court, a bakery, a tiny store selling a few canned goods. We wondered if the business of the inhabitants consisted solely of providing goods for one another.

Senor Godoy, black eyes also twinkling, spoke gently to the little sister, but she only hid herself within the skirts of the older girl, who was too busy practicing her schoolroom English to notice her. Abruptly he stopped the impromptu instruction.

"Here is our hotel," he pointed out. "We have to go now."

The little girl waved and called out "Good-bye," measuring each English syllable.

"I said we must go to the hotel because the little one was very cold," Senor Godoy whispered, as the children skipped back up the street. "The girl was so thrilled to talk English with you, but there was too much cold for the little one." He was the only one who had noticed her shivering in her light cotton dress. Darkness and the chill of Andean air had come quickly while we had been with the children. We did not enter the hotel but turned to walk on a different street that opened into a plaza, as large as one square block. Dim light from scattered lamps made specters of the trees and flowering shrubs. On one side was the expected church which, I presumed, housed the expected bedecked saint.

"Let us visit the church," I suggested happily.

"It is locked," he replied, happy in the thought that it might be.

Just then a bevy of nuns, in grim-faced determination, crossed the plaza and headed toward the church. I walked triumphantly across the plaza followed by the patient Senor Godoy. As we started to push open the church door, a gray-haired priest swept in before us. If the determination of the nuns was grim, his was savage. He seemed to have rushed away from something he would have preferred doing.

We pushed open the heavy church door. Candles throbbing faintly before shadowy statues were all we could see at first in the gloom of the large church. After our eyes adjusted, we could see a few women kneeling in the pews. One man, alone in a corner, was muttering prayers before a statue of the Sacred Heart. All at once, in a side chapel, a light was turned on so quickly that it made us blink. The women left the pews and shuffled quietly toward the chapel for the evening rosary. The lone man clung to his spot before the statue. "Only women go to the chapel, Senor," I whispered.

He sniffed. "Always."

I tiptoed away from the singsong voices coming from the chapel and quickly stopped. The saints had not failed me. There, in a gloomy corner, elevated on an altar, stood a saint in a kelly green wool robe, sporting an embroidered white silk hat that fitted him like an inverted bucket. The keys of St. Peter were in his hands.

"Aha!" exclaimed Senor Godoy, suddenly enthusiastic. I pulled out my camera and tiny tripod from its case and tried out various focusing positions that would imprison most of St. Peter, gorgeously costumed, in my camera. Finally I found that I could get all of him in the picture only if I focused my camera while lying on my stomach on the floor. I squirmed around awkwardly for a few moments trying to get him in the viewfinder.

"I can," announced Senor Godoy. He stretched himself out on his stomach, squinted through the viewfinder, wiggled into a different position, squinted again to get a good look, finally exclaimed, "*Perfecto!*" Snap! St. Peter was ready for transport to the U.S. Now it was Senor Godoy's turn to chuckle triumphantly. He loved to take pictures with my camera and his hand was far steadier than mine. He was a living tripod.

"Perhaps we will have a good dinner at the hotel," I said to Senor Godoy, as we walked back to it. "It is our Thanksgiving Day in America."

We went into the small dining room and sat down at a table. Rashly expecting a feast, we waited to be served. But we did not have hot roast turkey. In fact, we did not have hot anything.

"The stew is cold, Senorita," I told the the young waitress.

"Si, Senora, I know," she sighed. "The dinner is always cold here." I sighed with her. "Please ask the cook to heat up the stew," I begged. The waitress sighed again. "It is not possible, Senora." Unless the hotel were enveloped in a major conflagration, we would have to eat our dinner cold. I consoled myself by giving Senor Godoy the history of our "Day of Thanks."

"Yes, Senora," he said. "I know. I read in the periodical that your president is at his ranch in California today."

As we chewed like martyrs through our dinner, I noticed that the warmth and chuckle were fading away from Senor Godoy's face.

"Senora," he began. "When we are in Latacunga again, it is only two hours in the machine to Quito. I need to see my family. You will be all right in the hotel. I will come back the next morning."

Our revised plan now was that we would make a semicircle around nearby Mount Chimborazo, spend a night again in Ambato on the Pan American Highway, leave the highway at Ambato to make a looping detour to the southeast until we would get back to Riobamba for the night. From there we would go north again on the Pan American Highway, pass through Ambato without stopping, and return to our spartan, no-frills hotel in Latacunga. Heading due west from that city and crossing the cordillera, we planned a spectacular trip to *La Costa*, but we would not go as far as the Pacific Ocean. We would make almost a complete circle on this detour to the tropics and end up in Quito. All this was possible if the railroad strike was over for sure, as the newspaper claimed. Latacunga, which we would reach in three days, was indeed the best place from which Senor Godoy could make a quick overnight trip to Quito. Anxiously he awaited my approval.

I am no baby," I assured him. "I know you miss your family very much." He looked at me with relief, and his dark eyes danced with gratitude.

"Comprehend, Senora," he went on, "the children are males. They need their father. They are very strong." He poked at the miserable dinner reflectively for a few minutes. "Boys love more the

mother and girls love more the father," he continued, still thoughtful. "With the boys I must be strong. They are males, you understand. But with a girl I would be different." His face warmed. He
must have dreamed of cuddling the baby girl who persisted in not
arriving. Just as quickly he became somber again, and I knew he was
thinking of the boys who would be romping around the tiny house,
playing with their mother, not doing their homework.

"Ecuador needs propaganda, Senora." The change of subject
was not as abrupt as it seemed. Ecuadorians use the forceful word,
"propaganda," instead of our word, "publicity." Favorable "propaganda" would draw tourists to his country and increase his income.
Like men in all countries, he was fighting an inner battle—the need
of his boys for him and his need to earn money for them. Only when
he had taken me to the jungle and the Colombian frontier last year
had he ever been parted from his family. "I am always with the family at night," he had said to me once.

"Where do the tourists go? To Europe?" He was puzzled. Why
would anybody want to miss visiting his beautiful country?

"Yes, many," I ventured. "Perhaps they are afraid to travel in
South America, or they are not acquainted with Ecuador." He was
not the first person in the Ecuadorian tourist trade who had com-
plained to me that Ecuador needed "propaganda."

Suddenly he brightened. "Perhaps you can put a map of Ecuador on the wall of your agent for travel?" This was a solution. To a
map lover a map can only mean one thing—get there!

"No, Senor, it is not possible. She has no space on the walls." I
smiled at the thought of my travel agent attempting to plaster her
nonexistent wall space with a world supply of maps.

We continued eating the dismal dinner, one of us worrying
about life's problems, the other hungering for roast turkey in the U.S.
and hoping for a favorable digestion of what was taking its place.

When we returned to the parlor of the hotel we found the TV
playing quietly. A "Queen of Quito" was about to be crowned in
honor of some event of national significance. Two young men, bent
over a game of chess, sat in front of the TV and scarcely nodded

when we sat down to read the newspapers. I had just made my way translating the world disasters on the front page when I heard the sound of a band outside.

I jumped up and beckoned to Senor Godoy.

"*Vamonos!*" I called out.

He was on his feet in an instant, all smiles, temporarily forgetting the lack of tourists and the lack of wall space for maps. We clattered down the stairs and onto the dark streets. This was something new. It couldn't be a campaign parade or we would have known about it. Except for the music heard from a block away, the streets were too quiet and unconcerned.

We reached the plaza, shadowy under the street lamps, and found the brass band on a circular stand in the center. The twelve players had paused for breath and were rubbing their hands and drawing their jackets more tightly around themselves. Cold was sinking down from the Andes and icy Chimborazo, a few miles to the south. After a while twelve mouths closed themselves around twelve instruments, and twelve chilled lungs started blowing heartily. Their audience consisted of two people—ourselves—and we pulled our own jackets around us as we sat down on a bench in front to listen, clapping loudly at the end of each number. The end of each number also was the occasion for a long pause while the band glumly warmed themselves. A few more strollers in the plaza stopped to listen and then drifted off.

After the sixth long pause for resting and warming, I noticed that Senor Godoy, who was not bundled up in woolens as I was, had started to shiver. I felt that we should be loyal to the band members who had sacrificed their warm homes for the igloo of the Guaranda bandstand, but my loyalty would be misplaced. Senor Godoy needed to get back to the hotel. No, he insisted, I should not go up and thank the band for the music. Perhaps he felt that it was too bold to speak to them. Meekly, and without doing so, I followed him back to the hotel.

Next morning the washbowl was no closer than it had been to reaching a truce with its mate the drainpipe, and again I came down to the lobby half-washed. At the desk, the young clerk chewed on his pencil as he made his way through my bill. Standing on the other side of the counter, Senor Godoy was intent upon the clerk's upside-down figures. Laboriously the clerk continued figuring. Taut as a wound top, Senor Godoy continued watching.

"Look!" he interrupted. "It is not right."

Quickly he turned the paper around halfway, pointed out the mistakes, corrected the calculations, and saved me I didn't know how much.

"The clerk does not know how to calculate," he whispered as we went down the stairs. "Education is lacking to him."

It was already a brilliant day when we left the hotel and walked down the street to the walled-in lot where Senor Godoy had left the car. We started off, drove a few blocks to the edge of town, and stopped. "Look! Look!" we both cried out in delight. Ahead was Chimborazo, glistening, cloud free, the light of the rising sun pouring into its icy flanks. We were lucky. We sat in the car for a long time just looking.

"There are more vistas, Senora. More ahead," Senor Godoy said, and he started the motor.

We had truly stopped for Chimborazo on the "edge of town." The town ended at the top of a bluff. Slowly we followed the road over it and dropped down into the valley of the Rio Chimbo. At the bottom of the drop the road changed direction as sharp as a jackknife and soared skyward. Chimborazo disappeared and reappeared continually as we wound through the mountains. Just as spectacular were the tilled fields, waving quilts of brown and green, flowing over the foothills.

We were almost alone in that expanse without limit—rare cars, rare trotting Indians, rare trucks. One Indian woman was herding llamas up a steep hillside and, unusually friendly, she laughed and waved at us when we jumped out to photograph. We spun our way upward until the road leveled above gem-green valleys. Cupped in one tiny hollow, through which a stream flowed like a white ribbon, was a herd of llamas. Precipitously

Senor Godoy jumped out of the cab and I tumbled after him.

"*Crias!*" he shouted, and I looked down and saw two baby llamas close to their mothers' flanks. Senor Godoy grabbed his little Instamatic camera, jumped and hopped his way down the steep banks, took seven league boot leaps across the shallow stream, sprinted through the meadow and crept after the babies. They appeared to ignore him, but slipped away each time he was ready to snap the shutter. I sat for a while on the sun-warmed bank and watched the show of cameraman pursuing llama until something made me look up to the hill above. On the knife-edge margin of the hilltop, silhouetted against the blinding blue of the sky, was a man on horseback. Motionless, he was watching us. Dark hat pulled over his forehead, somber poncho thrown about his shoulders, he seemed so cloaked in mystery that I felt threatened. Silently he watched the antics of the photographer until he decided that not only was he harmless, but that he would have poor luck with the picture. Like a shadow he drifted away.

I decided to inch myself down the bank, but I stopped at the wide stream. Vaulting bodies of water was not my specialty. In the meantime Senor Godoy, satisfied with his picture-taking, was looking for a quicker way to get back to the road. He walked to the edge of a deep ditch of water that ran at right angles to the stream and measured its width with his eye. He backed up a few yards, crouched down for a running start, and dashed ahead. He leaped admirably at the edge of the ditch only to splash down unadmirably in the water. Laughing and shaking out his shoes after he pulled himself out, he scrambled up the bank again and sat down beside me at the edge of the road to dry off. Sun-warmed, we rested there for some time, watching the llamas in the meadow below, feeling the closeness of Chimborazo hidden behind the hill at our backs, looking at the picture postcard scenery all around. The true beauty of it all was that nobody had ever gotten there to produce picture postcards. Only a rare car passed by. "Nobody knows this road," Senor Godoy kept saying. Nobody knew the road that floated through the most spectacular scenery in Ecuador.

Dried off, we got back into the car and soon were below Chimborazo itself, driving beside the brown billows of cinders rolling down from its ragged snow line. The mass of the mountain filled the sky above us. A road in the cinders wound itself around the base of the mountain. It was no more than a wide depression in the mountainside and we braved it for a short distance. But as it dipped toward the east in an uncertain manner, we both cried out that we must turn back.

"I have no confidence in it," admitted Senor Godoy, and we got out of the car to walk about.

At that moment a large station wagon crawled toward us over a hump of the mountain, apparently with great confidence. It pulled up beside us and the driver, a cheerful blonde man with an equally blonde wife and child, leaned out to talk. He recognized me as another American.

"Hello!" he called out in surprise. "I'm from Minnesota. I'm a missionary here in Ecuador. We are exploring the country." As proof of his calling, he had two Indian converts in the back seat. His zeal was obvious, but he apparently had not heard of the parable of the wise and foolish virgins. Quite foolishly, I thought, he had been driving in this wilderness of mountains and *paramos* and had forgotten about his gas tank. It was nearly empty.

"Do you have any gas to sell, Senor?" he asked, switching to Spanish.

"No," Senor Godoy apologized, "I regret, Senor. I do not have extra gas."

"You can coast down about twelve miles south to Guaranda," I added. "There are several stations there." He might have preferred gas to advice, but he handed us some evangelical tracts and chugged away.

Inhaling what oxygen there was, I crept about, finding tiny gold flowers peeping and struggling through the rusty brown cinders. We were up above 4000 meters, about 14,000 feet. What I called "cinders" must have been ancient beyond memory. Chimborazo has been dormant for so long no human account exists of an eruption. We have only the geological evidence.

When we got back to the paved road, Senor Godoy lifted the bike from the trunk, where it had been stored during the long climb to the mountains, stationed it upright, and examined it critically. The descent would be long but gentle from that altitude to Ambato at 8435 feet. He tested the brakes, shook his head, then extracted his tools from the trunk. He tightened and tested, scrutinized and again shook his head, reminding me to get mine out of the way when I got too curious to see what he was doing. After a final test, he felt that the bike was safe for the downgrade. I retreated to the top of the pass a few yards away so that he could get a good photograph of me taking off and then, with a shout, I started down.

After a few minutes of cautious coasting and gripping the brakes, my hands were turning to ice. I had on a wool jacket, cotton sweatshirt underneath, wool scarf topped by my rain-sun hat on my head, but I had never thought to bring wool mittens to the equator. Soon the icy air, whipped up by my downhill speed, gnawed through my chest as if the wool jacket were no more than a cotton blouse. Down I kept spinning, getting blurred glances of huts sticking over the margins of the hills above, past a road crew, dismounting to walk up little hills, getting woozier every second. My stomach quivered with indecision—whether to ask for more food or to get rid of what it already had. I looked ahead to a small hill I would have to walk up and concluded I felt too shaky to do it. I stopped at the bottom of it and pulled myself off the bike. The taxi, quiet as a whisper, pulled up behind me.

"I feel faint, Senor," I said, and with a dramatic gesture I rested my head on the hood of the taxi. I should not have done that. Doubtless I would recover as soon as I got warmed up inside the cab and the blood returned to or departed from my stomach, whichever it had been about to do. Senor Godoy, on the other hand, was sure that I was just a few paces this side of the grave. He quickly settled me in the cab.

"It does not please me that you are ill, Senora," he kept saying, looking over to make sure that I was still breathing. I smiled wanly and tried to convince him that this had happened to me once in the Rockies at a mere 4000 feet after I had been in a sleeping bag overnight in the snow. The next morning I had gotten chilled dressing and even more chilled when I coasted down to Banff. I felt as faint then as I did now. I had to sit for several hours in a warm bus depot until I felt well again. This story did not convince Senor Godoy. It was obvious to him that whatever I had would soon be fatal. In the meantime the taxi rolled down a road that would have made a perfect descent for the bicycle: the downs were braked by ups and the ups were repayed by more downs.

By noon we had settled again into the Villa Hilda in Ambato. After lunch Senor Godoy announced to me that another presidential campaign had come to town. Surely there would be a parade, he said. This time it did not tempt me. I retreated to my room and slipped off into a warm afternoon nap that lasted for hours.

20
THE HOLY AND THE HYSTERICAL

FOR MANY YEARS pilgrims have journeyed to Banos, or "Baths," for the large pools of curative mineral waters that lie within the city. They came, too, to seek intercession at the shrine of the Virgin of the Waters beside the baths. Their pilgrimages must have cost them considerable pain. Even in the 1920s travelers told stories of struggling from Ambato to Banos on horseback, following a trail that scarcely existed, stumbling over rocks and ruts that did exist.

Now, in November of 1983, unlike the struggling pilgrims on horseback, I pedaled easily along a paved road. We were following the new highway that looped east of Ambato, through Banos and Riobamba, and then back to Ambato. But I did struggle to pass the market in Pelileo, so packed with booths, vendors, bargainers and tipsy people that I could do no more than thread my way through the edge of it and come away with my ankles black with fleas. The yellow taxi crept along behind.

Whenever I stopped for a photograph, I heard its radio beating out typical Ecuadorian music—a lively two-step rhythm.

I coasted down to the new bridge where the rivers Chambo and Patate tumble together to form the Pastaza, that churns along green and swollen until it roars over a 200-foot precipice about fifteen miles farther east from Banos, forming the cataract of Agoyan, one of the most magnificent in South America. We had seen this waterfall last year when we returned from the jungle and decided not to go there again this year.

I wheeled over this new bridge, rounded a minor mountain, and was soon in Banos, a leisurely twenty-five miles from Ambato. The taxi whipped past me and I followed it down a cobblestone street to a parking spot near a bridge at the edge of town. The Rio

Pastaza, with savage appetite, had sliced a deep gorge through the rocky cliffs. The waters of the two rivers, which had joined back at the bridge I had biked over, thundered through this chasm. I felt threatened by the power and tumult, and held tightly to the bridge railing as I looked down. Only tall yellow flowers in beds of ferns and tropical greenery braved the edge of the precipice. We watched the tumultuous river for some time.

I looked toward the crescent of mountains to the west of us and saw above the road, on a pyramidal hill, a saint enclosed in a glass case. Senor Godoy, with misgiving, saw me eyeing it and suspected that I was about to grab my camera.

"You can add it to your collection of saints," he sighed. He had no urge to climb all those steps to pay his respects to whoever the saint was.

I did and found that this was one celestial citizen who would feel at home in South America no matter how he was dolled up. He was St. Martin de Porres, the first saint of African descent in the Americas, and he had marched into heaven from Peru. His brown face was looking at mountains such as he had seen in his former home.

We stuck the bike in the trunk, and drove back up the few yards to the central plaza of Banos, noisy with people and cars. Vendors ringed the square, selling picture postcards, devotional statuettes and crucifixes, paste jewelry, fruits and vegetables. On one corner a man sold barbecued guinea pigs spread out on a small grate over burnt-out charcoal. "Guinea pigs. Delicious!" the man said as he beckoned to me.

Barbecued guinea pig is a specialty of Ecuador. Last year, not wanting to leave a forkful of a national dish unlifted, I had begged Senor Godoy to find me a restaurant specializing in this delicacy. His face had clouded.

"Si, Senora, I know of a place. But comprehend, it is not a presentable place. They do not have an elegant bathroom. But I eat there. No, you will not get sick."

When we had gotten there I had no trouble comprehending

that it was not exactly "presentable." The floor had not been swept since the first guest had eaten over it, I was sure. And the guests also must have had difficulty getting food into their mouths without spilling it all over. I had to screw the courage of my stomach to the digestion point when I saw the split-open guinea pigs turned on their backs over the flame and all their edible internal organs laid out in clinical order. It had been immaculately eviscerated. In the meantime, incongruously, a radio had played a concert of Brahms, Schumann, and Chopin. Senor Godoy and I had looked at the floor, smiled, and proceeded to dine on the just barbecued guinea pig. It was a treat that justified enduring any lack of sanitation.

More delicate than pork, but as mild and sweet as chicken, guinea pig doesn't taste like anything else. Still remembering my first one, I walked eagerly over to the barbecue here in Banos. The guinea pig was cold and dried up. Even in the clean, fresh air it was not going to be as succulent as the one a year ago. I shook my head and left it.

A young man in a small cubicle facing the plaza was vigorously pulling a long ribbon of molasses taffy attached to a hook on the portal. He gave us a small sample. It was irresistible. Squeezing by him to get into the shop, we bought a foot or two of the sticky, sweet stuff and soon had a layer of syrup on our faces and hands. Surely in a town named Banos there would be no lack of places to wash.

We found a place next to the taffy shop in the church, which for years had been the shrine to the Virgin of the Holy Waters. There we could accomplish two things: splash the water prayerfully over our heads or, less prayerfully, wash the stickiness from our hands. I watched the bike in the trunk while Senor Godoy went into the church to light candles and accomplish the first task. When he came back, I had the less devout task in mind. As I walked up two wide steps leading to the main doors of the church, I passed the outstretched hands of the beggars sprawled on the porch. Some had eyes too sore and swollen to see, some had withered limbs, some picked food out of dirty cups. They were all unwanted crumbs swept under the rug of humanity. Most worshipers entering the church tossed them coins.

I pushed open the heavy doors and went inside. I heard the murmur of pilgrims' prayers and their soft tiptoeing, everyone hushed in the expectation of something about to happen. It did. A black-robed priest swept in through a side door and strode with determination to the altar. The lights of the dim church flashed on, and the white altar became ablaze with reds, blues, and ebony painted in designs of geometrical extravagance. The people in the front pews settled themselves in for a service.

Hanging in rows along the two side walls were oil paintings attesting to the Virgin's miracles. One picture showed her extinguishing a fire in Guayaquil. In another painting she diverted ashes and lava from a village during a volcanic eruption. My favorite painting was of a man tumbling through the air, heading for a wild river below him because the bridge which he was crossing had split away on one side from the high cliffs. Calling out to the Virgin of the Holy Waters did not keep him from getting wet, but miraculously he found himself tossed up safely on the riverbank. Deliverance from nearly fatal illnesses was one of the miracles shown in homemade drawings on the walls of the cloister beside the church. In one, carefully made with color crayons, a patient lay on the operating table. The surgeon, long knife in hand, was poised above him. The words, "Save me, Virgin of the Waters!" were printed inside a cartoon bubble issuing forth from the man's mouth. It was not clear whether he was to be saved from the operation or the illness, but a tiny note in the bottom of the drawing expressed great gratitude.

I found the shrine with the holy waters in one corner of the cloister. A fountain bubbled into a pool at the feet of the statue of the Virgin. It reflected the ranks of flickering candles beside it. The Virgin looked gently down on a circle of worshipers. One kneeling young woman wailed without restraint, lamenting her sins, and making other entreaties, which were so smothered with sobs that I could not understand them. A woman companion beside her was embarrassed in direct proportion to the volume of lamentations. As the mourner, or penitent, pulled herself away, tears still gushing, her friend and I put our arms around her shoulders, imploring her not to cry. This seemed to have as magical an effect as the powers of the Virgin, and she quickly sniffed away the tears to a comparative drought and smiled. Later, every time I saw the two friends on the street, they greeted me as if they had known me for years.

Senor Godoy, still guarding the bike, smiled happily when I joined him. "The senora cried so much," I said, explaining my delay.

"They always cry there." He considered it all quite foolish.

"Si, Senor, but perhaps her baby died. She does not have a husband and wants a husband. Perhaps she has a husband and he beats her." I continued with a list of possible problems. He nodded slowly. Yes, it was a sad world.

We got back into the cab and began driving to a hotel for lunch. "I took pictures of the miracles, Senor. What do you think of them?" His reply was quick and firm.

"They are real."

"Perhaps the real miracle is faith, Senor."

"Ah, si!" He patted his heart with his hand. "When I touched the *Virgen de la Paz* in the grotto, I felt electricity pass." I would have explained all miracles as the power of adrenalin brought forth both by belief and emergency, but I respected my companion's faith and kept silent.

Not far from the central plaza a waterfall tumbles down a hill-side. It gives Banos its waters, both curative and holy. Not feeling rheumatic, I had no interest in the mineral baths, but the village washerwomen have found a practical purpose for the waters. Below the waterfall was a low, narrow white stucco building with open sides. On the end near the street was a large sign advertising *"Servicios Higienicos"*—Hygienic Services. Under the roof two long rows of tubs faced each other. At each tub a woman washed clothes and laughed with her neighbors every time she raised her head from the scrubbing board. A child ran around unencumbered by anything to cover his nakedness, happily enjoying his freedom while his clothes were being washed and air-dried. Meanwhile the bright skirts of his mother bobbed up and down over her hips in rhythm with her scrubbing.

We wanted to eat lunch at a tiny hotel across from the waterfall. It looked scrubbed itself and had an attractive dining room. That noon it had attracted a group of Swiss *Andesistas*, or Andean mountain climbers, who appeared to have just descended from the nearest peak and about to ascend the next. Their muscles rippled as they attacked the meal. At another table an Ecuadorian family was sampling the meal with restrained appreciation while they let an Indian nurse take care of their baby. The nurse was dressed all in white, even down to her bobby sox, and walked back and forth with the baby, cuddling it while she talked with the older children who had jumped down from their parents' table to play. I assailed my own hot soup with an eagerness midway between voracity and restraint, but observed that Senor Godoy was regarding his with unaccustomed languor.

"No, Senora, I did not sleep well last night," he sighed. "I could not get to sleep until four in the morning. The fog before Guaranda preoccupied me. I could not sleep." I sensed what he must have been thinking all night: What would his family do without him if he got killed showing any other crazy tourists the "vistas" in a thick fog?

After lunch we left Banos and started out on the paved road that climbed through a gorge alternately hung with greenery or scarred with landslides. The extinct volcano Tungurahua was not far east of us, but it teased us behind white clouds as we waited for that rare moment when it would poke its white head through for a photograph. I wanted to take the trip more slowly, to push my bike up the hill. But Senor Godoy seemed too tired to pull it out of the trunk. Worrying about fog all night had worn away the usual smiles and chuckles. Later I told him that I had been disappointed just riding in the cab, and this produced such contrition that for the rest of the trip he was offering me miles of cycling, no matter what.

Mercifully for him, it was a quick trip south on the new road that circled around a small mountain or two before reaching Riobamba. He assumed now that his wife had gotten the message sent four days earlier that we would not be at our original hotel in Riobamba and that she would not try to telephone him there. Wanting to save me money, he chose a cheaper hotel. It crowned a hill above the city, and had just been finished. I soon found out that it was more correct to say it was half-finished.

While Senor Godoy disappeared to his room for a nap, I began to explore my *habitacion*, as the Ecuadorians call a hotel room. To be specific, I wanted to use the amenities of my habitation. The bathroom had all the necessary equipment—beautiful shower, washbowl and toilet. I approached the latter trustingly. With no warning, the toilet seat flew off in one direction and I spilled off in the opposite. The seat, apparently, had not yet been attached to the rest of the apparatus. Placating overtures toward the seat would be necessary on my part in order to prevent future disasters.

Once I had established a truce with the bathroom fixtures, I decided to switch on the electric lamp on the headboard of the bed so I

could stretch out to read the newspaper before a nap. The wall switch cooperatively turned on the light but later refused to turn it off. I moved the wobbly switch up and down, but it responded like a piece of spaghetti. The light on the headboard burned on with blissful indifference. I looked for another switch, but saw only a piece of wire poking through the wall like a black snake that had gotten stuck midway. Like the bathroom fixture, it had no connection to anything whatsoever. I turned back to the wall switch and discovered that by holding it firmly in the off position, the light turned off. As soon as I let go of the switch, it flipped up again and the light flashed on. I left it on and abandoned the idea of a nap. Holding my "glasses of emergency" on my nose like a lorgnette, I propped myself up with the newspaper. Many amperes of electricity would have to flow anyhow before I finished translating it.

It was nearly dusk when Senor Godoy knocked on the door. He had taken a rare afternoon nap. Restored was the twinkle in his eyes and the laugh in his throat. When I described the peculiarities of the bathroom fixtures, he exploded with laughter. He held his side and gasped for breath. I laughed and gasped myself, and this started a chain reaction which triggered another attack of hysterics. He had just caught his breath when I asked him to contend with the light switch. He fiddled around but it also resisted him. Fresh whoops filled the room. "Now I have to stand here all the night and hold this so you can sleep," he gasped. He stopped laughing just on the safe side of cardiac arrest. We finally loosened the light bulb, slammed the bathroom door, and went out to explore the town.

We thought we might find an interesting restaurant for supper. We passed one with the unlikely name of *La Biblia*, and I wondered what sense of piety could inspire a restaurant to name itself in honor of holy scripture. I peeked through its front window and saw the forlorn proprietor brooding at a table, not only without Bible but without patronage. We returned to the hotel.

A brilliant succession of smiles greeted us when we returned. *La patrona*, worrying over her bookkeeping at the reception desk, lifted her head to smile broadly. The young waiter in the dining room, who up until that moment had been idling over a table, smiled in surprise when we entered and immediately started assembling knives and forks. The cook stuck her head out of the kitchen door and smiled as she waved a greeting. The cook's helper rushed through the room, smiling breathlessly. Having smiled ourselves at each one in turn, we sat down at a table, ready to receive the sole attention of the entire dining room staff. For a time we did, until four Americans came in who had the look of displaced tourists wishing they were somewhere else. They seated themselves without enthusiasm at a nearby table and wearily began complaining.

Hovered over by the amiable young waiter, we attacked our dinner of soup and roast lamb with marked enthusiasm and no complaint. We were still laughing over the whimsical behavior of the electricity and plumbing when there was a sudden cry from the reception desk.

"*Mi hijo! Mi hijo!*" the voice wailed.

We stopped to listen, forks en route to mouths.

"*Mi hijo! Mi hijo!*" The voice now rose to a shriek. Hastily depositing his tray, the waiter rushed out to the reception desk.

"What is she saying?" I asked. I had only understood "My son! My son!" Senor Godoy shook his head. He could not sort out the syllables from the sobs.

The waiter soon returned with the news that the son of *la patrona* had not come back from school. The boy was often late, he explained, but he had never been this late. The merriment drained from Senor Godoy's face, as if he had been doused with a bucket of cold water. He stopped eating and listened to the cries of *la patrona*, which filled the dining room.

"Many boys run away from home, Senora," he commented grimly. His next bite could have been soaked with tears. "Many, many." He seemed to be seeing his gentle, courteous eldest running off with a pack on his back. "The sons need the father," he went on. "They are very strong."

The waiter rushed again to the desk and returned to report that the boy was still at large.

"I tell the sons, 'Do not have bad companions,' " Senor Godoy said.

Soon the cook, brandishing a spoon, hurried out of the kitchen and ran to the source of sobbing. "*La patrona* fusses herself," she said as she returned to the kitchen. "She fusses herself."

We got through the soup as cheerfully as if we were dining at a funeral parlor. The wails became reduced in volume, but the latest reports, furnished by the waiter who kept running back and forth, were that the son was still not home from school. It was now nearly eight o'clock and school had been out since noon. The father, who was a policeman, had been commandeered into the search. In the meantime Senor Godoy continued to bemoan the hazards of raising sons.

"Girls need a father, too," I reminded him. He nodded slowly.

"I was alone with my girl," I said. "When she did not get home, I scolded her." I tried to explain to him how American parents "grounded" errant offspring by confining them at home for a specified number of nights. We picked away at the meat course, asking the waiter and the cook for the latest news, if we could catch them as they ran back and forth.

Midway through dessert, new shrieks came from the reception desk. "Where were you? I thought you were dead!" The sobs of relief swelled to the ceiling. By materializing, the presumed corpse had given unmistakable signs of life but not of reforming. By the time we were through dinner, he was off again with his companions.

"He needs to be scolded," I observed anew, but by this time, brightening as quickly as the switching on of a light, Senor Godoy was laughing again.

21
LAST SIGHT OF THE KING

TWO ROADS LEAD NORTH from Riobamba. Both tie together like a lasso over the mountains where they converge at the lower altitude of Ambato. The merged road crawls upward, north to Latacunga. Since we had already taken the lower route from Banos to Riobamba yesterday, we wanted to soar once again over the upper route today to catch our last glimpses of Chimborazo. I knew the road from our trip of ten days ago; but when you change directions on a bicycle, the sights and scenery also change. Nothing seems to look the same. The paved road floated upward from Riobamba, past fields of earth combed into swirling rows and dotted with huts of sun-baked bricks and straw roofs. We wound through a Sunday-quiet countryside that was still asleep. To the east, the brilliance of the sun washed out the colors of the Andes and Mount Altar. To the west, color saturated the distant green mountains, the rich brown fields. Still in the taxi for the climb to the plateau, I watched for Mount Chimborazo. Suddenly I shouted. Like a haughty god who has condescended to give us a last glimpse, the mountain appeared naked white in a sky of indigo. I could understand why the pre-Inca Indians considered these mountains deities. Speechless, we stopped for some time to look. Like a talking robot, Senor Godoy reminded me to check to see that the film was advancing so that Chimborazo would not escape me this time.

We were now at the highest point in the road—12,000 feet— and I was impatient to roll slowly through the grandeur. Senor Godoy quickly pulled the bike from the trunk, tested its brakes, and strapped the camera into place above the front wheel. I remembered the frigid ride I had taken down from Chimborazo before and rummaged in my suitcase for some sox slippers which I could put on my hands as mittens, a wool scarf, my sweater and wool jacket. Senor Godoy smiled in approval.

"Ah, Senora, now you have the head!"

Looking like a teddy bear, I started off. Few bicycle trips before this had rewarded me with so many miles of dramatic beauty. Other rides had rivaled the magnificence of this one, but only for short distances: pedaling beside Lake Garda in Italy through painted villages above sparkling Alpine waters; wheeling below the shaggy gray spires of the Dolomites on a sun-drenched day; or bicycling in New Zealand, through the composite beauty of many lands, a collage compressed into picturesque miniatures between the seas. But here in the Andes the splendor stretched as far as the eye could see.

The descent to Ambato was so gradual, the sun so warm, that I began doing a discreet striptease as we slipped into the trivial altitude of 10,000 feet above sea level. One by one I tossed my improvised mittens, wool scarf, sweater and wool jacket into the cab, trading them for suntan lotion, mineral water and hat. Long before noon I reached the last downhill before Ambato. The scenery had faded into the bedraggled border of the city. Dreary little stores of pink stucco, old and dust-caked, dozed beside the road. Meandering drivers roiled the peace of the highway. After we passed Ambato, the rest of the way to Latacunga would be less spectacular—and uphill.

"I do not wish to mount the bicycle to Latacunga," I explained after I had braked to a halt and Senor Godoy had instantly swished in behind me. "There is too much traffic."

A little surprised, he stuffed the bike into the trunk and we whipped off. Soon we were bumping over the cobbled streets of Ambato. We heard a distant roar, which became louder as we neared the soccer stadium at the north edge of the city. Waves of shouts and cheers rolled toward us. It was the day of the big soccer game between the *Nacionals* of Quito and the *Barcelonas* of Guayaquil. I wondered if the match was being played in the neutral city of Ambato to minimize the danger of an after-game riot. The action must have been at a continuous, frenzied pitch. The fans of each team screamed alternately, the noise rising and falling according to the action of the game. We rounded the corner to drive around the stadium. Its walls were festooned with boys climbing over, or perched astride, single legs dangling down one side. Two or three policemen, considerably outnumbered, ran along the street below the wall and threatened them half-heartedly.

Perhaps I was foolish for not fighting my way into the stadium to observe South America's greatest sport, but I knew Senor Godoy was anxious to drive to Quito to check on his family. One hour of the game would have sufficed, but we could hear the outcome over the car radio, now almost as noisy as the stadium. The screaming voice of the announcer, suddenly pitched decibels higher than usual, was the clue that someone had scored. I never understood his frantic language enough to know which team had actually made a point, but Senor Godoy, whose concern was only passive in the matter, always let me know who was winning. He seemed more impressed by the fact that the stadium had been filled by ten in the morning for a game that would not begin until one-thirty in the afternoon.

Slowly we wound our way through the Sunday traffic and up the hill north from Ambato over the route I had bicycled two weeks before. By early afternoon we could see the scrambled heap of the buildings of Latacunga ahead. We passed the straggling stucco stores, the white walls painted with election propaganda, the small shed where cockfights were held. We hurried along past the usual debris of life that towns try in vain to hide under their outer skirts. Here dust and decay, in America a junkyard of old cars. In Latacunga Senor Godoy would deposit me in the old hotel and then would drive two more hours to reach his family. He had not seen them since we had left Quito two weeks before to go south, nor had he been able to speak to his wife except for the one shouted phone call. He was as anxious to see them as if he had been gone a century. The drive between Latacunga and his family would seem endless to him.

The long, lazy afternoon had not yet started, and the morning's breakfast was past remembering. "Senor, I want you to have something in your stomach before going to Quito. Let us look for a restaurant." He smiled gratefully. I remembered his story of the bone-breaking miles he had driven to Cuenca with no lunch stop, when his passengers hibernated contentedly through the entire trip on stored fat while he had to keep himself alive with lima beans. We did not have to search for a restaurant. He already knew of one, and in a few minutes we were parked in front of it. We walked down a path past gardens and flowers and found a table inside near an open window that brought the outdoors in. The designer of the restaurant had created such a blend of architecture and landscaping that everything seemed to have grown from one judiciously planted seed. The other diners, even the children, conversed quietly among themselves, confined within a Sunday dignity. The solemn waiters bowed and served us *llapingachos* and other little deep-fried Ecuadorian pastries. I rejoiced in an immaculate ladies' room. Better restaurants in Ecuador, like this one, make a ritual of dining and a garden of the surroundings.

The afternoon was still in the midst of early drowsiness when Senor Godoy drove me to the tiny Latacunga hotel beside the tree-shaded central plaza. He first carried the bike up to my room so that I wouldn't have to worry about it and then, jumping into the car loaded with a bagful of shoes and sundry provisions for his family, waved himself off.

"I return at seven-thirty tomorrow morning, Senora!"

Latacunga was a ghost town of shuttered store windows, deserted arcades, empty cobbled streets, hushed as the tomb, as if it needed the sleep of death to recover from its violent past of earthquakes and volcanic eruptions. Mt. Cotopaxi, towering above, never lets the city forget.

I wandered about the old town, free to cross streets without any menacing traffic, hearing little beside the beat upon the pavement of my walking shoes. In only one spot, in front of a building housing offices of the province of Cotapaxi, did I hear the noise of human voices—shrill ones. I walked over to the noise. Squealing happily, little girls were sliding down the ornamental stone banisters which accented the building. Lacking better criminals to attend to, two policemen seemed to be supervising the activity. Like two mothers in a park, they were more interested in talking to each other, only now and then stopping to reprimand the youngsters, absentmindedly. For a few minutes I sat watching the girls play, then I strolled down a nearby sidewalk sheltered under an arcade supported by arches. The arches were restrained in their external decoration, graceful in their simplicity, as beautiful as Renaissance arches seen in Italy. Here, with no skillful restoration and upkeep, they showed their age.

Later on my walk, the hastening twilight filled Latacunga's streets with beauty. The shadows and pale light from the colonial lamps gently blanketed the dust of the old stones, masked the crumbling of the ancient buildings, hid the wind-scattered scraps of paper. Dusk in Ecuador covers all with tender pity.

Remembering that I had bought the Quito Sunday paper from a newsboy in Riobamba, I went back to my room to read it. Since it would have to take the place of night life in Latacunga, I labored through it slowly, thoroughly chewing all the news and articles, even those in which I had not the least interest. Its world coverage was surprising. In it I read a lengthy story about a girl in the United States who had been in a coma for months after taking drugs combined with alcohol. The case was well-known in our country, but never before had I learned so much about it.

After digesting the newspaper for an hour or so, I thought it might even be possible to digest the hotel dinner, so I went downstairs to the dining room. If I had thought the dinner was anonymous last time, I found that this time it defied identification. The only thing on the menu was a thin broth. The young man and woman who were keeping the restaurant open were carrying on a flirtation in the back of the room that promised to warm each other up, if not the soup.

Once Senor Godoy had listed in order of increasing seriousness all the words that Ecuadorians use to describe a relationship between a man and a woman: *amigo* or *amiga* for friends; *inamorato* or *inamorata* for sweethearts; *novio* or *novia* for persons engaged to be married; and *amante* for married persons having an affair.

"How can you tell if the *amante* is a man or woman?" I asked.

"With the article, Senora. You would say *el amante* for the man and *la amante* for the woman." I had observed that Latin Americans were very careful to use the right word.

As I took my mind off the liquid in front of me, which was supposed to be soup, I tried to figure out which term of endearment would apply to this couple. I remembered the children doing homework whom I had seen last time.

"Where are the children?" I asked the couple after I had at last finished the soup and went up to pay for it. They tittered and gave me a vague answer that I could not understand. Nodding to them with more civility than they deserved, I went out into the streets to forage for more food.

The lamps hanging down from the wrought iron lamp posts in the park across the street gave a tremulous light, and the dark side streets absorbed little of it. Looking down one narrow street, I saw a shaft of light cut across the deep shadows. I walked down to it and found that it came from a small shop that was still open. The old man in it was selling apples, chocolates, sticky taffy and other sweets to children. On his shelves were cans of fruits and vegetables, jars of jam, and other items that required a tool to open. No fast food place this. I joined the children, bought some ersatz fudge and munched on it for the rest of the evening.

Next morning I left word at the hotel desk for Senor Godoy to meet me at the little corner cafe we had gone to before, and then I walked the two blocks over to it. By this time the town had roused itself from its deep Sunday slumber and everyone was rushing off to work. Streams of pupils were flowing to school—girls in red one way, boys in brown another. One older girl had gotten adventurous and was wearing a t-shirt with the English words, "Here it is," slashed across the front. I wondered if the *colegio* had given up insisting upon uniformity.

I was in the restaurant and still waiting for my over-easy egg and glass of mora berry juice when Senor Godoy, face glowing, burst in. "Si, Senora, it is seven-thirty exactly!" he confirmed happily. He would shame even the most precise Swiss watch. Just as promptly he sat down and ordered his eggs.

"Si, Senora," he continued, "I got up at four o'clock. At four-thirty I helped my son with his studies." Monday was the fateful day when the eldest had to get to school at seven-thirty.

"Tell me all, Senor. How is the family now? Did the shoes please them?" I felt as if I were getting news from home after a long absence.

"Yes, the family is all well now," he answered between excited bites. "But the senora had to take two sons to the doctor—an emergency. My brother, he did not tell the senora that we would not be at that hotel in Riobamba. She tried to phone me. She went down to phone several times and was worried."

"Fine messenger!" was all I said, refraining from saying more about the irresponsibility of his younger brother, the silent one, who had caused so much trouble for his sister-in-law. Senor Godoy seemed less annoyed than I was, perhaps because he did not have complete faith in him to begin with. "My problem is I don't have confidence in anyone—not anyone," he had said to me once. "When I say be there at seven-thirty, I mean seven-thirty exactly! Someone else says 'I don't care. What difference does it make'." I had told him that what he called his "problems" were his virtues.

"And the shoes?" I asked again.

His face became incandescent. "The shoes pleased them all very much!" I thought of the glass slipper in the fairy tale Cinderella and could see each member of the family trying on a pair of shoes and passing it to the next if it did not fit.

"And your uncle with the problems?" I remembered that when I met him he reeled about drunk, trying to forget that his wife had left him.

"A divorce. He wants to work as a bus driver." A divorce would not be difficult. Ecuador legalized divorce at the turn of the century, the first country in South America to do so.

"Was your family glad to see you?"

"Si! Si, Senora!" Radiance burst from his entire body. Now I saw why his brother or uncle had not disturbed him. "The little one. He wanted me all the time. He wanted me even more than he wanted his mother." He grabbed himself around the chest to show how the baby had clung to him.

22

OVER THE LINE OF DEMARCATION

CONVINCED THAT THE FAMILY GODOY was surviving, we left the cafe and started on a road that climbed over the Western Cordillera. By late afternoon we hoped to be in Quevedo on the coastal plain, about a hundred miles from Latacunga.

In a few miles the road shot up the Andean range ahead of us with alarming abruptness.

"Hit me with a shout if you want a photo," Senor Godoy reminded me, repeating words he always said in the midst of "vistas." But in a moment he was the first to shout. "Look! The two! It is rare to see the two at one time."

I looked back to the northeast and jumped out of the car. Mount Illiniza, sharp as a needle, and Mount Cotopaxi, broader but higher, were both gleaming white against the blue sky. A few clouds brushed softly against them and then floated off. For a long while we watched as the mountains coquettishly hid and reappeared. First one peeked over its skirt of clouds, next the other, then both were bared.

We were parked on a road that looked back over Latacunga and that clutched the side of the mountain as it climbed upward. Perched below the road was a small hut presiding over a tiny garden, a rooting pig or two and a listlessly clucking chicken. Soon I saw a small boy clambering up the bank onto the road. He smiled at me uncertainly.

"*Buenos dias,*" I called out. He nodded with a whisper of a smile and padded in bare feet to the taxi. He stroked its bright yellow surface, feeling it as if it were a marble statue of rare beauty. He peeked inside and his eyes widened at the uncommon sight of its grandeur.

"Do you go to school?" I asked. It was mid-morning for a school day. He shook his head and lingered over a farewell stroke before pattering back down to his home.

"He is ashamed because he is not in school," I said to Senor Godoy after the boy had disappeared. "And he has no shoes."

"Si, Senora." He was thoughtful for a moment.

"I did not have shoes when young." Then he chuckled. "Just on Sundays we had shoes."

We got back into the cab and kept on winding upward, until we reached a crest high above Latacunga and the Ambato basin. A side road led off from the highway and we drove down it for a last look at the two flirting peaks which would soon disappear behind us.

Before we started back to the main road, I watched an Indian family tilling a field, children working beside their parents, hoes all scratching in rhythm. What appeared to be the family's dog ran on the road toward us, but cowered as soon as he caught sight of us. Tail between legs he sneaked under the wires of a fence. His coat, a threadbare rug, merely hung over his skeleton. We could count every bone.

"Dogs and cats do not please me," Senor Godoy said with disgust as we watched the animal slink out of sight. "Parents ought to feed children."

Clearly the family did not appear to have money to feed both children and animals. To feed a pet would be a burden even for Senor Godoy. For several minutes I leaned over the fence to watch the family hoeing the field.

"We do not know how much we have," I said under my breath, thinking of my own country. Senor Godoy overheard me but was puzzled. The poverty of the Ecuadorian Indian had been accepted by the country for so long that I wondered if it was unrecognized.

"The Indians get no diseases, Senora—nothing. No colds, no stomach aches, no grippe. Nothing!" Senor Godoy commented. I could not answer. Hard, recent data are scarce so I could not give him statistics that show how many Indian babies now die of dysentery and malnutrition during the first year. I knew that ten years ago it was over half. It is said that old age is the last thing an Indian expects to die of.

Back in the taxi we discovered that what we thought was the crest of the cordillera was a delusion. The road continued to soar up and drop down in a dizzy course as if it had been engineered by an eagle. Bleak, brown *paramos,* or lofty plateaus, such as we had not seen before, rolled off in all directions. At last we reached what we could safely consider the crest, and I mounted my bicycle, pumping along at cloud height beside the sweep of brown fields. The road was paved and gentle. No headlong dives toward the earth's center threatened me. Little huts were scattered along the way. As I passed, heads appeared in glassless windows but disappeared the second I looked in their direction. "They have never seen a bicycle here," Senor Godoy had said earlier that morning.

At a point where the road started to curve and dip, I noticed a hut above me. In front, the entire family was lined up, watching. I waved and stopped to greet them. The man of the family called out a *"Buenos dias"* and stepped out toward the road. His wife cautioned him, but he ignored her and soon was on top of the bank above me.

"Where are you going?" he called out. "Are you alone?" At that moment the little yellow taxi pulled up. By now the rest of the family had crept forward and lined up obediently beside the father.

"It is a beautiful bicycle, Senora," the man went on. "How many gears does it have? Only one?" He clucked in surprise. Only one gear was hard to believe. I complimented the two children, but they were deaf to the mother's rebuke that they should answer politely. They only hid their heads.

The road was still a waving ribbon on top of the world. It was now little traveled but once had been the main route to Guayaquil. Senor Godoy could remember going over it years before, when he was twenty. I pedaled along comfortably at a height that would have been congenial for condors, if rare ones had still been swooping about in Ecuador. I got a start when I looked up and saw a large herd of llamas on a field above the road. I all but fell off the bike, grabbed my camera and began climbing the bank. In a flash an Indian woman appeared from out of a hollow and waved her arms at me. "Leave them! Leave them!" she screamed.

"Just a photograph," Senor Godoy pleaded. But she continued chasing the llamas away and yelling, "Leave them!" The more he pleaded the more she yelled. I was contrite.

"Do not worry yourself," Senor Godoy said. "It is the way of the Indians." But I did worry. She must have been convinced that I would stuff all the souls of her llamas into my camera and leave the deprived creatures prey to endless disasters. It disturbed me that I had offended her and that I seldom could woo the confidence of the Indian women I met along the way south of Quito. I got no more than quick frightened glances.

I left the llamas behind, souls intact, peacefully grazing, and began to coast gently and carefully into the pleating hills. Rounding a bend, I skidded to a stop. The view of the cultivated fields startled me. A green and brown patchwork quilt, pieced together by an artist, fell from the blazing blue sky and flowed into the hollows below. I stopped a long time for photographs.

Huts of mud bricks and straw roofs huddled near the road, but only a few persons dared to look out the uncovered windows as I passed. An old woman, lying beside the road, face half-hidden under a felt hat weathered into shapelessness, stretched out a hand to me as I coasted past.

"Money," she wheedled.

"I have no money," I told her.

"Sure you have money!" She spat out the words. It was true, but all my money had been safely locked in the glove compartment of the cab.

I inched my way down a hill but was soon stopped by a dog, which had enough energy to raise the bristles on his scrawny back and bark at me. I froze, straddled over the bike frame, so that the motion of the wheels would not tempt him to sample my ankles. He was not threatened when I ordered him off, but seemed determined to devour me. In a minute a woman rushed out from the hut below the road to restrain him. She smiled broadly.

"He does not harm. Do not be afraid." Chastened, the dog retreated with a parting snarl. "Where are you going?" the woman asked, her smile broadening. "Ah! To *La Costa*. You are making a journey by bicycle all over Ecuador? Good luck, Senora, good luck!" she cried as she waved me off. I did not realize how soon I would need it.

By now the little-used road had turned into chunks of pavement with holes in between the chunks. One second I was bumping and twisting along with fists tightened over the brakes, and the next second I was tossed, bike and all, onto the side of the road. Conveniently, a soft dirt bank kept me from being hurtled toward earth's center, however far that was. I was trembling from shock, but had only skinned my leg when the bike frame crashed against it. There was scarcely a sign of blood. All my bones had remained in the prescribed number of pieces.

"What happened?" an alarmed Senor Godoy asked when he came down to me.

"I fell but it was not serious."

"Not serious!" He snorted in disbelief.

"The road is no good, Senor," I observed wisely, noting that not only had the pavement disappeared but that the road was continuing to drop, threatening to toss me off again if I kept riding. We looked across the valley and saw that far ahead the road was rising to the clouds again. We put the bike into the trunk.

Senor Godoy reminded me again that I must holler and whack him if I wanted a photograph, chuckling as he always did after such a reminder. We rose and plunged our way westward as the road slipped and twirled over, below, and beside the mountains. Now the spectacular scenery fell away behind us. The road, deserted by drivers who today take the good Guayaquil highway to the north, was almost our own. Now and again Senor Godoy stuck his head out of the window and asked a passerby the name of a rare *pueblo* we were passing through.

Our maps completely ignored these few villages. The road slipped through them without even widening, squeezing between the few huts and a rare schoolhouse. Shreds of fog drifted over us as we swooped down into the shadows of a valley, but the road soon labored up toward a bright sun. At the top of a pass I saw scattered white pillows of fog below us.

"More fog, Senora," Senor Godoy laughed and I looked down with fear. Unable to forget the fog on the way to Guaranda, I was ready to lie down on the floor of the cab in back and hide my head. I preferred not to know the exact moment when we dropped off the road into the bottomless bowl of skimmed milk. But the fog drifted harmlessly away, bits lingering here and there like pieces of gauze sticking to the mountainsides.

Suddenly Senor Godoy was the one to jar *me* with a shout. He stopped the taxi and we jumped out.

"Look, Senora! One side dry. The other green. The dry of the mountains and the wet of *La Costa*."

I looked across a canyon and saw what he meant. On the far

side was the brown, arid earth of the Andes. On the side near us was the green and moist vegetation of the coast. A giant knife could not have sliced the mountains more cleanly, dividing each side of the cut into wet and dry.

"Ah, the line of *demarcacion!*" I exclaimed.

"Ah, si!" He was impressed by my vocabulary, but demarcation is almost the same in English as in Spanish.

After passing the "line of demarcation," we descended rapidly into the green zone, diving through towering tropical trees into ravines, rattling over bridges that crossed small streams, passing a village or two struggling to get a toehold in the narrow defile. A few last twists and the road stretched out, as if abruptly dumped from a sack, and we were on the wide, flat tropical plain of *La Costa,* the rich food basket of Ecuador. Sweating and dripping under the equatorial sun, it was bursting with bananas, papayas, mangoes, pineapples, coconuts, cacao, coffee and rubber trees. I thought it could be one of the richest lands on earth.

The road made one straight run for the Pacific Ocean. I got on the bike again, and pumped through the flatness, finding variety in acres of rice fields or in haciendas of silvery-leaved pineapple plants, coconuts hiding in palm branches, hitchhiking egrets on angular cows that did not have enough fat to pad their arched ribs.

That afternoon I felt as if the temperature might be in the high eighties. But the motion of the bicycle made the heat tolerable. For an hour I pedaled along while Senor Godoy crept behind, the vegetation luxuriated, the cows munched, the egrets fluttered and all steamed pleasantly under the sun.

All at once I saw through a miasma of heat waves a large knot of people filling the highway up ahead. They appeared to be moving along slowly, now and then bunching to one side to let a car pass. I pedaled closer and saw that, in the midst of the group, eight men were carrying a wooden coffin on their shoulders, four on each side of it, bearing the deceased to wherever its last repose would be. The mourners were young people and, as I kept carefully behind them, I began to commiserate.

"It must be a young friend," I thought.

Cars were passing the procession in both directions with no apparent offense to the mourners so I began to do the same thing. As I passed I saw that the youthful mourners were uncommonly cheerful, all laughing and flirting with one another.

"It must be an elderly grandparent who is escaping to his just reward," I thought with relief.

I slowly left them all behind, still sauntering light-heartedly, except for the eight shouldering the heavy coffin under a merciless sun. Farther down the road was the hacienda of Senor Godoy's father-in-law, who was now in bed with a kidney infection.

"He does not please me," Senor Godoy had explained once with surprising rancor. "He does not please my wife, either." He shook his head.

"He did not let her go to school when she was a little girl. He made her wash all the clothes—a little girl of eleven years." Whether she bent over a board or scrubbed clothes against stones in the water, that job could have taken her all day, every day.

"The mother of my wife died and then he married a woman just the age of my wife. What a fool.

"But my wife worries herself because he is sick," he went on. "In all ways he is still the father. I must stop to see him." He was resigned to an unpleasant act of charity. I had to agree that filial concern was hard to destroy completely.

Within a few miles we had both halted in front of a large house, solidly built, with a veranda on the second story. The house and surroundings had a disheveled look. In back of it was a snarl of large trees and bushes. The bare ground in front, with its patches of grass, unkempt shrubs, and strewn debris, was like a dirty brown apron. Senor Godoy ran up to the front of the house, but I had no invitation to visit. I waited beside my bicycle on the road. The wife, carrying her baby, came out on the veranda and stared at me, pretending she was really interested in something else. Pretending I was more interested in finding yellow butterflies and iridescent birds in the tangle of bushes beside the road, I also sneaked looks at her. True, she was young enough to have been the sick man's daughter. Within ten minutes Senor Godoy trotted back to the taxi.

"He is very infirm," he explained, looking relieved at having performed his duty. "His wife will not let him go to the doctor in Quito. She says it is too much money. Too much money to help him. She does not care for him well." He had no more affection for the childlike wife than for the patient.

"As he makes his bed, so he must sleep," I said, paraphrasing our English proverb. Senor Godoy thought for a moment.

"Ah si," he nodded and jumped back into the cab to continue creeping after me.

My pedals revolved with unvarying rhythm for a number of miles until I looked ahead and saw that there was actually a right-hand bend in the road. Soon I was turning with it and coming into the city of Quevedo. On each side of the road were large yards for

drying cacao and coffee beans, long sheds for storage, and a few trucks for hauling. Workers moved about slowly.

We planned to find a hotel in Quevedo, but it would not be easy for me to follow Senor Godoy as he twisted about the streets looking for one. We put the bike into the trunk and soon were inching our way into the city. It was not possible to go any faster. A stirred-up beehive would have had less frenzy than this city of the coastal plain. People of all colors—brown, black, bronzed—made a babel of sounds and a flashing pinwheel of movement. They did everything with exuberance. They zigzagged across the street wildly, talked with each other excitedly, moved down the street like people rushing to a fire. Paradoxically, they were not really moving fast. It was an illusion of haste in an overheated atmosphere.

The two hotels we found were dingy. I groaned, imagining hot, shabby rooms, no bath for me, no air conditioning for Senor Godoy. He ran into them and found that those were exactly the amenities that were missing. I remembered passing a place outside of town where a winding driveway lost itself in a shelter of trees. A sign on the entrance gate announced a villa comfortingly named after some saint. I urged Senor Godoy to go back to it.

23

THE GREEN OVEN

WE DROVE BACK TO THE OUTSKIRTS of Quevedo and to the villa named after a saint. The hotel proper was tucked back among trees at the end of a winding driveway. My room was clean, had air conditioning and a shower. I peeled off my clothes and promptly entered it. It had no water. No matter. I put all my clothes on again, politely asked where the water might be, and was moved to another room.

We seemed to be the only guests and *la patrona* of the hotel was delighted to have us. A little later she was even more delighted. I was walking around the bare grounds in front of the hotel when I saw her run out to the taxi and scrutinize what was written inside the painted circle on the front door on the driver's side, the logo that identified not only the taxi *cooperativo*, but the hotel with which the driver was affiliated. She bent over to examine it more carefully. "Ah!" she exclaimed, having noted that the taxi came from one of the best hotels in Ecuador. Excited, she ran back into the hotel to spread the news.

She must have been impressed sufficiently to discuss the matter with Senor Godoy. Before supper, as the darkness dropped like a curtain, Senor Godoy and I were strolling along the hotel driveway under the shelter of the trees. He recounted his conversation with *la patrona*.

"Senora," he confessed. "I told her yes, you stayed at the Hotel Colon." Shocked that he would tell a lie, I plopped down abruptly on the curb beside the driveway. Here was the man whom I could trust so completely that I stashed all my money and possessions in the taxi and knew that he not only would protect them, but my life as well. Then I understood. Hurt pride sometimes makes us lie. An intensely proud man, he would not want to admit that I stayed at a

Quito hotel at a fraction of the price of his hotel. Like the man guarding the house in Ambato where three daughters each owned a Mercedes Benz, Senor Godoy wanted to boast about *his* senora.

The confessions continued. "Si, Senora, I told the senorita in the *cambio* in Ambato that you had cashed traveler's checks for three thousand dollars in Quito."

"No, Senor, not three thousand dollars!"

"Si, I was angry because she did not have confidence in you." True, the clerk not only studied my passport, but Xeroxed it in order for me to exchange two hundred dollars. I could never understand what use she was going to make of the copy. Send it to the police?

Nothing could be a worse insult to Senor Godoy than having someone not trust the senora. We continued pacing back and forth along the driveway, not venturing to leave for bushy areas where we would have to contend with assaults from bugs or snakes. Having confessed his fibs, Senor Godoy's thoughts turned back to his family.

"Ah, Senora, the son got eight out of ten on the grammar test!" He was elated. The hours of homework with his oldest son had paid off. "Si, the senora works with the son and he knows it all very well, but often when he is taking a test he is very nervous and cannot answer. But this time he did well." Yes, I understood. I always blanked out when confronted with tests in higher mathematics.

"He worries himself so much about the tests. My wife took him to the doctor. It costs 1000 sucres and all the doctor said was that he was nervous."

"One thousand sucres!" I cried. That would be about twelve dollars, his average daily wage.

"Si, Senora, the spouse spent 8000 sucres for food and emergencies while I was gone." This was a hundred dollars. He did not seem disturbed, but I was shocked.

"Senor, I am sorry. I am sad."

"Why, Senora? If I am here, I fall down and need a doctor. If I am home I fall down and need a doctor. Things happen if I am at home, if I am not at home." He was thoughtful for a minute. "I was thinking. Many men must be gone from the house for much of the time. It has been good for my wife to manage alone." I smiled to myself. I remembered suggesting the same thing to him. His wife, I knew, was a good manager, and on this trip he was learning to have confidence in her.

We strolled back to the little hotel, now dimly lit, front door closed against the night. There was a reason. A regiment of bugs was flattened against the window, struggling to reach the light inside. The ragtag army had uniforms and armor of all sizes and colors. One creature six inches long had a coat of mail like a grasshopper. A small cricket had managed to sneak into the hotel and was singing triumphantly.

At dinner two cooks hovered over us, their solitary guests, and served a fresh, tasty fish. But before I could stop it from happening, one of the cooks had put ice cubes in the mineral water I always ordered. I had kept well in Ecuador by not eating raw vegetables, not drinking the water, and avoiding ice cubes made from the water. I did not want to risk it now.

"Do you want my ice, Senor Godoy?" I asked. He drank the water with impunity.

"Oh, no, Senora! It is so hot here the mineral water will not remain cold. You need the ice."

I never hurt his patriotic feelings by explaining that I could not trust the sanitary inspection, or lack of it, in his country. It is impossible not to be thirsty on *La Costa*, but it was also impossible for the ice to last for more than a minute. It dissolved almost magically. In the woods near the hotel I had seen a high tower to collect rainwater, but I did not know whether the drinking water came from there or from a well. In the former case, the rain might manage to fall from heaven to here without contamination. I put my trust in rainwater, gulped the mineral water to the last drop, and survived.

The rapid melting of the ice surprised me. The coastal heat had not bothered me that day, but I would soon find out that it had only been delaying its fury. The next morning at breakfast we were still the only guests, but the cooks were busier. I could see one in the open kitchen getting her little girl ready for school: braiding her shiny brown hair, smoothing her white dress, inspecting her hands and face, tying a sash just so. At last the child looked like a paper doll that had never been handled and the mother surveyed her with satisfaction.

"Be a good girl," was her parting admonition as she kissed her and sent her off.

The other cook fussed over us, getting the egg plopped over just right, taking pains in such a simple item as toast. The breakfast was standard Ecuadorian except for an addition that was new to both of us—mixed papaya and maracuya juice. Maracuya is a tropical fruit that has the tartness of a lemon and the sweetness of an orange, a blend that hints of both flavors. It is olive-colored, the size and shape of a large lemon and has juicy pulp and many seeds. I had tasted maracuya marmalade when I was on the launch in the Galapagos. Once back on mainland Ecuador I had sought it with the intensity of a narcotics addict, but no grocery store sold such a preserve. We drank the juice with loud sighs of appreciation. It had a tang that would make the gods spurn ambrosia.

A morning drizzle was just clearing away when we stood in front of the hotel and considered whether we should put the bike into the trunk of the cab or whether I should put myself astride it. Quito was two days' pedaling away. We watched the steam rising from the ground as if water had been spilled on a hot stove and decided that the atmospheric conditions would be fine for cycling. Even if it had been pouring, I would have lost face if I had done anything else but fly off on two wheels. Within minutes the hotel family had gathered itself on the small front porch. The two boys not yet off to school, the two cooks, and *la patrona* had all assembled to watch the strange senora mount her bicycle. I gave a twist to my *pantalones maternales,* seized the handlebars, squirmed onto the bicycle seat, put my feet on the pedals and waved good-bye to all with a theatrical flourish. They waved back with a shadow of anxiety on their faces. It did not seem sensible to them to exercise so much under the equatorial sun.

They may have been right. When we left at eight that morning, the temperature was tolerable. But within an hour, the sun began firing up the flat coastland until it reached the temperature of a steam bath. Only an idiot would have considered it tolerable. With idiotic determination I pedaled on. The black rayon *pantalones maternales* sucked in the heat like a sponge, and I was thankful that I was not in the condition for which they were designed. I guessed that the temperature was at least a hundred degrees. Every time I stopped, Senor Godoy, trailing faithfully behind me, jumped out of the cab and held out the canteen of mineral water. He purchased liquid reinforcements every time he passed a roadside stand. I drank a liter an hour. If he did not hand me a bottle of water, he held out the container of suntan lotion and I slapped it over my face and arms. I forgot the back of my neck, and it slowly fried. Each time he stopped, Senor Godoy looked at my hair dripping over my forehead and chuckled, "You are in the bath of a Turk, Senora."

True, I was traveling through a Turkish steam bath, depending upon the little breeze of my movement to reduce the temperature slightly. I wondered if my hat was making me hotter so I took it off. The sun then bored through my skull like a drill under a magnifying glass. I put the hat back on my sopping hair.

On I pedaled, in somnambulistic rhythm, drinking *minerale* and slapping on lotion, agreeing a dozen times that I was in "the bath of the Turk," looking on all sides for scenery that wasn't. When I looked far ahead, the highway seemed to bend and promise a novel view. When I got there, I found that the highway went on as straight as it had been doing for the past fifteen miles and that the view was the same as it had been for the past fifteen miles.

On the side of the highway was a wide ditch choked with marsh grasses. Green and blue birds and yellow butterflies darted in and out among the reeds—a naturalist's dream. I imagined snakes of all kinds and did see one that had ventured out onto the road only to be squashed. Now and then I got a whiff of something dead, rotting in that steamy crematorium. Beyond the ditch were plantations of pineapples, avocados, coconuts, an exuberant assortment of tropical fruits. Even a bicycle is too fast for all the abundance of this lush coastal plain. I yearned for a walking tour, poking along with a naturalist.

I passed displays of papayas, maracuyas, bananas, sometimes

spread out in orderly lines on the ground and arranged according to size, sometimes dumped into a plastic bucket. Salesmen were nowhere to be seen until we stopped. They then appeared by magical and spontaneous generation, ready to bargain. I looked back and saw that a mountain of green bananas had materialized just as astonishingly on the top of the cab. Later I saw a bushel of papayas stuffed inside. When he was not busy getting me water and handing out suntan lotion, Senor Godoy had scurried around in behalf of the family larder. The appetite of his boys for bananas was only slightly less than that of a jungle full of monkeys. His mother particularly loved papayas, and I succumbed to maracuyas.

Along the way we saw huts elevated on jerry-built stilts and reached by long ladders—a tropical structural style that achieves air conditioning. No walled foundation kept air from circulating under the house. No doors or glass on windows shut out a rare breeze or the view from passersby on the road. The occupants lived openly and unashamedly, safe above floods, snakes, and other creatures crawling about on the ground underneath.

Few people were walking along the road. We saw no Indians in felt hats and hot brown skirts, only women in cotton dresses with wide-brimmed straw hats, and men in faded khakis and small straw hats. All had bronzed faces.

Yet one was different. He was a man on horseback, a dark felt hat pulled over his forehead at an insolent angle, a face rock-hard, with eyes steel-cruel. He glared at me as if he had a whip in a clenched fist.

"He is a *montubio. Agresivo,*" Senor Godoy explained. "Very aggressive." *Montubio* is the name for an itinerant laborer on the coast, but this man looked like an overseer, a Simon Legree. The English word "aggressive" would be too mild. In Ecuador it could be translated as "ready to attack." A belligerent sea lion on the Galapagos was called *"agresivo."* I returned the horseman's riveting stare and wheeled on, just as arrogantly.

By noon, we had piled the raw material for a salad in the cab. Senor Godoy selected a foot-long papaya and carefully split it in two lengthwise. He picked out two maracuyas, cracked them open, and squeezed the juice over the papaya, as near as we could come to achieving the ambrosial juice we had drunk that morning. We slurped noisily, spreading a crescent of juice from ear to ear, attacking the papayas as we would a watermelon but without wasting time for spitting out seeds.

After lunch I hoisted myself onto the bike for the last ten miles of the way into Santo Domingo, the city of the Colorado Indians with the red-plastered hair and many-colored striped costumes, whom we had visited the previous year on our very first excursion.

As I neared Santo Domingo large plantations disappeared, little houses clustered closer together, more cars chugged by. A large sign proclaiming the skills of an herb doctor tempted me to swing off on a side road. The Colorados are famous for their skill with herb cures, attracting wealthy patients from all over Ecuador. The old-fashioned witch doctor is supposed to work spells here, but he may exist only in travel books, like the topless Colorado woman. The jungle furnishes many of our drugs and cures. Some day the herb doctor might receive the approval of modern medicine.

I was disappointed that no Colorado Indian emerged from the roadside bush as I bicycled along. We would have regarded each other with amusement, wondering which one of us was more bizarre.

By late afternoon we reached our hotel just east of Santo Domingo. It sprawled over flat terrain near the highway and then spilled over the hillside, ending in a fringe of new rooms under construction. My room opened onto a veranda, which was shaded by high trees that were filled with an orchestra of tiny, piping, red and olive-green birds. Across the veranda was a yawning excavation eventually to be transformed into a pool. Taking part in the transformation was an old man, no more substantial than a blade of grass, who was shaking gravel through a screen over a heap of sand near my door. He slid the screen back and forth until nothing was left but stones, which he cast aside. With trance-like motions, he shoveled more gravel on top of the screen, leaned the shovel against a post, and then shook the screen back and forth, back and forth, until nothing but stones remained. This went on without variation for an hour or so until he looked over at me.

"Good day, Senorita, what time is it?"

"Five o'clock, Senor."

He thanked me softly and said his work was ended. He placed the screen against the wheelbarrow of gravel and padded off, nodding good night.

A woman with a pile of fresh towels on her arm came down the veranda, padding along quietly in worn sandals. She tapped at my door.

"Good evening, Senora, what do you need?" When she saw the bicycle parked trimly against a wall, she exclaimed, "Ah! You mount the bicycle in Ecuador? How good!" Her eyes twinkled warmly. "You are of the United States? Where do you live? On *la costa* or in *la sierra*?"

"*La costa*," I answered, relieved that I did not live on the plains of Kansas, which would have necessitated a trip to the little man's gravel pile so that I could construct ridges and flat places to demonstrate the topography of my country. She checked the towels in the bathroom, pulled back the covers of the bed to make it inviting for the night, and left me a bottle of mineral water. With a gentle "*Buenas tardes*," she moved softly on down the veranda.

The dining room of the hotel was an overgrown gazebo, closed off from the tropical outdoors only by a low wall. A roof kept out the sudden downpours. But close to us were the birds, trees, flowers, and the fragrance of the moist, warm earth. Senor Godoy, who had a room at the top of the hill near the entrance of the hotel, managed to find me, and we climbed up the hill to have dinner in the midst of this lushness. We should have dined solely on the sights and aromas outside. Trustingly, we ordered the first course. Just as trustingly, we started eating it.

"This meat is spoiled, Senor," I said, putting down my fork and not risking another bite. He took a cautious taste, wrinkled up his nose, and called the waiter. Senor Godoy may have been able to survive his country's water and lettuce, but he had a bloodhound's instinct for the scent of ptomaine poisoning. "Do not buy from the Indians on the street," he had said to me once. "They lack refrigeration. If you eat their marinated fish, you go to the hospital for three days." The waiter was offended that we did not trust his meat, but finally brought a small steak that was cooked to such a point of desiccation that even the strongest germ could not have survived. We did not get sick.

At breakfast next morning I looked out toward the highway and saw the little man again whose job it was to sift gravel all day. This time he was facing a different gravel pile than the one beside the excavation that was to be a swimming pool. He was standing to one side while his boss was demonstrating to him how he would shovel the gravel onto a screen and then shake the fine sand onto a pile underneath. Two men, casually observing the demonstration, were standing near. The boss kept on for several scoops of gravel while all three men watched.

"Look," I pointed out to Senor Godoy with some annoyance. "Four men for that job."

He shook his head. "That is the problem with my country."

We were wrong. After a few minutes, the three men left the little old man with his shovel, gravel, screen and sand-pile. The problem was that every morning he had to be shown anew how to shake the gravel through the screen so that he could start the task again, shaking and sifting all day long. Where would he be in a highly mechanized society?

24
LAST DAY ON TWO WHEELS

SANTO DOMINGO WAS ONLY one day's cycling away from Quito—the last day I would ride. The night before we were to start out Senor Godoy had been listening to the radio. The news made him excited.

"Senora! It is raining very hard in Quito, very hard!"

At once we both thought of the same thing. A very hard rain meant landslides, and what could keep the land from sliding down upon us in the same place where it had slid down a year ago? Would rain-loaded earth bury us all as we waited for the bulldozer?

Luckily, there was merely an early morning drizzle when Senor Godoy knocked on the door and was ready to carry the bike up the hill to the taxi. He looked it over wistfully.

"I was thinking last night, Senora. I regret that the trip is over."

"I regret it, too, Senor."

For me the trip had been unique. Wheeling through a country always lets me see it closely, but here I had also seen the land through the lively eyes and intelligent interpretation of another person. Poking behind me, sometimes over strange roads, sometimes having to cast aside old notions, he had seen his country anew through me—a companionable partnership as symbiotic as that between dough and yeast. It had leavened both of our lives.

He slipped the bike under his arm and carried it up the hill to the taxi, an exercise that made only casual demands on his muscles. He stopped before he opened the trunk and looked critically at the gray sky.

"Ah, the rain is stopping. You can mount the bicycle!" True, a wet-looking sun was trying to shine, struggling with dirty clouds that clung to it like wet sheets.

When I started to pedal off on the level highway the sunlight made crystals of the raindrops on the tropical shrubs. The same sun would soon make them vanish in a cloud of steam and illuminate the fuchsias, orchids and exotic flowers I could not name that were festooning the trees beside me. I did not have to pedal far before I saw a waterfall spilling from a high cliff down to the road and under a bridge. The cliff had appeared suddenly. Just as suddenly, the road rose to climb over the Andes. Reluctantly, I let Senor Godoy put the bike into the trunk and I crawled into the front seat. I always sat there, of course, but this time there was no other spot left. The back seat was piled with tropical fruits. Even the luggage rack on top was heaped with bananas. Later, when we reached the farms of the *Sierra* a bushel of carrots and a cabbage as immense as an elephant's head joined the mountain of produce from the coast.

As we passed through this Western Cordillera the steep mountains were emerald lush. Shuddering with the memory of it, we also passed the mountainside still scarred by last year's muddy convulsion. Now, for a time, it was glued together by dry weather.

In an hour we were at the top. We got out to look at the rolling valley below us and at the road ahead, which slipped through the

pillows of hills until it dropped into the long basin that held Quito. The descent was gentle, not precipitous. The sun was straight overhead and gloriously warm. We pulled the bike out of the trunk, tested its brakes, and I gave a hitch to my *pantalones maternales*. Off I sailed, weaving through the hills. This was not like climbing up from Riobamba far south of us, through mummy-colored peaks jumbled together. Instead these green hills rippled and rolled in equatorial incandescence, coaxing me onward, promising a drama of snow-crowned mountains.

As the road began to level out into the Quito basin, which itself is rolled into gentle folds, the traffic on the two-lane highway began to increase and brush perilously close to me. I could feel Senor Godoy behind me becoming sick with fear, seeing me hit by every passing truck. I found a wide place beside the road and braked to a stop. He was soon beside me.

"Are you nervous, Senor? Are you worrying about me because of the traffic?"

He groaned, relieved to hear that I was afraid also. As he began getting the bike ready to put into the trunk, a constellation of admirers who had seen me spin down the hill gathered around us. The men stood around silently, not presuming to ask questions, but obviously dying to do so. Senor Godoy strapped the bike to its usual place in the trunk, never looking in their direction. No one said a word. As we drove off I saw them whispering among themselves.

Threading our way through the ascending and descending cars, we started dropping down to the basin. I looked happily in all directions, forcing from my mind the thought that this would be the last time I could indulge in such raptures.

Suddenly I shouted, "Ah, Senor! *Manjar de leche!*"

We were passing a dairy, and it would be my last chance to slobber over spoonsful of caramelized milk. I thought it would make a fine lunch with papaya. He whooped.

"No, Senora. It is not possible. Papaya with *manjar de leche* and we need a very private bathroom, very rapidly."

My zinc-lined stomach so far had been resistant to such inconveniences, but nothing could be more distressing than needing a very private bathroom, rapidly or otherwise, in a picnic spot where none was to be found. I did not question one who had doubtless suffered unmentionable embarrassment in order to come by this useful knowledge. Sensibly, we left the dairy behind.

One-half hour later we were settled down comfortably on a grassy meadow, cupped in by green wooded mountains, and our mouths were about to span another foot long papaya doused in maracuya juice. We slurped voluptuously, burying our chins in the soft fruit. I had been warned about combining sugar with fresh papaya, but I had not been warned about papaya itself. What we would need shortly was not a bathroom, but the dose of salts which our grandmothers used to give small boys who ate too many green apples. Later I almost wished I had eaten the papaya with *manjar de leche* as the lesser of two afflictions. Foot-long fresh papayas settle in the stomach as questionably as the green apples, defying digestion and refusing to go either up or down. A ravaging army of enzymes attacks the stomach, and twists it into tight, agonizing coils. Within an hour we were grabbing our middles, trying to press out the pain. It took the papaya twelve hours to call a truce and be incorporated into my digestive system.

Sitting in the sun-drenched meadow I was innocent of future agonies and only stopped slurping to inhale the beauties about me. Mid-slurp, Senor Godoy shouted, "Look, Senora, the train!"

There, off to the west, was a freight train, tiny as a toy, snaking along with its line of cars. It was true, then. The strike was over. The freight train could make its way to Guayaquil in peaceful leisure, commandeered by ex-strikers still hoping for promised benefits: the train company promised to rebuild the rail line with the help of German or Japanese engineers, who, they claimed, would make such a safe railroad that it again could carry passengers. (The tragic derailment of the previous year had made the train dangerous for passengers.) The company further promised that all the men who had been thrown out of work because of the derailment would be rehired to help rebuild the railroad. When the rail line was rebuilt, the company promised to rehire the men to take care of the increased load of passengers. Pie for the railroad in the sky!

"How good," I commented to Senor Godoy. But he had no faith in it.

"It is not possible," he said. "It is too complicated." I had to agree.

Later Senor Godoy picked out a paved road for me to bicycle on that left the main highway and wound and rolled through farms and fields. I could pedal along with no trucks hissing at my rear tire. By this time schoolchildren were poking along home. As I started up a hill, I passed a group of little girls. They greeted me joyously and soon were running along beside the bike, laughing and having no trouble keeping up with me. I had slowed down puffing and pumping up the short hill, and could not disgrace myself by getting off to walk. My camera was in the car, and I motioned for Senor Godoy to take a picture. But by the time he had the camera out of its case and focused, the children were too far away. I would have to carry in my head a picture of grinning faces and black eyes sparkling with mischief.

A few miles from Quito I stopped. I remembered the crowded highway that sprawled over the land like an elevated roller coaster as it made its way into the city. It was no place for any vehicle that did not have four wheels to fight with. I found a parking place and for the last time I pulled myself off the bicycle.

"It is enough, Senor," I said, and carefully we put the bike back into the trunk where I planned that it would stay. With the help of Senor Godoy, who constantly checked its brakes, nuts, bolts and other vital hardware, it had been reliable. The fat tires never got any punctures once they recovered from the first explosion in Quito. It had carried me along without incident. Its conservative behavior coasting down mountains had been its greatest virtue. It was like a plodding laborer who had gained my respect if not my eternal affection. Remembering the glories of the Andes, I would become nostalgic for the bicycling but not the bicycle.

Together in the taxi, we rolled past the groves of eucalyptus trees imported by Ecuador years before, past the stable of horses belonging to the affluent, past the groups of black-hatted Indian women working in the fields with digging sticks. By late afternoon we were twining through the streets of Quito, its colonial churches defying decay, its modern buildings rising incongruously above its ancient streets. Twisting and turning around one-way avenues, we finally pulled into the parking lot of my hotel.

"Senor, we have arrived!"

I sighed with all my being. I had not been pitched headlong from a road into a bottomless Andean chasm. I had not been tossed into a ditch by a truck. I was sound, and because of Senor Godoy's constant inquiries as to the whereabouts of *la cabeza*, my head was still in place. I was as sane as I could expect to be. Senor Godoy had not been rear-ended as he crept behind me. We had survived and arrived. Senor Godoy sank back into his seat without a word. I could see candles flickering in thanksgiving in front of his favorite saints.

"I will see you in the morning. Eight-thirty exactly," was all he had energy to say. Once I had asked him if he would want to take care of another cyclist. He had paused. "I would need five years' rest!"

I did not make him pull the bike from the cab and haul it up to my room. In the morning I had only one day left in Ecuador and I could not waste it. Senor Godoy and I were taking a trip that he said was impossible for a bicycle. It could rest in his father's house.

Not far north from Quito, a little beyond the monument to the Middle of the Earth, are some simple ruins, simple because all that might explain their purpose was still under the earth. What had been unearthed was a rectangle of fitted stones surrounded by a partially preserved stone wall, each stone adhering to the other as if they all were one solid piece. The ruin is visited by almost no one except possibly the Banco Central of Quito, the institution that is watching over it in its underfinanced zeal to preserve historic sites. The bank's Archaeological Museum has one of the finest collections of art and archaeology in South America. Some of its 23,000 artifacts are 10,000 years old.

Whatever else the Inca builders had in mind, whether a dwelling or a fort, they did manage to build a room with an unsurpassed view in a land where spectacular view lots are plentiful. Look to the east and your eye sweeps over the entire sky, bitten by the jagged teeth of the Andes. Step to the edge of the stonework and you look down into a deep canyon, where a maddened river twists and slices its way into the rust-tinted mountains. To the southwest, a ridge of hills scarcely hides the obelisk pointing out the equator. Below us on the west the earth stretches out like a brown, shaggy rug until it runs into the Western Cordillera.

On the western edge of the rug was a little white school. That morning the voices of the children reciting in singsong unison were all that broke the silence of that lonely place, hidden by mountains, yet still so close to the city.

Below us not far from the school a man was plowing the brown earth with a crude wooden plow pulled by a bullock. Stooping down from time to time, his wife patiently followed him. I pointed them out to Senor Godoy, but he saw nothing novel in the scene.

"Si, Senora, I worked in that manner with a bullock when I was young."

From that isolated ruin, the road descended to the Rio Guayllabamba. It fell recklessly, as if it were chasing a ball that had been tossed down the mountainside. It would have been sure suicide for a bicyclist. To catch our breath during the downward dive, we squeezed into a rare flat place to photograph the brilliance of a blooming red cactus. The arid spot looked like the Arizona desert tilted sideways.

At the bottom of the canyon, perhaps more safely reached by parachute, a strong but narrow bridge spanned the thundering river. We crossed the bridge to the other side of the canyon only to find that our perils were reversed. We had to creep upward, inching away from the drop at the edge of the road. We caught our breath after a kilometer when we found a flat place just large enough for the taxi to park. We got out to admire the view and trembled when we saw the spirals that we had spun down on the opposite canyon wall.

We peered fearfully over the precipice to see where we would have landed if the car had not had good brakes.

At the top of the canyon we reached a small village squeezed onto a wide place away from the canyon's edge. Even here the perils were great. The road into the village nearly had reached the state of impassability. The ruts were not ruts but gullies. I did not expect even Senor Godoy to keep balance on the ridges between the gullies without shattering the taxi to pieces. Concentrating intensely, he slid in and out. If we had had eggs in a bushel basket, he could have negotiated the passage without breaking a single one.

We crawled into the village square, idle in the noon hour, and watched over by a solitary policeman. Senor Godoy jumped out of the cab and ran to him. I could hear them discussing the whereabouts of an obscure village with an equally obscure, polysyllabic Indian name.

"The road there is bad, Senor," the policeman kept saying. "It is the worst road." He declaimed the word "worst" so dramatically that no wingless creature would dare go there. Senor Godoy trotted back to the taxi, quite convinced that if the policeman, who was serenely standing in the midst of the roil of ruts in the village plaza, considered the road to the the other village even worse, it must be no road at all. Senor Godoy had wanted to visit his sister who taught there. How she managed to reach the school in the first place and then take a bus home to Quito every weekend, was a feat to defy a condor.

When we started to leave the village, we were stopped by a small truck blocking the narrow road. In front of it, a man stooped over to attach one end of a cable to the front axle. Apparently needing technical improvement, a telephone pole stood upright on the side of the road about ten feet away from the truck. Gripping the other end of the cable and dragging it behind him, a second man hitched himself up the pole. When he reached the top, he eased the cable down to a third man who was standing by a transformer on the ground. Shortly the truck, the cable draped over the pole, and the transformer were all attached to each other. The truck backed down the road, pulling the long cable taut and slowly hoisting the swaying transformer to its destination. Stumbling into holes and falling over rocks, a number of spectators, not wishing to miss a thing, backed up with the truck. In the meantime the children, who had just been sprung from school and considered the operation set up for their own amusement, began jumping back and forth across the cable, challenging each other, daring the trembling, moving cable to trip them and toss them on their heads into the ditch. No one shooed them away.

After half an hour the transformer was secure in its place. The spectators and machines slowly drifted away, all assuming that this was the most sensible way to hoist transformers into place in a spot which small cars could scarcely reach, to say nothing of an immense truck with crane, block and tackle. The Andes demand ingenuity.

We drifted away also, leaving behind the precariously perched village, the road fighting for survival in the mountains, the river like Niagara turned sideways, the land of unending excitement. Within an hour we were back at the hotel, and in a different world.

Now came the moment I had been planning privately all during the trip, even before I left home.

"Senor, I do not mount the bicycle any more."

He shook his head.

" Keep it at your father's house," I continued. "It is yours."

If it was possible to collapse all at once from gratitude, he was doing it. "Oh, Senora, *muchas gracias!*"

"Sell it. Whatever you wish. It is yours."

He recovered from his paroxysms of gratitude sufficiently to think of what he might do with his newly acquired "Mercedes Benz."

"Oh no, Senora. I will mount it near my house and ride it up and down the street in memory of you."

I was surprised. But I knew from experience that he would get little of what the bike was worth if he tried to sell it, which was difficult to do in Quito because there were few bicyclists. I was also planning to tip him in useful Ecuadorian currency. He deserved it. For a moment I saw him riding plumply up and down the rutted street near his house, but this would not happen often. Then I saw the bright black eyes of his boys when he showed it to them as a special Christmas present. Few boys in Ecuador would find a present like that beside a miniature tabletop Christmas tree.

The next morning I was not eager to leave Ecuador. I would miss the perpetual spring of the Andes, the steepled peaks puncturing the sky, the sudden drama of a heaven roaring with black clouds. I would miss the lilt of Spanish speech and the challenge of conversing in it. We creatures seek light and I would go home to long, dark days and cold, gray rain.

We drove out to the airport and Senor Godoy was soon bustling about, reserving my seat, moving from one line to another, arranging for things that I always had to arrange for myself, supervising and advising me as I stood meekly behind. In line number three he turned around to me.

"Senora, they need American dollars. I will care for the things. Go into the bathroom and get the money."

Obediently I went into the ladies' room and furtively extracted the money from my "bosom bag." I would not embarrass him again by pulling it out in public.

After nearly an hour he had all the tickets, passes, permits, identifications and receipts necessary for me to leave the country and stop in Panama on the way to Miami. Carefully he handed each item to me one at a time, explaining its importance and cautioning me as to the need for its safekeeping. As usual our roles were reversed: he was the septuagenarian and I was the innocent in need of admonishment and protection.

I carefully stowed all the documents in an inside jacket pocket. At last I stood ready, tiny suitcase held by my right hand, an Otovalo Indian *bolso* stuffed with a twelve-and-a-half-pound book about Ecuador hung around my neck and, balanced on my left hip, a plastic shopping bag spilling over with gifts. Senor Godoy regarded me wistfully.

"*Muchas gracias*, Senora!"

For a second he flapped his arms about uncertainly. To give the senora an American hug would be improper, and the senora had no spare hand to shake.

"*Adios*, Senora. Good journey! Write me," he called, and waved as I started to disappear irretrievably through the forbidden doors leading into the security system. I waved back with an elbow I was able to maneuver and shouted that yes, I would write. I smiled as I squeezed my way through the narrow hallway to the waiting lounge. Already I could see his letters, written in a careful hand on his children's lined notebook paper. After first making sure that I was "encountered in good health," he would tell me of his struggles to build a new house for his family. Chuckles would ripple noiselessly through the letter as he described the "battles" to raise his five *hombres*.

Not future chuckles, but past chuckles made me smile after I settled into my window seat on the plane and looked down upon the mountains I had crossed on two wheels with a taxi. "Water for the Colombians!" I heard Senor Godoy say as I imagined I was flying over the hotel on the frontier and saw the men in their bathrobes wandering around with their loaded toothrushes looking for water—just one of the many remembered moments of laughter.

Too soon the plane had left the Andes and was over the sea. Gone were the snow-topped peaks, fields plowed into patterns, and rolling highways that had once been so close.

"I have been over every road in the Ecuadorian *Sierra* possible for two wheels or four," I thought contentedly. Then I remembered. I would have to go back to the base of Mt. Chimborazo, layer myself in woolens, put on warm mittens, and sail again down that magnificent road to Ambato—this time on two wheels.

"Ah, Senora, now you have the head!" I know Senor Godoy would say.